MENTAL ILLNESSES AND TREATMENTS

SELF-FRAGMENTATION AND SELF-INTEGRATION IN PEOPLE WITH SCHIZOPHRENIA

VOLUME II

INTERPRETATION AND RECOVERY OF POSITIVE AND NEGATIVE SYMPTOMS

Mental Illnesses and Treatments

Additional books and e-books in this series can be found on Nova's website under the Series tab.

MENTAL ILLNESSES AND TREATMENTS

SELF-FRAGMENTATION AND SELF-INTEGRATION IN PEOPLE WITH SCHIZOPHRENIA

VOLUME II

INTERPRETATION AND RECOVERY OF POSITIVE AND NEGATIVE SYMPTOMS

KAM-SHING YIP

nova
Medicine & Health
New York

Library of Congress Cataloging-in-Publication Data

ISBN: 978-1-53613-323-3
Library of Congress Control Number: 2015931179

Published by Nova Science Publishers, Inc. † New York

CONTENTS

PREFACE

THEORETICAL UNDERPINNINGS OF SCHIZOPHRENIA

Schizophrenia has long been regarded as one of the most important mental problems since the twentieth century. There are numerous theoretical underpinnings in explaining and describing the formation, cause, process, and treatment of schizophrenia. Apart from the biochemical model of dopamine (Healy, 1993) as well as the genetic models, there are in fact many psychosocial theories explaining the cause of schizophrenia. These include psychodynamic, cognitive behavioral, phenomenological, existential, biochemical, as well as social construction perspectives. Psychodynamic concepts stress the conflicts of the id and superego to a stage that the individual distorts the sense of reality in order to settle this. It is also a diffusion of ego boundary with the external environment (Freud, 1924/1983; Blatt & Wild, 1976). Cognitive perspective emphasizes the cognitive impairment in hallucinations and delusions in which external stimuli are wrongly perceived, interpreted, and responded to (Costella, 1993). In negative symptoms, individuals even lack the abilities to have emotional responses (blunt affect), to forsake pleasure (anhedonia), to express his/her idea clearly (alogia), and to have clear purpose and behaviors (avolition) (American Psychiatric Association, 1994). Phenomenological and existential perspectives affirmed that persons with schizophrenia face intensive ontological emptiness and insecurity to an extent that the self of the individual is fragmented and split. Individuals with schizophrenia also strive for their own meaningfulness as well as attitude in life (Jaspers, 1946/1963; Laing, 1960). Related studies and literature affirmed that individuals' mental illness, including psychosis, are generated by highly oppressive social environments such as prolonged bullying, previous life trauma, and related cultural context (Al-ssa, 1995; Laing, 1960; Walker, 2005). Within all these perspectives, schizophrenia is interpreted as the manifestation of problems occurring in various layers of a full human being, including the ontological insecurity and meaninglessness of life in existential phenomenological perspective, diffusion of self boundaries, conflict in self-system in psychodynamic schools of thought, cognitive impairment in cognitive perspectives, and interpersonal oppression in social construction and interpersonal perspectives. All of these have strong implications to the recovery of persons with schizophrenia. It implies that for a full recovery of schizophrenia, individuals need to deal with difficulties and problems that occur in their meaning of life, self-system, mind, and social environments.

MENTAL HEALTH RECOVERY MOVEMENT

Recovery is an upfront trend within this decade, regarded as the most important ideologies and practice orientations in providing service and intervention for persons with mental illness, including those with schizophrenia. In 2004, December, the National Consensus Conference on Mental Health Recovery and Mental Health Systems Transformation was launched in the U.S.A. Related parties in this conference had successfully formulated the National Consensus Statement of Mental Health Recovery (U. S. Department of Health and Health Services, 2004). This statement became the overriding guidelines in mental health services in the U.S.A. Following this statement were various technical papers, reports, studies of recovery processes for different types of clients, in different life spans as well as in different social sectors such as family, community, organizations and society (Yip, 2012). Mental health recovery, defined by the Consensus statement, is as follows:

> Mental health recovery is a journey of healing and transformation enabling a person with a mental health problem to live a meaningful life in a community of his or her choice while striving to achieve his or her full potential. (U.S. Department of Health and Human Services, 2004)

In this definition, several personal components include:

1. Personal Journey
2. Healing and Transformation
3. Living a Meaningful Life
4. In a community
5. Individual's Choice
6. Achieve the full potential

The Consensus statement consists of ten principles in recovery. These ten principles can be regarded as ten fundamental principles for mental health recovery. They are self-direction, individual and person centered, empowerment, holistic, non-linear, strength based, peer support, respect, responsibility and hope.

The recovery movement, which happened in this decade, can be described in terms of three main types of recovery, personal and subjective recovery, functional recovery, and social recovery. It started with personal experiences and narration of clients with various mental illnesses, in particular those with chronic schizophrenia. All these personal experience narrations affirmed that recovery is a highly subjective and personal journey in which hope and will to recover occurs for patients who are determined to get well. Since it is highly subjective and personal, every person may have his/her own pace and process, as well as one's own interpretation of recovery. It seems that subjective and personal recovery is very good in asserting one's own will responsibly, and experiences in getting well from mental problems. However, it creates difficulties for policy makers and practitioners in measuring their input and outcomes in a recovery based mental health service.

To input objective measurement in related services, related scholars tried to develop various types of scales in ensuring the effectiveness of services and programs in implementing principles of recovery for clients with mental illness. All these objective scales assume that people with mental problems undergo similar stages, processes, and outcomes in recovery in which measurement can be imposed. It enables service providers and policy makers to ensure proper implementation of services. The outcome of these services is measured by the social functioning of clients with mental problems as well as their drug compliance. All this literature implies a focus on functional recovery of clients with mental problems. However, an objective articulation of recovery, in many ways, is contradictory to subjective paradigm in interpreting recovery of persons with mental illness. The assumption of a unified path for every client with a mental problem is a highly reductive and simplified articulation about the complex natures of human beings and mental illness. It violates the uniqueness of clients in terms of individuality, and self-directedness.

Apart from subjective personal recovery and the objective functional recovery in the development of the recovery movement, related pressure groups organized by mental health consumers attempted to advocate an accepting social environment as well as related policies and services, which are accessible and adequate in ensuring a holistic recovery for clients with mental illness. They disclose the conspiracy of pharmacological companies and psychiatry in advocating psychiatric drugs as well as electric shock therapy. They criticize related stigmatization and discrimination of people with mental illness in accommodation, employment, and other aspects of life. They also advocate for sufficient social support, respect, and acceptance for persons with mental problems. Coupled with this mental health consumer movement is the continuation of the self-help movement, flourishing since the 1970s. Within the 12-steps self-help wisdom, self-help groups have been developed for different sorts of people with mental problems. Together with this is also the spontaneous development of relatives and friends support groups. Within these self-help groups are individuals' own wisdom, insight, and experiences in helping members to recover from various types of mental problems. The mental health consumer movement can be described as a development of social recovery in which consumers advocate for a better and more acceptable social environment for recovery of mental problems. Whereas the self help wisdoms can be considered a social environment formed by the clients and patients to combat their own mental problems.

Within the recovery movement in this decade, there seems to be unresolved theoretical dilemmas and controversies within the development of subjective personal recovery, objective functional recovery, as well as social recovery. The subjective personal recovery considers that every one's recovery process is unique, subjective, and individual based. The functional recovery stresses objective measurement and scales assuming the recovery process and outcomes can be commonly observed and measured by related scales and measurement. The social recovery presumes that individuals with mental problems have to fight for their own rights in counteracting adverse social labeling, stigmatization, inadequate mental health services, and social control oriented mental health legislation and policy. They should create their own social environment and self-help group for their own recovery. While subjective recovery is contradictory to the objective oriented 'functional recovery', social recovery provides no answer in which this dilemma can be resolved. In many cases, even if there is a good and accepting social environment, without appropriate clinical help or support, clients with mental problems with traumatic and experiences and memories may feel reluctant to come from their pathological subjective experiences of mental symptoms. The whole recovery movement tends to neglect the importance of clinical recovery for persons with mental symptoms, in particular those with schizophrenia.

Clinical Recovery for Persons with Mental Problems

All these developments have a vital impact on clinical practice and psychosocial intervention for clients with mental problems. Within the influence of post-modernist thinking, studies of resilience, as well as the recovery movement, intervention models such as the empowerment model, strengths based orientation, positive psychology, narrative therapy, solution-focused therapy, or brief therapy are evolving. In all these intervention models, therapists presume that related approaches and theoretical frames could be applied to people with different types of mental problems. In comparison with traditional models of psychotherapies, such as psychodynamic approaches, cognitive behavioral approaches, as well as existential approaches, these post-modernist and recovery based models are good if assuming that people with different mental problems can embrace their own strengths, abilities, and resilience to recover from their mental problems. However, they have the problems of neglecting the rich traditions and profound conceptual underpinning in every type of mental illness.

The situation is particular problematic in persons with schizophrenia. The traditional psychotherapeutic interventions for people with schizophrenia are still well known for their richness and depth in describing and analyzing clients with schizophrenia. However, they presume deficits, deterioration, and even impairment in the process of intervention. Some may even deny the subjective and personal recovery of clients with schizophrenia. They presume that over-whelming professional authority and power is the only magic in helping clients to treat their mental problems.

Unreachable Theoretical Gap in Recovery from Schizophrenia

That means, up to now, a huge theoretical gap exists between concepts research in schizophrenia and mental health recovery. This theoretical gap makes related intervention and services for recovery of patients with schizophrenia become shallow and superficial in theoretical underpinnings. They may follow the recovery orientation closely but they cannot connect with the rich and solid foundation of related theories in schizophrenia in past centuries. It also makes traditional in-depth clinical practice, for people with schizophrenia, fail to meet the challenge from the upfront trend of mental health recovery.

Self-Fragmentation and Self-Integration Dilemma in Recovery from Schizophrenia

This book serves to bridge this theoretical gap by a profound revisit of different perspectives and concepts in self-fragmentation of persons with schizophrenia. Within a phenomenological and existential orientation, the writer re-articulates clients' intense urge for an integrated self-system and ontological existence behind their fragmented psychotic experiences. The writer revisits psychodynamic theories to search the urge of ego in attaining its integrity and harmony within intensive conflict of superego and id in psychotic manifestation. The inclination for consolidated ego boundaries behind the diffused ego boundary is also articulated. The inherent search for meaningfulness within ontological meaninglessness, and the emptiness of psychotic experiences are described. The prevailing urges and needs for an accepting, empathic, and genuine social environment for people with schizophrenia, in facing their highly oppressive reality, are clearly expressed. The inherent urge and potentials of self-integration behind various symptoms of self-fragmentation, once fully recognized and developed, assist in mental health recovery of clients to become clinically valid and effective. It also facilitates related professionals, clients, and their significant others to participate in a multi-dimensional recovery within supportive and caring social and service contexts. The self-fragmentation and self-integration dilemma can be further elaborated into three dynamic forces, self-splitting versus self-cohesion, self-preservation versus self-destruction, as well as self-visibility versus self-concealment. These three dynamic forces have a crucial influence on positive, negative, and first rank symptoms of clients with schizophrenia. In this book, the writer describes the details and process of self-fragmentation in terms of self-concealment, self-destruction, and self-splitting on one hand. On the other hand, he points out how every client with schizophrenia contains an intense urge for self-preservation, self-visibility, and self-cohesion. However, within a highly oppressive environment, self-preservation, self-visibility, and self-cohesion can only be attained within a self-constructed delusive reality. If related professionals can nurture and provide a supportive, caring, and developmental social environment, the client with schizophrenia can actualize his/her self-preservation, self-visibility, and self-cohesion within an actual reality. Then, related psychotic symptoms in self-fragmentation are gradually alleviated and the client is on the road to mental health recovery.

THE LAYOUT OF THIS BOOK

Since the self-fragmentation and self-integration dilemmas in schizophrenia are highly complicated, they can hardly be covered in one volume. This book is divided into three volumes.

Volume One is a multi-dimensional interpretation of self-fragmentation and self-integration dilemmas in people with schizophrenia. Its implication to mental health recovery is also fully discussed. It consists of three chapters.

Volume Two consists of eight chapters. It is a full and comprehensive interpretation of positive and negative symptoms including diagnosis, etiology, psychosocial causes, and how they contribute to, as well as are influenced by, the three dynamic forces in psychotic self-fragmentation.

Chapter 1 is a description about the diagnosis and a multi-dimensional articulation of positive symptoms in people with schizophrenia. In fact, for every client with schizophrenia, his/her delusions and hallucinations represent an endless struggle to their unavoidable but highly oppressive or even abusive social environment.

In Chapter 2, the writer begins with a full articulation of related psychosocial concepts and theories of paranoid delusions and hallucinations. The self-fragmentation and self-integration dilemma in paranoid delusions and hallucinations is fully mentioned. Its implication to mental health recovery is also suggested.

In Chapter 3, the writer reviews various psychosocial theories in grandiose delusions and hallucinations. Their relationship with paranoid delusions and hallucinations are also discussed. In what ways they are influenced by the three dynamic forces, self-preservation versus self-destruction, self-visibility versus self-concealment, as well as self-splitting versus self-cohesion are fully described. Related implication to mental health recovery for clients with schizophrenia is also suggested.

Chapter 4 is a comprehensive account of catatonic stupor and fixation in people with schizophrenia. Related literature shows that catatonia in clients with schizophrenia is not a stagnant and inert state of mind. Instead, clients are trapped with a dilemma of existence and non-existence from external threats within a highly oppressive environment.

In Chapter 5, the writer gives a comprehensive description of how people with schizophrenia shift and interchange among paranoid, grandiose, and catatonic delusions and hallucinations. Related interventions for mental health recovery are also discussed.

Chapter 6 is a description about the diagnosis and etiology of negative symptoms in schizophrenia. The related literature is dominated by concepts of cognitive difficulties and impairment. However, in 2006, the NIMH had induced a project on the measurement and treatment research to improve cognition in schizophrenia (MATRICS). The findings illustrated that negative symptoms are not correlated to cognitive impairment and difficulties.

Thus, in Chapter 7, the writer provides a multi-dimensional articulation of negative symptoms including existential, phenomenological, and psychodynamic concepts. The writer formulates a comprehensive mechanism in negative symptoms in terms of dissociation, detachment, fixation, regression, and fixation. The self-fragmentation and self-integration dilemma in negative symptoms is then fully articulated in Chapter 8. Related implication to mental health recovery is fully mentioned in this chapter.

Volume Three is comprehensive articulation of self-fragmentation and self-integration dilemma in first rank symptoms. It consists of 6 chapters.

References

Al-ssa. I. (1995). 'The illusion of reality or the reality of illusion, hallucination and culture' *British Journal of Psychiatry*, 166: 368-373.

Blatt S.J. & Wild C.M. (1976). *Schizophrenia: a Developmental Analysis*, New York: Academic Press.

Costella, C. G. (1993). (Edited) *Symptoms of Schizophrenia*, New York: John Wiley

Freud. S. (1924/1983). *'Neurosis and Psychosis' in Sigmund Freud: on Psychopathology*, London: Penguin Books.

Healy D. (1993) *Psychiatric Drugs Explained*, London: Mosby

Jaspers K. (1946/1963). (7th edition) *General Psychopathology*, (J. Hoenig, & M.W., Hamilton trans.) Manchester: Manchester University Press (Original work published 1923)

Laing R.D., (1960) *The Divided Self*, London: Tavistock Publication.

Walker, M. T. (2005) 'The social construction of mental illness and its implications for recovery model', *The International Journal of Psychosocial Rehabilitation*, 10(1): 35-64.

United States Department of Health and Health Sciences (2004) *National Consensus Statement on Mental Health Recovery*, Washington, DC: United States Department of Health and Health Sciences.

Yip, K.S. (2011) 'Resilience and recovery: Implications to clients with mental problems' in K. S. YIP (Ed.) *Recovery and Resilience of Persons with Mental Problems: Interpretation, Interaction and Intervention*, pp. 15-210. New York: Nova Science.

Chapter 1

Diagnosis and a Multi-Dimensional Articulation of Positive Symptoms in Schizophrenia: An Endless Struggle with the Oppressive Environment

Introduction: Diagnosis of Positive Symptoms in Schizophrenia

DSM IV Diagnosis of Positive Symptoms in Schizophrenia

According to the DSM IV, schizophrenia is diagnosed by the following criteria:

A. *Characteristic symptoms*

Two (or more) of the following, each present for a significant portion of time during a one-month period (or less if successfully treated):

1. Delusion
2. Hallucination
3. Disorganized Speech
4. Grossly disorganized or catatonic behavior
5. Negative symptoms such as: affecting flattening, alogia, or avolition

   Note: Only one criterion, a symptom is required if delusions are bizarre, or hallucinations consist of a voice keeping up a running commentary on the person's behavior or thoughts, or two or more voices conversing with each other.

B. *Social/occupational dysfunction*

For a significant portion of the time since the onset of the disturbance, one or more major areas of functioning (such as work, interpersonal relations, or self care) are markedly following the level achieved prior to the onset (or when the onset is in childhood or adolescence, failure to achieve expected level of interpersonal, academic, or occupational achievement).

C. *Duration*

Continuous signs of the disturbance persist for at least six months. This six-month period must include in at least one month of symptoms (or less if successfully treated) that meet criterion A (i.e., Active phase symptoms) and may include periods of prodromal or residual symptoms. During these prodromal or residual periods, the signs of the disturbance may be manifested by only negative symptoms or two or more symptoms listed in criterion A present in attenuated form (e.g., Odd beliefs, unusual perceptual experiences).

D. *Schizoaffective and Mood Disorder Exclusion.*

E. *Substance/general medical examination exclusion.*

F. *Relationship to a pervasive developmental disorder.*

G. *Classification of longitudinal course* (can be applied only after at least one year has elapsed since the initial onset of active phase symptoms) (American Psychiatric Association, 1994: 275).

From the symptoms listed in DSMIV, there are three main groups of symptoms. They are positive symptoms, negative symptoms, and the first rank symptoms. Positive symptoms include delusion, hallucination, catatonia, and disorganized speech. Negative symptoms include alogia, avolition, anhedonia, and blunt affect. First rank symptoms are thought insertion, thought broadcasting, and two voices arguing with one another. In clinical diagnosis, delusions and hallucinations are the most explicit positive symptoms in people with schizophrenia.

According to DSM IV, delusions are erroneous beliefs or misinterpretation of perceptions:

> Delusions are erroneous beliefs that usually involve a misinterpretation of perceptions or experiences. Their content may include a variety of theme (e.g., Persecutory, referential, somatic, religious, or grandiose) . . . . The distinction between a delusion and a strongly held idea is sometimes difficult to make and depends on the

> degree of conviction with which the belief is held despite clear contradictory evidence . .' Delusion are deemed bizarre if they are clearly implausible and not understandable and do not derive from ordinary life experience . . . . Delusion that expresses a loss of control over mind or body (those included among Schneider's first rank symptoms) are generally considered to be bizarre . . . thought withdrawal (taken by others) . . . thought insertion (thought input by others) . . . delusion of control (mind or body control by outside force).' (DSM IV, 1994: 275)

According to the above definition, delusions should consist of the following components:

1. Erroneous belief
2. Misinterpretation of perceptions or experiences
3. Various themes in contents (persecutory, referential, somatic religious or grandiose)
4. Hard to distinction between delusions and strongly held idea

Once the delusions are bizarre, it is classified as first rank symptoms. In terms of self fragmentation, bizarre delusions are more severe than positive symptoms.

Hallucination is defined by DSM IV as follows:

> Hallucination may occur in any sensory modality (e.g., auditory, visual, olfactory, gustatory, and tactile, auditory hallucinations are by far the most common and characteristic of schizophrenia. Auditory hallucinations are usually experienced as voices, whether familiar or unfamiliar, that are perceived as distinct from the person's own thoughts. The content may be quite variable, although pejorative or threatening voices are especially common. Certain types of auditory hallucinations (i.e., two or more voices conversing with one another or voices maintaining a running commentary on the person's thought or behavior) have been considered to be particularly characteristic of schizophrenia and were included among Schneider's list of first rank symptoms. If these types of hallucinations are present, then only this single symptom is needed to satisfy Criterion A. (American Psychiatric Association, 1994: 275)

In other words, hallucinations consist of the following characteristics:

a. As a sensory modality (auditory, visual, olfactory, gustatory, tactile)
b. Auditory one is the most common one
c. It can familiar or unfamiliar voice
d. It is distinct from one's thought

The above definitions on delusion and hallucination clearly show that that is not a clear distinction between strongly held ideas and delusion, and between over-sensitive perception and hallucination. Also, both definitions do not provide a description of linkage of reality. It tends to presumes that people with schizophrenia embrace a faulty interpretation, belief, and perception of reality.

Disorganized thinking, according to DSM IV is interpreted as follows:

> Disorganized thinking (formal thought disorder, "loosening of association" has been argued by some (Bleuler, in particular)to be the single most important features of Schizophrenia Because of the difficulty inherent in developing and objective definition of "thought disorder" and because in a clinical setting inference about thought are based primarily on individual's speech, the concept of disorganized speech . . . Because mildly disorganized speech is common and nonspecific, the symptom must be severe enough to substantially impair effective communication.' (American Psychiatric Association, 1994: 276)

Disorganized thinking according to DSM IV consists of the following:

1. Loosening of association
2. Based on client's speech
3. Impairment in effective communication

Again, the definition of disorganized thinking is hard to make clear. As mildly disorganized speech is common and nonspecific, it is quite hard for related professionals to have a clear diagnosis in this area. In fact, clinically speaking, related professionals may fail to have a clear and precise picture of positive symptoms in terms of delusions, hallucinations, catatonia and disorganized speech. Very often, psychosis and insanity is defined by its consequence rather than by its actual features. Thus, in criterion B, all clients with psychosis should have a marked impairment in psychosocial functioning. It can be problems and difficulties in employment, family life and communication with others. In some severe cases, it can be severe problems in personal hygiene and very confused mental state.

DSM V Diagnosis of Positive Symptoms in Schizophrenia

In DSM IV, there are some changes in the diagnosis of schizophrenia. These changes are listed as follows:

Two changes were made to Criterion A for schizophrenia:

1. The elimination of the special attribution of bizarre delusion and Schneiderian first rank auditory hallucination (e.g., two or more voices conversing), leading to at least two Criterion A symptoms or any diagnosis of schizophrenia.
2. The addition requirement that at least one of the Criterion A symptoms must be delusions, hallucinations or disorganized speech.

The DSM IV subtypes of schizophrenia were eliminated due to their limited diagnostic stability, low reliability and poor validity. Instead, a dimensional approach to rating severity for the core symptoms of schizophrenia is included in DSM 5 Section III to capture the important heterogeneity in symptoms type and severity expressed across individuals with psychotic disorder.' (American Psychiatric Association, 2013: 810)

From the above description, it is clear that first rank symptoms are omitted in the diagnosis. Instead, positive symptoms such as hallucinations, delusions, and disorganized speech put more emphasis in the diagnostic criterion. Following this is the domination of positivistic language in terms of reliability, validity, and reliability but an ignorance of content, details, and process of delusions, hallucinations, and disorganized speech. That means, subjective experiences such as the loss of self boundary and confused sense of reality in first rank positive symptoms are ignored in the process of diagnosis and assessment.

From Positive Symptoms to an Endless Struggle in Oppressive Environment

Positive Symptoms in Terms of Paranoia, Grandiosity, and Catatonia

In people with schizophrenia, delusions, hallucination, and disorganized speech manifested in three forms such as paranoia, grandiosity, or/and catatonia. All these represent an intense need for the individual, in facing the prevailing external oppressive environment, to protect his or her residual self system in the process of self fragmentation. Paranoid delusions and hallucinations may represent an intense and overwhelming urge for the individual to avoid or prevent any hypothetical dangers from the very oppressive environment. Grandiose delusions and hallucinations may mean a prevailing need for the individual to defend and empower him- or herself from possible attack by being delusively omnipotent and superior. Catatonic delusions and hallucinations as well as physical and mental fixation may imply individual's very nervous and intense defensive posture, awareness and reaction to any external intrusion. All these refer to a continuous inner mechanism to protect the genuineness of the inner, true self from being polluted, intruded as well as destroyed by external objects. The struggle of inner, true self within the self splitting versus self cohesion, self visibility versus self concealment as well as self preservation versus self destruction within grandiose, paranoid as well as catatonic delusion and hallucination are fully discussed. Their impact to self system, mind, body and social functioning of the individual with schizophrenia are also mentioned.

A Multi-Dimensional View of Positive Symptoms

As mentioned above, within the diagnosis of schizophrenia, there are three crucial groups, the positive symptoms, the negative symptoms and the first rank symptoms. Positive symptoms are grandiose, paranoid and/or catatonic delusions, hallucinations, and related behaviors. Strictly speaking, despite their odd, bizarre, and pathological contents, delusions and hallucinations, as well as related behaviors, they are a full manifestation of one's inner urge to reach out to the external world, to defend oneself from hurt and harm, to strive a sense of agency and a sense of cohesiveness. It also represents a sort of self constructed and delusive power to empower the individual to face the oppressive environment (Glass, 1995). In terms of Foucault (1968, 1980) truth, knowledge, and power, positive symptoms are also a self constructed, delusive reality so as to replace the unavoidable, very dominating, capillary, and circulatory powerful, but oppressive, social environment.

In terms of Arieti's (1974) orientation, the oppressive environment is the family in which the parents are very critical and/or detached to an extent, the individual develops poor self image as well as confusing interpersonal relationships. Because of that, he or she has to develop schizoid personality, in which he or she tries to dissociate emotionally and mentally from their distressing others. In stormy personality, the individual tries to be very sensitive and reactive to the unstable, but very stressing, others (Arieti, 1974).

In terms of Sullivan's (1953) dissociation mechanism, schizophrenia is a failure of the dissociative mechanism in which psychosis starts when all these over-whelming, but specific and concrete fear turns into a well organized, but confused, paranoid and grandiose delusion and hallucination.

In Garland (1998), psychosis occurs when traumatic experiences create a determined breaking effects on the ego system in which internalized and traumatic fear finally turned into overwhelming psychotic delusion and hallucination. The ego is split into two parts. One split parts of ego finally turns into the lost object that the individual needs to totally identify with in a delusive and psychotic way.

In cognitive and behavioral terms, schizophrenia can also be a result of traumatic experiences such as sex abuse, domestic violence, bullying, and oppression by others (Larkin and Morrison, 2006; Bebbington et al., 2004). Fowler (et al., 2006) tried to speculate the pathway from trauma to psychosis within four cognitive routes.

1. Direct associations between intrusive memories of traumatic or stressful experiences and delusion and hallucination.
2. Indirect association between trauma and persecutory delusions and hallucinations mediated by negative evaluation of self and others (the schema route).
3. Indirect association between trauma and hallucination mediated by negative and self critical rumination concerning relationship between the voices hearer and the voice identity.
4. Speculations about potentially catastrophic interactions between trauma processes and information processing abnormalities which characterize psychosis which may magnify vulnerability to psychosis. (Fowler et al., 2006: 100)

Similarly, in terms of Laing's concept of divided self in psychotic self splitting, it is clear that positive symptoms are a representation of inner, true self. It also represents a strong, inner force for the individual to push out the overwhelming, oppressive force from the external environment. That means the implosion within ontological insecurity gradually turns into a powerful, inner pushing force for the individual to push back internalized oppression from the adverse environment. All these have crucial implications in the formation and development of positive symptoms in terms of paranoid, grandiose, and catatonic delusions and hallucinations.

Isolated and Split Inner Self with a Very Oppressive Social Environment

Normally, individuals facing external oppression have only two alternatives, either fight against it or avoid and escape. However, as what Foucault (1968, 1980) the powerful and dominating environment is very intense, circulatory, and with a penetrating capillary-oriented network all around the individual in which he or she cannot escape or avoid. Among various social contexts, the family context is the most unavoidable and influential to an individual, in particular in babyhood, childhood, and adolescence.

In Artieti's (1974) terms a very critical or detached parent is very distressing. The individual may develop two mechanisms to cope with that. The first mechanism is to internalize all these negative and critical comment, and the second mechanism is to externalize and fight back all this negative and critical comment. However, prolonged internalization of negative comment is far too damaging and unbearable for the individual. The only way out is to suppress or even to repress all this internalized, negative comment but at the price of a damaging effect on the individual's ego function, self identity, and image. In fact, prolonged dissociation and repression are the basic form and roots of negative symptoms. If the oppressive force or the critical parents are too intense and distressing in a way the individual cannot fight back. Or any fighting back may lead to more severe criticism and oppression. The only way or the individual to cope is to transfer the fighting back in an indirect way such as gossiping out of earshot, thinking, planning, and waiting for the chance to fight back. In fact, positive symptoms such as paranoid or grandiose delusions and hallucinations can be interpreted as imaginative ways in fighting back the oppressive others.

Prolonged and unavoidable oppression turns all these imaginative responses into delusions and hallucinations that are out teach of reality. Within prolonged, oppressive experiences, some are intensely fearful and traumatic. In Fowler's (et al., 2006) terms, all these traumatic experiences directly and indirectly create the contents of hallucinations and delusions. Directly, all these traumatic experiences such as being physically or mentally abused by others are being maximized, accumulated, intensified, and generalized and finally become prevailing paranoid delusions and hallucinations. Indirectly, all these traumatic experiences greatly humiliate the individual, making his or her self image become really inferior, weak, and diffused in a way that is very vulnerable to others' oppression. Finally, all this leads to the development of hallucinations and delusions.

From an existential perspective as mentioned by Laing (1960), the self system, in the process of self splitting, in facing ontological insecurity, is split into the inner self and unembodied false self in which the inner self is being isolated from external reality. The isolation is dreadful for the active inner self with an intolerable sense of emptiness. To compensate for this, the inner self has to undergo a secondary splitting in relating the inner self to the unembodied self, and the individual harbors an intense sense of insecurity and loss of control.

> The isolation of self is a corollary, therefore, of the need to be in control. He prefers to control, rather than to be given. He prefers to give, rather than have anything, as he feels, stolen from him; ie he has to be in control of who or what comes into him, and of who or what leaves him . . . . (Laing, 1960: 83)

Together with the sense of losing control comes an inner world of loneliness and being untouched by love as well as profound fear of the external world.

> The substitution of an interaction with other results in the individual coming to live in a frightening world in which dread is unmitigated by love. The individual is frightened of the world, afraid of letting anything of himself go, of coming out himself, of losing himself in any experience, etc. because he will be depleted, exhausted, emptied, robbed, sucked dry. . . . (Laing, 1960: 83)

Within the frightening world, the inner self gradually becomes empty and not touched by love and care, the individual feels dreadfully lonely and fearful. He or she tries to protect themselves from anything inside coming outside and anything from outside coming inside. That means, he or she loses his or her ability to keep his or her self identity and boundaries.

UNSETTLED STRUGGLE IN POSITIVE SYMPTOMS

Unsettled Struggle for Existence and Identity

On the one hand, the individual, in the process of self splitting fails to keep his or her own identity and sense of being and existence because of the lack of contact created by the false self in a very oppressive world. On the other hand, the inner self harbors an intense urge to strive for existence and its own identity. However, the existence of one's being needs to be sustained by a sense in the actual world that is unreachable due to the separation imposed by the false self system.

> The unrealness of perception and the falsity of the purposes of the false self system extend to feelings of deadness f the shared world as a whole, to the body, and in fact, to all that is, and infiltrate even to the true self. The inner self becomes entirely unreal, split and dead and no longer able to sustain what precarious some of its own identity it started with. In one way, the schizoid individual may be desperately trying to be himself, to regain and preserve his being, yet it is very difficult to disentangle the desire to be form the desire for no-being . . . (Laing, 1960: 139)

In other words, the individual is trapped within a dilemma that on the one hand he or she is afraid of external oppression and needs to separate itself using a false self system. On the other hand, prolonged separation from substantially reality make the individual have a strong urge to sustain his or her identity within the substantially reality in which he or she can be attained because of the false self system. Laing (1960) summarized the consequence of the inner self in the self fragmentation process as follows:

a. It becomes unreal or volatilized and has hence loss any firmly anchored identity (boundary and identity of inner self).
b. It becomes unreal (substantiality of inner self).
c. It becomes impoverished, empty, dead, and split (content of inner self).
d. It becomes more and more charged with hatred, fear, and envy (feeling of inner self). (Laing, 1960:140)

The Gradual Loss of Boundary and Self-Identity

Within the continuous separation from the external contact with an oppressive outside world, the individual's inner self undergoes four aspects of change. First, before the self fragmentation, the individual usually has a concrete self identity in terms his or her name, sex, family, and educational standards, as well as other references in the society. However, in the process of self fragmentation, after the splitting from inner self and false self, both the boundary of the false self and inner self are diffused and ambivalent. As a result, ingredients of inner self can easily flow outside. The speed of flowing outside can be various. In time of a strong urge to relate to outside, the loss and the flowing outside of important ingredients from the inner self can be high and intense in a form of volatizing. If this urge is lessened, the individual loss of the flowing will be decreased.

The Loss and Emptiness of Content of Self

Coupling with diffusion of the self boundary and flowing outside of the internal ingredient of the inner self, there should a drastic loss of emptiness of content of the inner self. The quicker the speed of flowing and the more diffused the ego boundary is, the more empty and greater the loss the individual feels will be. In psychotic self fragmentation, the sense of loss and emptiness is not actual physical loss. Instead, it is a perceivable, or even imaginative, loss. It can be a delusive loss or threatening sense of losing of one's sex organ, eyes, hands, and legs. It can also be a fantastic loss of one's ideas, the theft of one's thoughts or insights. It can be a sudden absence of one's wisdom, memories, and past experiences.

The Loss of Substantiality of the Inner Self

The spontaneous sense of loss of content, uniqueness, and identity as well as the ingredients of the inner self means that the inner self is under a constant threat that it will become dead, split, and ontologically empty. The multi-dimensional functioning of self such as maintaining a substantially self image, sustaining a clear self boundary, distinguishing between oneself and others, and having a sense of existence are all gradually diffused, diminished, and erased.

The Intolerable Fear, Hatred, and Envy in the Loss

The sense of losing one's substantiality of self is very threatening to the individual. Together with this comes an intolerable and overwhelming fear that the individual will finally burst out or explode into nothing as into dust. It is also a dread of vanishing completely in this substantially world. This intolerable fear may also bring along a strong sense of hatred and envy toward external objects and persons that may trigger or speed up the loss of the substantiality of the inner self. As a result of this, the individual is in a super urgent need to preserve the existence and uniqueness of the self. In doing so, the individual may involve the following three forces:

1. The first force is to *push back* the oppressive others delusively *(positive symptoms)*: That is the pushing force of the inner true self.
2. The second force is to *dissociate the internalized negative influence* from the oppressive environment *(negative symptoms)*: That is the pulling force of the false and unembodied self.
3. The force to diffuse individual's self boundary, consciousness, and sense of reality so there is *no differentiation between oppressive others and the oppressed self (first rank symptoms)*: That is the confusing force of the diffusion of the self boundary.

In this chapter, the writer will focus on the positive symptoms. That is the force used in pushing back the oppressive others delusively. In fact, this force can have three types of directions and functions:

1. Assuming that the oppressive others are everywhere and trying all means to identify them and avoid them *(Paranoid Delusion and Hallucination).*
2. Transforming oneself into a powerful and omnipotent figure in order to fight back the oppressive others *(Grandiose Delusion and Hallucination).*
3. Full attention and concentration on oneself and one's environment in order to prepare to response or defend oneself from an oppressive environment *(Catatonic Delusion and Hallucination).*

This process of changes in the inner self is shown in Figure 1.

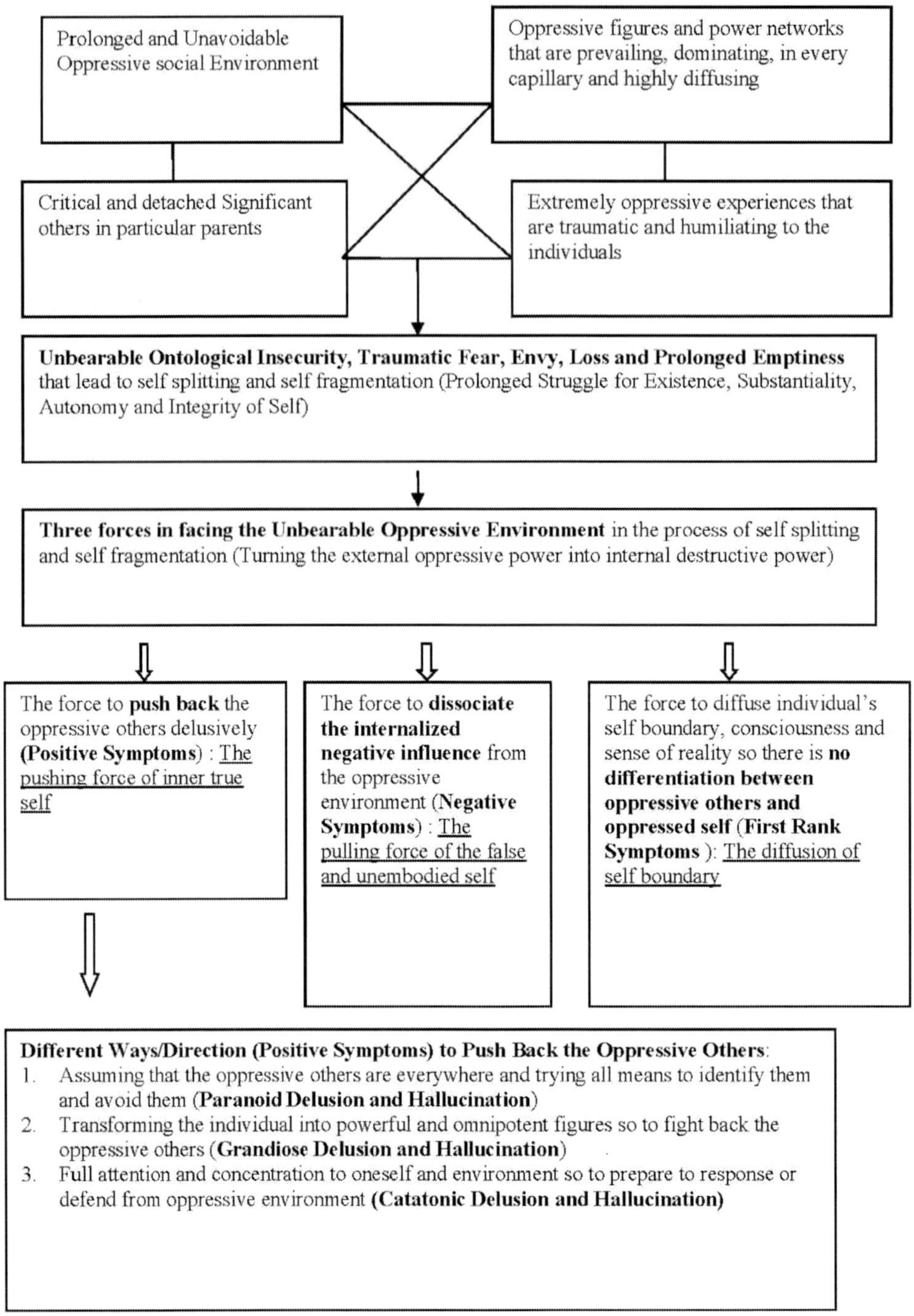

Figure 1. Sources, Processes, and Forces in Self-Fragmentation in Persons with Schizophrenia.

From Implosion to Psychotic Positive Symptoms

As mentioned in the previous chapter, implosion can gradually lead to the formation of positive symptoms. It is a denial and deprivation of one's sense of agency and cohesiveness with a result of being absorbed in continuous confusion and uncontrollability in reaching out to the external environment. Under normal threat or usual stress, the individual may be able to exercise his or her psychic energy in pushing back by a full-fledged exercise of his or her sense of agency in changing an adverse external environment or pushing back at least to gain an external position and space for his or her own survival and existence. The more cohesive the individual in perceiving him- or herself, the more focused the pushing force in facing the external threat and risks. Nevertheless, in facing insurmountable, prevailing, and overwhelmingly crushing forces, the individual faces three difficulties: The first difficulty is that the crushing forces come from all directions; the second difficulty is that the crushing forces are far too powerful for the individual to overcome; the third difficulty is that the crushing forces are spontaneous and continuous over a very long period of time. Because of these three sorts of difficulties, the individual gradually loses his sense of cohesiveness and sense of agency in dealing with crushing forces in actual reality. This is an impingement of reality. It is also an accumulation of individual anger, frustration, and loss of power that cannot be released as the prolonged crushing forces suffocate his or her pushing back. Instead, the accumulated anger, frustration and loss of power become pushing out forces that may store up to a maximum degree leading to an internal explosion and a potential fracture of the self system and sense of existence.

According to Laing (1960), implosion contains the following elements:

a. impingement of reality
b. external world collapse
c. explosion of identity
d. possible internal vacuum
e. a state of nothingness
f. struggle between emptiness to be filled as well as being taken away
g. internal explosion

That means, this sort of inner explosion cannot burst outward as it is suffocated and surrounded by a crushing, oppressive reality. It only explodes inside the self system, making related elements in the self system fractured and fragmented with a prevailing feeling of emptiness and vacuum. In facing the collapse of reality and the result of implosion with its unbearable sense of emptiness and vacuum, the individual may have several ways to respond by:

- Assuming that the oppressive others are everywhere and trying all means to identify them and avoid them *(paranoid delusion and hallucination).*
- Transforming the individual into powerful and omnipotent figures in order to fight back the oppressive others *(grandiose delusion and hallucination).*
- Fully attending and concentrating on oneself and one's environment in order to prepare to respond to, or defend against, the oppressive environment *(catatonic delusion and hallucination).*

With these three changes, all of them imply a process of fragmentation of the self system in which the true inner self is trying its best to reach out and become:

- very alert to external threat (developing of paranoid and assuming others are bad).
- omnipotent and illusively powerful to resist from external threat (extremely powerful self).
- shifting from one aspect of an implosion to another that is not so powerful until all aspects are being absorbed by others.

CONCLUSION

In conclusion, this chapter is a discussion of the diagnosis and multi-dimensional articulation of positive symptoms. In DSM IV, schizophrenia is defined by its positive, negative, and first rank symptoms. However, the first rank symptoms are omitted and the positive symptoms of delusions, hallucinations and disorganized thinking are stressed. Within a multi-dimensional articulation, positive symptoms actually represent an endless struggle for existence and being for people with schizophrenia. They are also a painful and splitting response and way of coping with a very oppressive social environment. Within R. D. Laing's perspective, positive symptoms can be interpreted as a delusive, but fragmented, response to a very oppressive social environment. Paranoid delusions and hallucinations can be interpreted as a delusive mechanism that achieves avoidance by assuming oppressive others are everywhere and trying all means to identify and impose oppression on the client with schizophrenia. Grandiose delusion and hallucination is a delusive transforming mechanism that makes the client feel powerful and omnipotent enough to fight back the oppressive other delusively. Catatonic delusions and hallucination is a full attention and concentration in preparing an appropriate response to delusive oppressive others.

References

American Psychiatric Association (1994). *Diagnostic and Statistical Manual of Mental Disorders, 4th Edition*. Washington, D.C.: American Psychiatric Association.

American Psychiatric Association (2013). *Diagnostic and Statistical Manual of Mental Disorders, 5th Edition*. Washington, D.C.: American Psychiatric Association.

Arieti, S. (1974). *Interpretation of Schizophrenia*. New York: Basic Books Inc.

Bebbington, P., Bhugra, D., Brugha, T., Singleton, N., Farrell, M., Jenkin, R. et al. (2004). "Psychosis, victimization and childhood disadvantage: Evidence from the second British National Survey of Psychiatric Morbidity." *British Journal of Psychiatry*, 185: 220—226.

Foucault, M. (1965). *Madness and Civilization*, Translated R. Howard, New York: Routledge.

Foucault, M. (1980). *Power/Knowledge: Interview and Lecture by Michael Foucault*, New York: Pantheon Books.

Fowler, D. Freeman, D., and Steel, C. et al. (2006). "The catastrophic interaction hypothesis: How do stress, trauma, emotion and information processing abnormalities lead to psychosis?" in W. Larkin, W. & P. Morrison, (Edited) *Trauma and Psychosis: New Directions for Theory and Therapy*. pp. 101—124. London: Duckworth.

Garland, C. (1998). "Thinking About Trauma," in C. Garland (Edited) *Understanding Trauma: A Psychoanalytical Approach*, pp: 9—31, London: Duckworth.

Laing R. D., (1960). *The Divided Self*, London: Tavistock Publication.

Larkin, W. & Morrison, P. (2006). (Edited) *Trauma and Psychosis: New Directions for Theory and Therapy*, London: Routledge.

Sullivan. H. J. (1954). *Clinical Studies in Psychiatric*, New York: W.W. Norton & Company.

Chapter 2

SELF-FRAGMENTATION AND SELF-INTEGRATION IN PARANOID DELUSIONS AND HALLUCINATION: INTERPRETATION AND RECOVERY

INTRODUCTION

As mentioned in the previous chapter, positive symptoms are hallucination, delusion, and disorganized thinking. There are three forms of hallucinations and delusion. They are paranoid, grandiose, and catatonic delusions and hallucinations. In this chapter, the writer outlines theoretical underpinnings of paranoid delusions and hallucinations. Then, the process of self fragmentation and self-integration in paranoid delusions and hallucinations are discussed. Finally, related implications to mental health recovery is mentioned.

THEORETICAL UNDERPINNINGS OF PARANOIA

Self-Attention and the Feeling of Being Watched

Fenigstein and Vanable (1992), by reviewing three studies on undergraduate students discovered that self attention was related to feelings of being watched. The awareness of oneself as an object of attention leaves people susceptible to the idea that other people are more interested in the self than is actually the case.

Self-Consciousness and Self-Reflection in Paranoia

Von Geemmingen, Sullivan & Pomerantz (2003) found that individuals with mild levels of paranoia are prone to inflated levels of both private and public self consciousness. Self reflection, in terms of paranoia and self consciousness may make people to misconstrue and exaggerate any imagined or identified imperfection. Such self recognized imperfection and externalizing bias are projected to others (Bentall, Kinderman & Kaney, 1994).

Defense for Self-Esteem, Ideal Self, and Actual Self

Kinderman and Bentall (1997 & 2000) further articulated that this sort of externalizing bias is a self defense toward low self esteem. The development of persecutory delusion and paranoia seems to be a resolution of related discrepancies between the individual, ideal self and the actual self, especially when the individual is exposed to threatening events. Such a paranoid attributional style is an external attribution for threatening events and internal attributions for positive events (Campbell & Morrison, 2007).

Self-Retreat Vs. Projection

In psychodynamic theories, Fairbairn (1944) affirmed that there is a defensive aspect to paranoia involving internal retreat. From a similar viewpoint, Bentall et al. (1994) articulated that persons with paranoia experience conflicts in terms of self discrepancies, but their strategy to defend the self is to project the blame externally rather than to retreat internally. The conflicts in self may be further deteriorated and intensified to nurture schizophrenia.

Related Emotions and Paranoia

Freeman et al., (2002) interpreted paranoia in terms of its related emotions. They discovered that emotional experiences are directly related with contents of paranoid delusions. Such delusional beliefs and ideas sustain or intensify related emotional experiences. Freeman et al. (2003), by means of involving subjects in virtual reality, they found out that anxiety is crucial in generating related persecutory delusions.

Themes and Components of Paranoia

Campbell and Morrison (2007) tend to have a good summary of related themes in paranoia. Theme 1 is the phenomena of paranoia including the content of the paranoia and the perception of paranoia (intention of harm, type of harm, and acceptability of harm); the nature (confusion, dynamic process, and origin of paranoia); and the insight into paranoia (insight cause and insight remoteness from reality). Theme 2 is the beliefs about paranoia including positive belief (re-evaluation and protection) and negative belief (control issues and conflicts). Theme 3 is related factors that influence paranoia, including unusual perceptional experiences (control, promote paranoid); biased information processing (loose association and personalizing), past experience (severity and impact), alleviating factors (safety, -reappraisal, setting limits, and medication). Theme 4 is consequences of paranoid including emotions (anxiety, fear, and anger); the self (self perception, self esteem and splitting of the self); behavior (defense, controllability, and harm to self).

A Multi-Dimensional Perspective in Paranoia

Within all above perspectives, the formation of paranoia seems to consist of the following components:

Diffused and Confused Awareness

1. A constant awareness of being watched
2. An awareness of self as an object

Problems in the Self System

3. Discrepancies between the ideal and real self
4. An inflated level of private self and public self

Related Negative Emotions

5. Anxiety
6. Fear
7. Anger

Interpretation and Accumulation of Past Experiences

8. Unpleasant past experiences
9. Accumulation and intensification of traumatic experiences

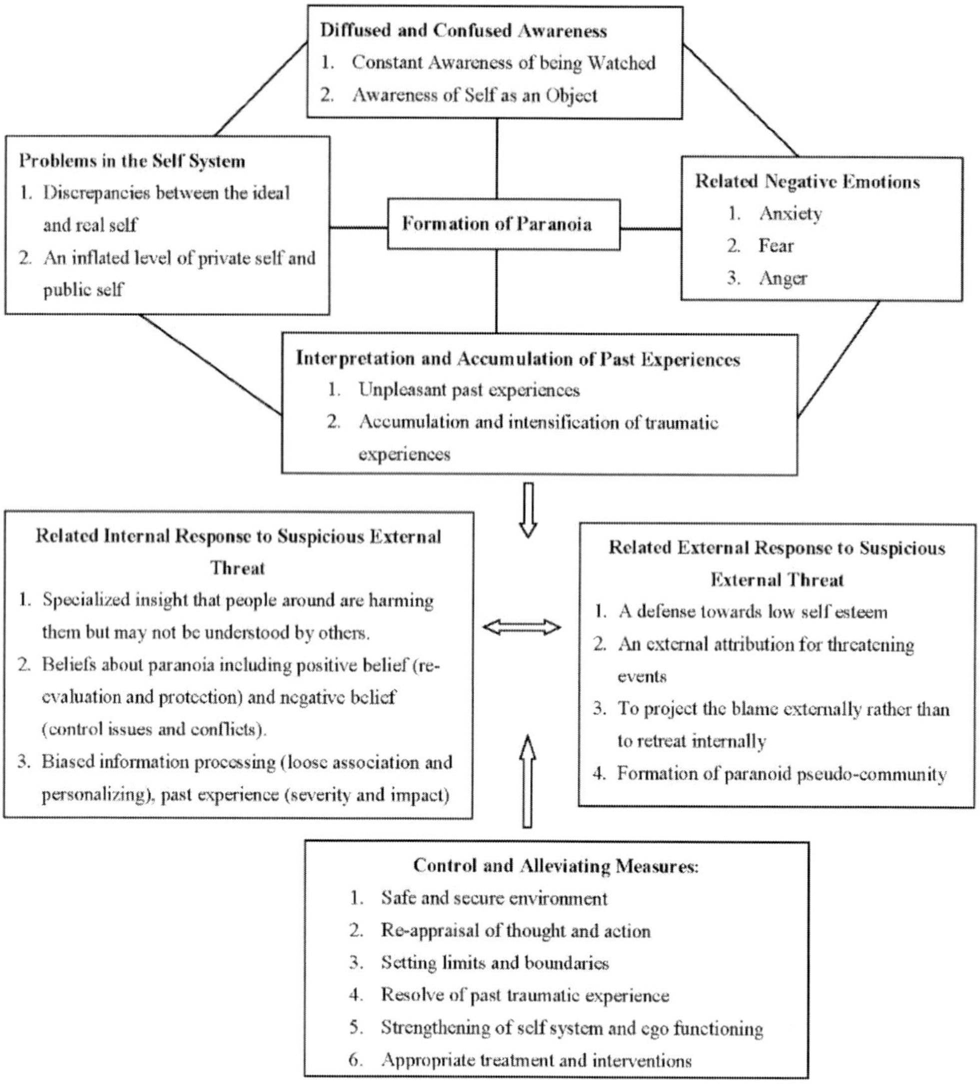

Figure 2. Connections of Different Dimensions and Components in Paranoia.

Related External Response to Suspicious External Threat

10. A defense toward low self esteem
11. An external attribution for threatening events
12. To project the blame externally rather than to retreat internally
13. Formation of paranoid pseudo-community

Related Internal Response to Suspicious External Threat

14. Specialized insight that people around are harming them but may not be understood by others
15. Beliefs about paranoia including positive belief (re-evaluation and protection) and negative belief (control issues and conflicts)

16. Biased information processing (loose association and personalizing), past experience (severity and impact)

Control and Alleviating Measures:

17. Safe and secure environment
18. Re-appraisal of thought and action
19. Setting limits and boundaries
20. Resolve of past traumatic experience
21. Strengthening of the self system and ego functioning
22. Appropriate treatment and interventions

Despite all these recent perspectives in understanding paranoia, there is a still a lack of understanding and consideration of the subjective experiences in paranoia experiencing by individuals. Rethink (2006) and Paranoia Network (2006) tend to be only organizations that are keen in sharing all these subjective experiences. All these experiences that may not be believed by others are very unique and subjective.

The dimension and components of paranoia are shown in Figure 2.

Implications to Mental Health Recovery

A Deficit Orientation Ignoring the Various Dimensions of Paranoia

All these perspectives and understanding on paranoia have strong implications in mental health recovery for clients with paranoid schizophrenia. Within a deficit orientation, a client with prevailing paranoid delusion and hallucination is easily regarded by related professionals as being very confused and insane. Instead of embracing an empathic stance in understanding the emotions, many professional tend to neglect clients' emotions (anxiety, fear, and anger); diffused and confused awareness; and a problem in the self system and the interpretation and accumulation of past experiences behind paranoia. They simply regard paranoia as meaningless and non-understandable. They may try to clarify whether the paranoid ideation/delusion can be diagnosed as paranoid personality disorder, delusional disorder, or paranoid schizophrenia. All these are distinguished by other symptoms together with paranoid ideation/delusion. Once the diagnosis is made, what follows is only delivering appropriate medication such as anti-psychotics and -antidepressants.

A Multi-Dimensional Understanding of, and Intervention for, Clients with Paranoia

Within a multi-dimensional perspective, paranoia in various forms and degrees is not meaningless and non-understandable. Instead, underlying this is related emotions, diffused and confused awareness, problems in the self system and in the interpretation and accumulation of past experiences. All these have strong implications to mental health recovery for clients with paranoid schizophrenia. Related professionals should beware of the following in the process of intervention.

1. Related professionals should understand various dimensions underlying clients' paranoid ideation and delusion by relating its contents and process to clients' unfulfilled needs, past pleasant and unpleasant experiences in life.
2. Related professionals should help clients develop a proper awareness and consciousness of related issues, objects, and persons in reality by engaging clients with meaningful and positive activities and relationship with others in the immediate physical and social environment.
3. Related professionals should help clients resolve problems and difficulties within different dimensions of paranoid ideation/ delusion. Once these problems and difficulties are resolved, related paranoid ideation/delusion can be alleviated. This includes the following intervention strategies:
   a. Facilitating the ability of clients to express and ventilate underlying negative emotions such as anxiety, anger, and fear. In doing so, clients do not need to use paranoid ideation/delusion as a symbolic expression of repressed negative emotions.
   b. Enable clients to understand the discrepancies between what they expect and what they encounter in reality to help them to nurture and construct an accepting and supportive reality and social environment. This can be done by joining in supportive self help groups or constructive activities in social services units. Related professional should help clients to resolve their conflicts and negative emotions and relations with their significant others.
   c. Facilitating the ability of clients to ventilate and describe their unpleasant past experiences including traumas, suffering, torture, and hardship in life within an empathic, genuine, and supportive social environment. Help them to understand and feel that, despite all that, there are still people who really care, concern, support, and love them.

4. When the above interventions are rendered, related internal factors leading to paranoid ideations or delusions are clarified. Then, related professional should help clients to resolve related external factors to nurture paranoid. This includes the following:
   a. Help and facilitate clients to acknowledge their defense toward their low self esteem.
   b. Enable clients to acknowledge their unnecessary formation of a paranoid pseudo community.

c. Facilitate clients to assess external threats, challenges, and difficulties in an accurate and realistic ways.
d. Help clients to find or create safe and secure working, family, and peer environments in which clients are accepted, supported, and nurtured.

5. Related professionals should facilitate clients to strengthen their self control mechanism in alleviating future paranoia. It includes:
   a. Setting realistic boundaries and limits in work, in taking responsibility, and in accepting new challenges.
   b. Building up confidence and the ability to have an accurate assessment and articulation of related issues, and persons.
   c. Strengthening of the client's self image, self identity and self boundaries so that he or she will not be vulnerable to others' comment and oppression.

All these may be shown in the following case illustration. Related parties' consensus in using their stories for academic purpose was sought. For the sake of confidentiality, their personal identities and information were appropriately disguised.

Beautiful Woman and the Watching, Nasty Man

P was a middle-aged, Chinese woman. She came from a conservative family in which her father was a teacher, and her mother was a lawyer. Both of them were very strict with P. They demanded that P be very obedient to all commands given. Under their influence, P became self demanding and rigid in her school life as well as in relating with others. At first, she was able to get good results from her performance in primary school. As she became more and more anxious and rigid, her school performance declined accordingly in secondary school. Together with this came bullying from other classmates because of her strange and rigid behaviors. Her parents did not care for her much. Instead, they demanded her to perform better academically.

This was very stressful for P. She began to develop paranoid ideation that someone was saying in her ear that she was bad, and no one liked her. Once, she encountered an old woman on the street, she suddenly broke into anger and attacked the old woman, saying she cursed her as useless and seductive. P was then sent to a nearby hospital and was diagnosed as suffering from paranoid schizophrenia.

P stayed in the mental hospital for several months. Her condition was stable, and she was discharged home. P finally finished her secondary school education, and the scores of her public examination were fair. Despite her parents' objections, P chose to work. She worked as a clerk in a large business firm. At first, P was hardworking, responsible, and sociable. After two years' hard work, she was promoted to senior clerk. At that moment, she fell in love secretly with another senior clerk in the same company. She tried to approach this colleague for courtship. He refused her bluntly. One year later, he resigned from this company and never returned.

From then onward, she always became deluded that other male colleagues were in love with her. This delusive thought really disturbed her and made her appear odd. Colleagues in her company teased her as a "seductive witch." She was very angry with this nickname and was furious when other teased or bullied her. Once when a male colleague teased her, she hit him on the nose and was thus hospitalized. One year later, she was discharged home. At the same time, her mother died of cancer, and six months later, her father had a stroke. All these were a great shock to her. P had to stay at home to take care of her father. She was sad, lonely, and desperate.

She always harbored a prevailing paranoid delusion that men around her, including her neighbors and any men on the street, were deeply attracted by her beauty. Every one of them wanted to have sex with her. Thus, they tried every means to watch her and seduce her in particular when she was in her bedroom or in a restroom. To prevent this, she sealed up every window of her bedroom and bathroom. She even thought that adult males nearby, including those next to her flat, those on upper floors, and those in the opposite block, all watched her day and night. To counter all these, P called the police and urged related policemen to warn or impose a legal charge on related adult males. At first the police investigated the case by interviewing adult males nearby. These calls were very disturbing to her neighbors. Gradually, the police refused to take her complaints. It made P furious. One day, she rushed toward a male neighbor and cursed him. When the male neighbor tried to escape, in intense rage, she came along and hit him. At once P was taken to a nearby mental hospital and diagnosed as having paranoid schizophrenia. She stayed there for six months and transferred to a psychiatric halfway house for rehabilitation. The social worker (M) there sought the professional consultation of the writer. Under the supervision of the writer, M performed the following intervention on P.

Understanding P's Paranoid Delusion in Relation to P's Past Experiences and Unfulfilled Needs

Under the supervision of the writer, the social worker. M, began to understand that P's paranoid delusion was closely related to her unfulfilled needs and unpleasant experiences in life.

P harbored the following delusions:

1. She deluded that someone was saying in her ear that she was bad, and no one liked her (in her secondary school). (D1)

2. She always deluded that her male colleagues were in love with her. This delusive thought really disturbed her and made her appear as odd. Colleagues in her company teased her as a "seductive witch."(D2)
3. She always harbored a prevailing paranoid delusion that men around her, including her neighbors and all men on the street were deeply attracted by her beauty. Every one of them wanted to have sex with her. Thus, they tried every means to watch her and seduce her in particular when she was in her bedroom and in the bathroom .(D3)

It was clear that D1, D2, and D3 were related to P's unfulfilled wishes as well as her previous unpleasant experiences and traumas in life. In D1, the content of the delusion clearly reflected that as she was rejected by her parents because of poor academic performance in addition to being bullied by others, she harbored a strong need to be accepted by others. At the same time, the traumatic experiences of being bullied by others and being blamed by her parents made her feel that she was spontaneously blamed by others. All these formulate the content of her auditory delusion. In D2, it clearly appeared that P harbored a need to have a normal courtship and marriage as an adult. However, all these needs were totally suppressed by being refused by her male colleague. In a paradoxical way, she deluded that her male colleague fell in love with her to satisfy her unfulfilled need for courtship and marriage. These unfulfilled sex and courtship needs prevailed and very intensified in D3, deluding that neighbors and men on the street were deeply attracted by her beauty. They watched her and seduced her everywhere including her bedroom and bathroom.

Facilitate P to Develop a Proper Sense of Reality

Under the supervision of the writer, the social worker, M, helped P to develop a proper sense of reality. Instead of merely fixating on the irrational response to her paranoid delusions, P was helped to have a proper engagement with issues, objects, and persons in reality. M visited P and got a good recognition and understanding of her emotions and the needs behind her paranoid delusion. She did not question the validity of P's delusion. Instead, she listened carefully, nodded and smiled as P asserted that all males around her tried to watch her bathe. After that, M invited P to go to a social center in M's psychiatric rehabilitation service agency. At first, P refused to go there. She insisted on staying at home and fixated on her paranoid delusion. M did not push her to go there. Instead, she simply had a causal and happy chat with P. In the next visit, M brought a female client, V, from her service center. V was a young, energetic, and active client. She recovered from schizophrenia and served as a peer mentor in the service center. With her help, V enabled P to develop a proper sense of reality by engaging in meaningful activities and relationships in the service center. What follows is a verbatim recording of M and V's home visit to P.

P opened the door upon M's visit.

M: How are you, P? This is V, our peer mentor in our center.

P: Nice to meet you all. Try to be quiet. I can sense that someone is watching over us. This is a male neighbor next door. He is such an ugly and nasty guy who always tries to watch me. (It was clear that P was engaged in her paranoid delusion again).

M: I can understand that you are very attractive to men around you. (Instead of going into P's paranoid delusion, M tried to pull out M's unfulfilled but paradoxical needs. P aspired to be attractive and hoped that men around her would start a courtship and even sex with her).

P: I don't want to be so attractive. But I cannot prevent others from liking me and having sex fantasies about me.

M: I can understand that. Nevertheless, men are always attracted by beautiful woman. So I think it is normal that they focused the attention on you. (M tried to normalize P's delusion in terms of males being attracted to beautiful females).

P: Yes, men are so annoying. It is not sinful to be attractive. But it is sinful to gawk over others and act seductively.

V: So, it is not sinful to be beautiful. But it is really a waste to spend time on such nasty and immoral males. (V came in. M had already told V to encourage P to come to the rehabilitation center to build up a proper sense of reality)

P: I agree with that. But I had no way out.

V: Better not stay at home all day. You can go out and let them stay home where they cannot watch over you.

M: I think this is really a good suggestion. It can make you feel less stressed and more at ease in life.

Finally, P agreed to go the rehabilitation center with M and V. Without delay, they escorted P to there.

Under the supervision of V and M, P stayed in the rehabilitation center every day. At first, P still harbored paranoid delusions in connection with males there, thinking they seduced her to have sex with her. To alleviate her paranoid delusion, M encouraged her to join in various activities there. From casual chat, V knew that P had various talents such as drawing and knitting as well as cooking. V and M encouraged P to join in a cooking class first. It made P feel interesting and involved in the process of cooking. Once P did so, her focus on paranoid delusion decreased proportionately and her sense of reality increased proportionately.

What follows is a verbatim recording of this process:

V brought P to watch over a group of female clients who engaged in cooking a Chinese dish.

V: Hi, P. See, they are making a Chinese dish of fried fish balls mixed with vegetables. It should a yummy dish.

P: Frankly speaking, they are not so skillful in doing that. (P seemed to involve herself in the cooking. It aroused her interest and attention. That means, she began to establish substantially connection with objects, persons, and issues in the immediate reality).

V: Oh, that is wonderful, you are skillful in doing that. How is it made?

P immediately demonstrated how to deep fry the fish in a proper way. Other members in the cooking group were amazed by P's talents. They began to have a good chat with P. All these made P feel happy and engaged. With that sort of engagement and involvement, P clearly took a break from her prevailing paranoid delusion.

Enable P to Resolve Problems and Difficulties Behind Her Paranoid Delusion

Gradually, P tuned into related activities and groups in the rehabilitation center. She joined in the cooking group and members there regarded her as a mentor for cooking good food. They began to have constant and regular sharing with P. With the help from M, they enabled P to elaborate her negative emotions behind her paranoid delusion. This could be demonstrated from the following verbatim recording:

P was sharing some cooking skills with V, M, and R and S, two other female clients in the cooking group.

P: Hi, R. You are really good in cooking. I loved your dish very much.

R: Thanks for the compliment. I love your dish, too.

S: By the way, where and whom you taught you to cook so well? Did you learn from your mum and dad?

R: I think your dad must be a good cook, too.

P: My father was a senior teacher in a secondary school. My mum was a solicitor. They did not want to cook. (P answered in a low and repressed voice. She did not want to speak much about her demanding and rigid parents)

R: Ha, your parents were so smart. My mother was a waiter in a Chinese restaurant, and my father was a security guard. You were so lucky to have parents with good social status.

P: Don't talk about them, I hated them, , , , (P was able to ventilate her anger toward her parents).

M: I can understand your stress in having demanding parents.

P: Ya, my parents were really demanding. They expected me to be the best in my school performance but I could never fulfill their standard. (P began to air out her anger and sadness toward her parents' unreasonable demands).

M: I can understand your sadness. My parents expected me to be a doctor, but I now I can only be a social worker. They always look down on my profession and make me feel really upset. (M disclose her own experiences so to establish empathy in facilitating P to air out her deep-seated anger and sadness).

P: Indeed, my whole life was ruined by them. Their unreasonable demands made me so stressed that I could not concentrate on doing my work. I was so anxious in fulfilling their demands. (P began to weep. At that moment, V, R, and S came along to embrace her).

R: By the way, you are such a good cook. We all admire your distinguished cooking talents.

P: In fact, I learnt my cooking from my grandmother. Every Saturday I went to her house, and she taught me to cook good dishes, but my parents always criticized her since they thought it was useless to learn cooking. They thought I should concentrate on studying. My grandmother loved me so much, and I enjoyed the time cooking with her. She always told me she loved me no matter how I performed. But she died when I was only fifteen years old. (P was so sad in losing her grandmother and she wept bitterly).

S: Don't cry, your grandmother is now in the heaven. She must be proud of your cooking skills, and she is watching and smiling at you in sharing good cooking with others.

P: Throughout the year, I was stressed. Even now, I do think that I am just a total failure in the eyes of my parents. In fact, I have already tried my best. I am so anxious to gain their actual acceptance. They never accepted me.

R and S embraced P together. They sat on the chair of the kitchen for quite a long while. After that, they shared the food they had prepared in the cooking session.

Interestingly, after the deep ventilation of unresolved emotional complex, P was much released. From that time onward, P's paranoid delusion of being watched by the males around her was much alleviated.

Facilitate P to Understand and Accept Her Discrepancies between What She Expected and What She Encountered in Reality

When P's love/hate dilemma with respect to her parents was ventilated, her related paranoid delusion was much reduced. She became more and more open and social in relating to others. From P's delusion it was clear that P embraced conflicts and discrepancies between her expectation and actual reality. They are the following:

1. Being accepted and appreciated by her parents vs. being pressured, criticized, and even rejected by her parents.
2. To be a high performer in every aspect of life vs. repeated failure in school performance, work, and courtship.
3. To be attractive, loveable, appealing, and welcomed by others, in particular handsome males vs. being excluded and labeled by others.

For P, all these discrepancies certainly made her feel very unacceptable, annoying, and frustrated. They were also a breeding bed for her paranoid delusion and psychotic fragmentation. To bridge these discrepancies, it was crucial that P be able to accept that she was a normal human being. That means, for every normal person, there are some people who accept and some who reject him or her. Similarly, everyone can give a good performance in some areas and a poor performance or even fail in some other areas. Finally, everyone can be attractive, loveable, appealing and welcomed by others in some social contexts but be excluded, criticized, and labeled by others in other social contexts.

To achieve acceptance of these principles, several measures were taken. First, M let V, R, S, and P become a small and cohesive mutual support group. Within this mutual support group, they not only supported one another in daily social functioning, but also in searching for work, as well as doing volunteer work in serving clients with special needs such as disabled elderly and children with intellectual disabilities. With the help of M and V, P was able to find a job as a junior clerk in a nearby factory in which V was the manual worker there. M organized some volunteer service in an elderly service unit. P and R were invited to organize a birthday party for elderly clients there. P and R cooked many delicious dishes and baked a birthday cake for them. Their work was fully appreciated. All the companionship, job opportunities, and volunteer work greatly enhanced P's self image. The above-mentioned discrepancies in her life were partly resolved.

What follows is a verbatim recording of a conversation among M, P, R, and V showing how P's discrepancies were partly resolved. At the time, they were sitting in the sitting room discussing the feedback in doing the birthday party for clients in a nearby elderly service unit.

M: Thanks for your efforts. All of you performed very well at the birthday party. The center in charge was very happy about your performance saying that she would invite you all to organize the birthday party in the coming month.

R: I can understand how happy the elderly clients are. Many of them smiled, and some even clapped their hand when P's favorable dish appeared.

P: It was not my own performance. V also helped me in preparing this dish.

M: Now, P, we all know you are an excellent cook. Not only do we know but everybody in the neighborhood knows you are the best cook in the community.

P: They appreciated me, but my parents still considered me as rubbish and impotent as I performed poorly in every aspect of life. (P narrated her discrepancies between what her parents expected and what she could achieve in life).

R: Certainly, your parents did not discover your potential. But we discovered it. It is so valuable and good. We all like it; now you are an adult. You should have your own views and values.

P: Thanks for your appreciation.

V: One day, we should invite them for the birthday party and let them look at your performance and let them see how well you are appreciated by us and by the elderly in the neighborhood center.

M: I agree with R and V's comments. . . . Anyway, P, be proud of yourself.

P's cooking was fully appreciated by clients in the halfway house as well as members in the elderly center. P was very happy and regained her self confidence and self image of a person with talent and welcomed by others. From that time onward, interestingly, P's paranoid delusions as being rejected by others or being seduced by handsome man were greatly reduced. Instead, she regained her normal functioning in life. She worked as a junior clerk in a nearby factory. On the weekends, she served as a volunteer helping elderly clients and clients with intellectual disabilities. She no longer appeared anxious and delusive but calm and cheerful.

From Paranoia to Paranoid Delusion in Schizophrenia

From Paranoia to Paranoid Delusion in Schizophrenia

Criteria for a Delusion to Be Classified as Persecutory

Freeman & Garety (2000) affirmed paranoia can turn into a persecutory delusion if the following criteria are met:

> "A: The individual believes that harm is occurring, or is going to occur, to him or her.
> B. The Individual believes that the persecutor has the intention to cause harm.
> There are a number of points requiring clarification:
> Harm concerns any action that leads to the individual experiencing distress.
> Harm only to friends or relatives does not count as a persecutory belief, unless the persecutory also intends this to have a negative effect upon the individual.
> The individual must believe that the persecutor at present or in the future will attempt to harm him or her.
> Delusions of reference do not count within the category of persecutory beliefs." (Freeman & Garety, 2000: 410)

This means that the persecution delusion has already had substantially effects on the normal daily functioning of the individuals. He or she fully believes that the persecutor is doing and going to do actual harm to him or her. To avoid being hurt or to alleviate the harmful effect by the persecutor, he or she must do something. Actions include avoiding seeing some persons, not going to some places, and doing some odd and bizarre acts that cannot be understood by others. In doing so, his or her sense of reality, social functioning, along with ego boundaries are gradually diffused and confused. This is also the basis of self-fragmentation in the psychotic process.

Formation of Paranoid Delusion as the Threat Increase

In the formation of paranoid delusion in the psychotic self-fragmentation process, the more intense the belief that people around are threatening the individual, the wider is the pseudo paranoid community, the stronger the paranoid delusion is, the greater the self-fragmentation will be, and the less is the individual's ego strength to distinguish the actuality of his or her paranoid delusion. Gradually, the individual becomes totally absorbed in his or her self constructed paranoid pseudo community. Most of his or her activities in daily life are confined to response and development of this paranoid pseudo community. Freeman (2007) has summarized various degrees of threat in the following table.

Table 1. The Paranoid Hierarchy (Summarized from Freeman, 2007)

Severe Threat (e.g., People trying to cause significant physical, psychological, or social harm, conspiracies, known to wider public)	Increase in Threat ↑	Decrease in Possibility ↓
Moderate Threat (e.g., People going out of their way to get you)		
Mild Threat (e.g., People trying to cause minor distress such as irritation)		
Ideas of Reference (e.g., People talking to about you, being watched)		
Social Evaluative Concerns (e.g., fear of rejection, feeling of vulnerability, thoughts that the world is potentially dangerous)	Decrease in Threat	Increase in Possibility

Paranoid Delusion in a Form of Anomalous Experiences

From Freeman's (2007) description, it was clear that paranoid delusions in persons with schizophrenia presumed threats are severe in which the individual presume that people or even the wider public tried to cause significant physical, psychological, or social harm, conspiracies to him or her. The dreadful thing is that the wider public grouped together to hurt the individual. He or she feels him or her has less and less chance to escape from the conspired public and community that try every mean to harm him or her continuously. In that situation, the individual may get into a state of anomalous experiences in which he or she feels very confused, anxious, puzzled and helpless. In such a confused mental state, individual's sense of reality also deeply challenged and blurred. Freeman (2007) further articulated these delusive anomalous experiences are intermingling effects of:

1. Emotion, Beliefs about the Self, others and the World
2. Cognitive Biases Associated with Psychosis
3. Precipitating Events and Stimuli
4. Selection of An Explanation and Meaning (being mediated by beliefs about illness, social factors and belief flexibility)

Mahler (1974, 1988 & 2003) emphasizes that delusional ideas spring from unusual internal experiences. Many people with psychosis have clear anomalous experiences such as hallucinations, thought insertion, and replacement of will, and also a range of more subtle perceptual and attentional alterations in experience and often a period of arousal.

Cognitive Behavioral Interpretation of Persecutory Delusion

Freeman (2007) articulated that persecutory delusion composes of affective process, reasoning and threat.

Affective Process

1. Paranoid Concern fear. Anxiety help create thoughts of a paranoid content and anxiety-related processes contribute to the maintenance and distress associated with the experience.
2. The most common type of suspiciousness is that of a social anxiety or interpersonal worries theme, ideas of reference build upon these sensitivities; persecutory thoughts are closely associated with the attributions of significance; and as the severity of the threatened harm increases, the less common is the thought.
3. Worry thinking Style: Worry in individuals with persecutory delusion is associated with higher levels of distress and with delusion persistence.
4. Depression, Self Esteem and Paranoia: Poor me Paranoia (defend from negative emotion and Bad me Paranoia (reflect from negative emotion).
5. Paranoia is associated with symptoms of anxiety, depression, victimization experiences and recent stressful life experiences.

Reasoning

1. Biases in information gathering may make individual to jump into conclusion.
2. Acceptance of false memories and knowledge corruption.
3. External attribution of negative event are made in paranoia.
4. Misreading of the intention of other people.

Threat

1. Estimation of threat and action on threat

Affective process, reasoning and threat work together in forming the schema of persecutory delusion. Stressful and anxious social environment intensifies individual's worries, suspiciousness and inferiority making that he or she easily accepts and internalizes his or her false memories, ignores his or her knowledge corruption, and misinterpret a safe environment as an over-whelming harmful environment.

Implications in Working with Clients with Paranoid Schizophrenia

According to Freeman's (2007) hierarchy of paranoid threat, it is clear that clients with paranoid schizophrenia suffered from *severe threat continuously in their life.* This sort of severe threat may exist in several ways.

First, it can be continuous engulfment from their significant others in which the client found no way to escape from others' control and manipulation in childhood and adolescence.

Secondly, it can be *very oppressive others.* They bully, physically, mentally or even sexually abuse, exploit and/or depersonalize the client. All these oppressions are so severe, frequent and continuous that clients' normal evaluative mechanism is in vain and even totally breaks down. That means, even all these oppressive others are not there, clients with paranoid schizophrenia may still presume that related oppression, abuse, exploitation and manipulation is still existing.

Thirdly, related *oppressive experiences are so traumatic* that make the individual's internal and external system shatters. Even a minor stimulus in the outside environment can fully trigger clients' intense fear, anxiety and related threatening traumatic memory. The breaking of internal and external system as well as the evaluative system may finally result in *delusive affect, delusive reasoning and delusive threat. Delusive affect* implies that the effect of the individual are entirely delusively constructed. Even within a safe environment without the presence of threatening events, persons, issues and objects, the individuals still feels threatened, fearful, inferior and very anxious. *Delusive reasoning* means that the individual presumes that threatening objects, events, persons and issues are everywhere and exist in most social contexts, entirely out of the control of the individual. Once this delusive assumption is consolidated, he or she can justify the content of his or her paranoid delusion as logic, reasonable, and meaningful. *Delusive threat* means that the individual feel that the threat from related objects, events, persons, and issues are continuous, uncontrollable, and increasing. Delusive affect, reasoning, and threat link and intermingle together forming the paranoid delusion. In other words, while others perceive clients with paranoid delusion as unreasonable, delusive, and illogical, *their delusive affect, delusive reasoning, as well as delusive threat, work together justifying the reliability and validity of the paranoid delusion.* What follows is a detailed illustration of this. Related parties' consensus in using their stories for academic purpose was sought. For the sake of confidentiality, their personal identities and information is properly disguised.

Pinky was a client with paranoid schizophrenia. She worked as a lecturer in post-secondary college. In her delusion, she deluded that the secret agents in China were very powerful. They could control our minds everywhere in the world through the computer. Whenever anyone started the computer, they could work through the computer waves and control the user's brain. By means, of this, anyone in the world could be manipulated by them. She even correlated all sorts of natural disasters to delusive computer control of the secret agents in China. Facing all these powerful delusions, Pinky was very threatened. So whenever she opened the computer to work, she wore a self made aluminum cap. She said by means of this aluminum cap, she could successfully exclude her from powerful influence of the computer wave.

Of course, all these appeared as strange and bizarre to her colleagues and her students. To justify her delusion, she gathered a lot of information from the Internet showing that human brain consisted of electromagnetic waves that could be controlled and maneuvered by others. She also opened a website discussing this overtly with people in other countries. Finally, she used her money to publish a booklet illustrating how many natural disasters and deaths of famous international figures were, in fact, controlled by secret agents both in China and in Russia.

From Pinky's case, it was clear that she harbored paranoid delusion. She perceived delusive threat from delusive secret agents from China and Russia. The *delusive threats* existed everywhere. Because of that, Pinky felt extremely intense insecure. To cope with the sort of *delusive affect* she had, she engaged in *delusive reasoning*. She tried to clarify all the delusive threats by means of scientific explanations connected to electromagnetic waves and brain functioning. She also allied herself with others with similar views and experiences on the web. By doing that, her delusive affect and threats become explainable and predictable, as well as controllable.

All these can have implications for intervention. Related professionals should not challenge, debate, or argue with the client with paranoid delusion. In fact, once the delusive reasoning is being challenged, the client will defend his or her delusive reasoning by refining the content and details of the paranoid delusion. In Pinky's case, her paranoid delusion once was challenged by her colleagues and students, who teased her, saying that her behaviors were odd, bizarre, and meaningless. Facing their criticism, Pinky further refined her delusive threat and reasoning. In fact, her paranoid delusion had three stages of development:

Stage 1: Secret agents in China were very powerful and ubiquitous.
Stage 2: Secret agents in China were very powerful and ubiquitous and could control one's mind though the computer.
Stage 3: All severe disasters, accidents, warfare, or even deaths of important figures in the world were caused by secret agents in China through the computer.

In Stage 1, other people might argue with Pinky about how secret agents in China controlled others. To bridge this logical gap, Pinky further extended her delusive reasoning by bringing in the computer which could connect everyone in the world through the Internet. She thus extended her delusive threat by saying that anyone using the computer could be controlled through electromagnetic waves. In Stage 2, while others might challenge Pinky that it did not sound logical and reasonable, Pinky developed her delusive reasoning further, arguing that all disasters, accidents, warfare, and deaths of important figures in the world happened by secret agent in China controlling electromagnetic waves through the computer. By doing so, she could cite many examples to illustrate her delusive reasoning and confirming that the power of delusive threats was indeed everywhere and uncontrollable. Interestingly, the more she engaged in such extension of delusive threat and reasoning, the more her delusive affect was intensified on one hand. On the other hand, the prevailing fear pushed her to cope with that by engaging in more unrealistic activities or relating to more people for help. She engaged in creating a comprehensive network on the Internet, sharing her delusive reasoning and ideas about delusive threats. The response of other people on the Internet with similar delusions greatly enhanced the creditability of her delusive threat and reasoning and alleviated her delusive affect and fear.

All these symptoms have the following implications for related psychosocial intervention with clients with paranoid delusion:

1. It is harmful to engage in cognitive disputes with clients with paranoid delusions. This only increases clients' defense mechanisms and further elaboration and justification of their delusive reasoning. In doing so, their delusive threat and delusive affect increase accordingly.
2. Clients with paranoid delusion easily build up their own paranoid pseudo community (Cameron, 1959) in which they regard people around them conspiring together to hurt, to control, and to do harm to them. Thus, professionals connected to helping them should be prepared to be included in that

community. That means, they may face counter-transference by clients with paranoid delusion.

3. Clients with paranoid delusion are overwhelmed by their delusive threats. They feel dreadfully insecure and fearful. Related interventions should focus on establishing their sense of trust, security, and predictability in relating to others within well recognized social and physical environment.
4. Within delusive threats and delusive reasoning, there are two major components. One is an exaggerated, as well as delusive, aspect. Another is an element from actual reality. It is important that related professionals can pull out and reflect on, as well as consolidate, elements from actual reality and ignoring those exaggerated and delusive aspects. In doing so, clients' sense of reality and contact of reality can thus be increased with a result of decreasing the delusive aspects of paranoid delusion.
5. No matter how confused and intense the delusive reasoning and threat is. The clients' affect behind delusion is still real and substantially. It symbolizes the clients' repressed senses of frustration in past and current life. Very often, in their whole life, they fail to find someone to recognize, comfort, and care about such negative emotion. Thus, related professionals should facilitate clients to ventilate, challenge, and ease out of intense emotions such as intense fear, inferiority, and anger behind paranoid delusion. In doing so, intensity and frequency, as well as duration, of paranoid delusion decrease accordingly.

All these could be briefly showed by the following verbatim recording in Pinky's case. Walter was a social worker at Pinky's college. Under the supervision of the writer, he had the following meaningful chat with Pinky.

Pinky: Walter, nice to meet you. I would like to share something with you.

Walter: You are welcome to. (Walter showed acceptance but avoided reinforcing the delusive reasoning and threat).

Pinky: You know the secret agents in China are very powerful. They can control nearly everything in the world. They deliver electromagnetic waves through computers.

Walter: They are really powerful. They should be very frightening to us. (He did not question Pinky's delusion. Instead, he tried to pull out her fear underlying frightening delusion).

Pinky: Of course, they are able to control the human mind. You know many disasters are actually controlled by secret agents in China.

Walter: I can imagine that. (He used short and accepting remarks to illustrate that Pinky's delusion came from her imagination but he avoided showing doubts that might stimulate Pinky's further development and elaboration on that delusion).

Pinky: They utilize electromagnetic waves to confuse the human mind. In doing so, they could disturb the consciousness of a pilot, a driver, or anyone controlling the engine. In doing so, they cause accidents and disasters. In a very complicated way, some have even been able to disturb the magnetic forces of the Earth and caused serious disasters.

Walter: You are very knowledgeable about science. Certainly, you are an expert in science. (Walter focused on Pinky's strengths and ability within a reality context).

Pinky: Sure, I am a lecturer on science in this college. I am an expert on science and computers. Apart from me, many people in other countries know that. We shared our discovery on the Internet.

Walter: So you find a lot of friends on the Internet? You must be very insightful and sociable. (Walter focused on Pinky's ability and strengths. He tried to ignore related details in Pinky's delusive reasoning and content).

Pinky: We carry out many investigations to find out how powerful these electromagnetic waves are. Walter, even now as I am talking with you, they can still control our mind if you open your computer.

Walter: Then it must be very threatening. How can you deal with such a threatening life? In what ways do you cope with it? (Walter focused on her coping and delusive affect so as to relax the emotions underlying her delusion as well as her connection to reality).

Pinky: Thanks for your understanding. Indeed, this is a life full of threatening issues and events.

Walter: You must spend a lot of effort on coping with that.

Pinky: I need to wear a special hat made of metal to isolate the control of electromagnetic waves. (Pinky showed a photo of her aluminium hat to Walter. In fact, she looked really bizarre wearing this).

Walter: Thanks for your photo. Wow! You are so creative. You are really a scientist. You must have very good training in physics. Did you do many scientific experiments? (Walter did not comment on the oddhat and the delusive content. Instead, he shifted Pinky's attention to her talents and strengths in scientific inventions).

Pinky: I am a scientist. In fact, I have spent my whole life doing scientific experiments and writing scientific papers. I am a good scientist. My doctoral supervisor, who was a world-renowned science professor said that I had a lot of talent and the potential to be an excellent scientist . . . Wow . . . . (Pinky seemed to elaborate on her deep-seated frustration with life).

Walter: Life does not always go our way! (He tried to help Pinky pull out of the life frustration underlying her paranoid delusion).

Pinky: After my graduation from my PhD Program, I was employed as a research assistant to my supervisor. I participated in a huge, international, scientific research. I was responsible for conducting an important part in it. At that time, I had full confidence that sooner or later, I would become a world-class scientist. Unfortunately, two years later, my supervisor got cancer. He died, and the project was taken up by another professor who was a racist. He had severe, racial discrimination against Asian scholars. Under his leadership, all Asian scholars, including me, were sacked by him. I lost my chance to be an excellent scholar in science. In fact, on this project I had already done a lot of work in scientific investigation. I just needed another year to have remarkable and innovative findings. This professor stole our research findings as his own scientific inventions. (Pinky, with Walter's encouragement, was able to air her frustration in life).

Walter: What's a pity! You nearly became a great scientist. By the way, what sort of topic had you investigated in your great research?

Pinky: It was a very important investigation in electromagnetic waves. (Pinky began to reveal the background of her delusion).

Walter: I have no knowledge about electromagnetic waves. I think it must be a very important area in scientific study. Is it?

Pinky: Sure. Even our brain is related to electromagnetic waves. (Under Walter's guidance, Pinky is finally to express unfulfilled needs, functions, hidden emotions, and the meaning underlying her paranoid delusion).

Walter: Are you still doing similar research at our college? It would be a pity if you do not continue working in this area!

Pinky: Our college is too small to house such an important study. That sort of study requires large and expansive equipment. Only a college in the US can do so.

Walter: It is really a pity that you could not continue this study.

Pinky: My whole life was ruined by this bad professor.

Walter: Why didn't you continue your study at another university.

Pinky: I tried to do so. But similar studies at other universities in the United States were all controlled by this professor.

Walter: So, you did not have any chance then. I can understand how frustrated you are by all these matters. You are a real scientist, but things in life did not occur in the way they should. (Walter successfully reflected Pinky's feeling, unfulfilled needs, and the frustration in life underlying her paranoid delusion).

Pinky was very impressed by Walter's comfort. She began to get tears in her eyes.

Walter: Then you returned Hong Kong to this college.

Pinky: Thank for your comfort. I went to China and continued my PhD studies in a famous university in Beijing.

Walter: By the way, the facilities of a university in China could help you continue your research. (Walter began to explore in what way Pinky's paranoid delusion related to China and in particular to a "secret agent in China/".

Pinky: Not really, but I was dreadfully frustrated by the cunning Americans. I returned to my mother country hoping that I could contribute my talents to serve China.

Walter: That was good. As Chinese, we should commit to China and contribute our talents to the well-being of fellow citizens in China. So, they ought to appreciate your return and contribution deeply.

Pinkly: I continued my PhD study in Peking University.

Walter: Peking University is the tope one in China. So they should welcome you and give you plenty of opportunities to develop your scholarship in this area.

Pinky: At first, they did, but later, things changed . . . .. (Pinky was deeply disturbed emotionally, it seemed some traumatic memories were triggered).

Walter: Things don't always happen our way. Men are always unpredictable. (Walter tried to elaborate and open up Pinky frustrations).

Pinky began to cry, and tears ran down her cheeks.

Walter: I can understand your feelings.

Pinky: The professor at this university was also a bastard. At first he welcomed my research. Later, he borrowed all my ideas, published his own article, and was recognized as an international expert in this area. I tried to make complaints about his misconduct. But he conspired with all the senior staff. He even said I was unethical in my academic pursuit and disqualified my PhD status . . . .

Walter: It was really frustrating. It was really unfair.

Pinky: In Beijing, the National Security Agent was very powerful. Whenever anyone came into this city, within half an hour, the security agent could detect whether or not this person on the blacklist of people who were harmful to China.

Walter: They were so powerful. It was really threatening. (Walter tried to reflect Pinky's fear instead going into the details of this delusion).

Pinky: Thus, after years of investigation, I finally discovered that they detect and control others by electromagnetic waves. (Pinky finally disclosed how her paranoid delusion was formulated by her frustration and difficulties in life, in particular in facing her unfair treatment in her academic career).

Freeman (2007) has summarized various degrees of threat in the following table:

Table 2. The Paranoid Hierarchy (Summarized from Freeman, 2007)

Severe Threat (e.g., People trying to cause significant physical, psychological, or social harm, conspiracies, known to wider public)	Increase in Threat ↑	Decrease in Possibility ↓
Moderate Threat (e.g., People going out of their way to get you)		
Mild Threat (e.g., People trying to cause minor distress such as irritation)		
Ideas of Reference (e.g., People talking to about you, being watched)		
Social Evaluative Concerns (e.g., fear of rejection, feeling of vulnerability, thoughts that the world is potentially dangerous)	Decrease in Threat	Increase in Possibility

Psychodynamic View of Paranoid Delusion in Schizophrenia

Apart from a cognitive behavioral perspective, paranoid, or persecutory delusions in schizophrenia are comprehensively described by Sullivan (1956) and Missinner (1974).

Sullivan's Paranoid Dynamism

Sullivan (1956) affirmed that paranoid delusion is a form of dynamism for the individual to face interpersonal anxiety and worries. It is rooted in two things. The first one is that individual experiences a strong sense of awareness of inferiority and putting the blame on others. Sullivan (1956) described that there were two types of paranoia. The first one is a paranoid slant on life in which the individual need this mechanism to adapt minor interpersonal conflicts and frustration in daily life. The second one is a full blown paranoid state. That is the misinterpretation of events to constitute an explanation, usually rather transcendence in nature. Gradually, under unfavourable psychosocial condition, such full blown paranoid state can become active persecutory delusion.

The Process of Paranoid Dynamism

Sullivan (1956) articulated that there are three, important, inter-related factors that lead to a full-blown paranoid state. They are an intense self awareness of inferiority, a habitual mechanism in putting the blame on others, and a sense of interpersonal insecurity and anxiety since childhood. They can be listed out as follows:

A: Awareness of inferiority (Sullivan: 1956:146)

1. It means one is unable to keep out of consciousness that formulation of some chronic feeling of the worst sort of insecurity.
2. One suffers from anxiety, or even worse, jealousy.

3. The fear that others can disrespect a person because of something is shown in his contact with other people.
4. Anxiety arises from something the individual knows they can- not fix. It also represents a consciousness of a deficit in the self system.
5. The self cannot disguise and exclude the feeling that "I am inferior; therefore people will dislike me, and I cannot be secure with that." (The sense of insecurity in extreme cases can turn to a kind of ontological insecurity).
6. The failure of the self system calls out for effort as an unresolved need for satisfaction of the self to attain security. (In extreme cases, it also means a sense of ontological security).

B: A transfer of blame to others (Sullivan, 1956: 146)

1. The refined cognitive operation of the self system develops the group process that makes up the paranoid dynamism
2. The cognitive process may appear in the form of a sudden insight and illumination such that the individual finally comes to the conclusion that, "And then I saw it," (X is actually jealous and/ or harming me, I have to do something about it).
3. An awareness that "It is not that I have something wrong with me, but that the other does something to me."
4. One is the victim, not of one's own defects, but of a devilish environment.
5. One is not to blame; the environment is to blame
6. That is the transference of blame.

C: Interpretation of security and insecurity in childhood and in culture (Sullivan, 1956: 146)

1. That the person can make the sad transition from unhappy sanity to the relatively more comfortable psychosis of the paranoid state is not very surprising.
2. It builds on the entities of culture as a working system of adjustments and compromise and not as a rational way of life.
3. The evaluation which establishes our security or insecurity has come to us very early in our life by empathetically experienced, significant people.
4. One cannot reach back to that time, to the origins of our security and insecurity and say: "I would be perfectly happy and entirely content if it were not for the significant people in my infancy and their evil effect on me."
5. One can reach back into late childhood when, certainly, significant people blamed the individual him or her at times, taking out their disgruntlement with their own carelessness, their own miscarriages, their lack of judgment and one thing and another. They are unfair to the individual, and in case one

was secure enough with them to attack their unfairness, they compounded the felony by defending themselves, by claiming that they were fair, and so on.

6. The recall of this makes the individual feel this as a double offenses to have an awareness that, "I would not have the horrible feeling of discomfort with others if they were not there, and If I had not been educated the way I have been educated by other people," or "And I would not have this sense of discomfort if other people did not treat me unfairly."
7. The feeling of discomfort is unstable and gradually becomes more intellectual by cognitive transference of blame in "It is not I who am undeserving but these people who make me undeserving."
8. The sense of inferiority makes the individual also feel very powerless and helplessness in life. Thus, the cognitive transference of blame is the only way to retain the sense of power and mastery.

D: A full-blown state of paranoia (Sullivan, 1956: 147—148)

1. (In addition to sense of inferiority and transfer of blame, the individual needs to go further into action by formation of a pseudo community). Paranoia appear in the form of a conspiracy, which may have most exquisitely built up plot, supported by an amount of introspective falsification that would produce stunning, mysterious stories and permit him to live in the lap of luxury on royalties for the rest of his life.
2. A very systematized paranoid state may appear under the guise of litigious paranoia, revolving around the business of the courts, or in the person who is simply shot through with insecurities in dealing with people.
3. It may be a nightmare of practically transcendental persecution.
4. The paranoid dynamism make the individual think that, "I feel more insecure; therefore it become more necessary for me to see how you have persecuted me."
5. Anything that increases, or threatens to increase, insecurity calls out more vigorous operation of the paranoid dynamism of misinterpreting events to show that one is all the more unutterably correct in the paranoid formula. "I am a very important person against whom certain more or less devilish people are engaged in a destructive plot."

Table 3. Natures of Different Types of Paranoia

Type of Paranoia	External Threat	Inferiority and Self Deficiency	Sense of Insecurity	Transference of Blame onto Other
Occasional and situational paranoia, excuse, and lying	Temporary threat that could be properly tackled	Sense of inferior is only a reactive response to external threat	Light sense of insecurity	Putting the blame into other so as to avoid being blamed in certain issues or event
A paranoid slant on life	Constant awareness of threat in life. Or one's life is full of unpleasant events	Constant sense of inferiority and self deficiency but do not affect one's overall social functioning in daily life.	Constant sense of insecurity and is unable to seek for a good, secure social environment in life	Habitual response to one's fault by putting the blame on others. In doing so, one is fully beware his or her own faults and wrongdoing.
A fully blown paranoid state	External threats are well-organized in forms of conspiracy and social network	Intense sense of inferiority and self deficiency in which individuals feels intolerable and unbearable. He or she also tries to hide his or her senses of inferiority and deficiency	Intense and prevailing sense of insecurity, most social and physical environments are full of threat and insecure issues, persons, and objects	The individual puts the blame on others by assuming that all persons around is planning to hurt them. Even though all these persons have not done anything or said any words, they are still gossiping or planning to harm them.
Stable and organized schizophrenic paranoid state	External threats exist in a form of unrealistic or even supernatural paranoid system such as evil spirit, demons, electronic waves or computer. This well-organized supernatural paranoid network exists in everywhere in the world.	Individual's intense inferiority and self deficiency are unbearable and intolerable to a stage that he or she needs to use a well-organized and supernatural based paranoid delusion and hallucination system to show one's uniqueness and importance.	Being closely watched and hurt by a well-organized supernatural paranoid network, the individual should harbour an extreme sense of insecurity that is intolerable to the individual. To tackle that he or she employs specific measures (usually odd and bizarre behaviors)	The individual tries to attribute his or her life long misfortune in life to related persons, issues, events within he well-organized supernatural paranoid network. He or she also attributes his or her present difficulties and frustration in everyday life to the destructive power of the prevailing paranoid network. In doing so, individual feels that once this paranoid network can be controlled, he or she can regain his or her hope and luck in the future.

Table 3. (Continued)

Type of Paranoia	External Threat	Inferiority and Self Deficiency	Sense of Insecurity	Transference of Blame into other
Acute and confused schizophrenic paranoid state	The well-organized external threats exist in a form of well-organized, supernatural, paranoid network. It suddenly turns into an acute and intolerable state in which all related persons and objects create immediate harm to the individual.	Individual faces acute and intense senses of inferiority and self deficiency to a stage that he or she is totally absorbed in the dreadful, well-organized, paranoid network. To escape from this dreadful network, the individual needs to change his or her self identity so that he or she can be free from related harm. Also, he or she may develop a grandiose and supernatural identity to fight back all related and conspired harm as well as destruction.	The intense sense of insecurity increases to a huge intensity that sparkles the shift of self-identity. In the development of grandiose self-identity, his or her sense of insecurity may gradually vanish and decrease accordingly.	The intense projection of blame onto others increases tremendously to a self destructive and fragmentation effect. After the development of the grandiose identity, individual prepares him- or herself to fight back by supernatural power and defense.
Substance Induced Paranoid State	External threat exists in actual reality. It relates to substance abuse in two ways. First, the individual greatly suppresses and represses it in their mind by substance abuse. Secondly, the individual has already suppressed and repressed it in their minds. However, it re-bounces in the process of substance abuse	Individual embraces intense senses of inferiority and self deficiency aroused by external threats. All these are deeply intolerable and unbearable. Thus, the individual needs to suppress and repress all these senses by substance abuse. Even if all these painful experiences and unpleasant feelings are re-bounced by one type of substance. Individual may use another type of substance to further dissociate all these painful feelings and senses.	Individual embraces intense senses of insecurity that can be intolerable and unbearable. Thus, the individual needs to suppress and repress this sense of insecurity by substance abuse. Even if this sense of insecurity is re-bounced by one type of substance. Individual may use another type of substance to further dissociate this sense of insecurity	The projection of putting the blame on others as someone near is going to hurt the individual tends to occur in time of substance abuse. When the individual does not take drugs, all the blaming stopss.

E. From paranoia to schizophrenia (Sullivan, 1956: 148-149)
   1. The paranoid system works in a self operation system under the pressure of the circumstances provoking insecurity in this general way: The greater the insecurity, the more risk there is of schizophrenic process appearing.
   2. Even in most reasonable types of paranoia, such as litigious paranoia, the more people-may express some pretty far-fetched, practically dreamlike elements in the process of fitting events in the paranoid system.
   3. In paranoid schizophrenia, the greater the pressure, the more incomprehensibly schizophrenic will be the content that comes forth.
   4. The cognitive validation process is invented, developed, and utilized for the sake of maintaining a sense of security.

Within Sullivan's (1956) articulation of external threat, inferiority, self deficiency, and transference of blame to others may exist different degrees and forms of various types of paranoia. All these can be shown in Table 3.

Projective Identification

Good and Bad Self as Well as Good and Bad Others

As mentioned in the previous chapter, both paranoid and grandiose delusion and hallucination can be explained in terms of projective identification in the process of psychotic fragmentation. As mentioned by Bion (1984) and Klein (1946), in terms of *projective identification,* both the self system and others can be identified into two ways: the bad self and the good self, as well as the bad others and good others. In paranoia, the individual's bad self is projected outside and identifies with the bad others, so that the individual's good self can be concealed and protected from the oppression. Facing prolonged, external oppression, there are two representations of the bad self (BS). The first representation s regarding oneself as bad and deserving of being punished by others (BS1). The second is one's deep-seated anger and urge to take revenge and diminish others (BS2). Similarly, the good self (GS) can exist in two ways. The first one is regarding one is tolerable, endurable and surviving within prevailing oppression (GS1). The second one is regarding one is good should not be oppressed other (GS2). The bad others (BO) can also exist in two ways. The first is those who substantially and overtly oppress the individual (BO1). The second is those who seem to, are going to, are planning to, or covertly oppresses the individual (BO2).

Combinations of Projective Identification in Paranoid Delusion

There can be various combinations of projective identification in the formation of paranoid delusion.

The first one is BS1 + BO1 + GS1. The individual internalizes the substantially, negative comment from the oppressive others (BO1) admitting that he or she is deserving of being punished and oppressed by the bad others (BS1). In doing so, the individual's good self assumption that one is tolerable, endurable, and surviving (GS1) within this oppression-can be concealed and protected. That means the individual appears as if he or she is deserving of being punished. He tends to reflect the opponent's form and style. The more he or she is punished, the more he or she ensures him- or herself they can tolerate and endure the oppression. Within this type of projective identification, the individual tends to develop a very developed and well-organized network of paranoid delusion and hallucination. The more the individual thinks that he or she is deserving of being punished by others (BS1), and the more he or she feels he or she can tolerate and bear the punishment, the better organized and well-developed the delusive paranoid network is. For example, an adult male with schizophrenia, P, may develop a well-organized paranoid network, feeling and thinking his bad boss and his colleagues are trying all means to kick him out of the office. His bad boss and his oppressive colleagues actually exist (BO1). Gradually, within the profound influence of BS1 and GS1, his paranoid delusion network prevails. Underlying this well-organized, paranoid delusion is his unconscious assumption that he is deserving of being punished by many the same as he can tolerate any type of harm and suffering he gets from his bad boss and colleagues.

The second combination is BS2 + BO1 + GS2. The individual harbors an intense anger and a strong urge to take revenge (BS2). He or she identifies with the substantially oppressive others (BO1). He or she joins with the oppressive others. He or she becomes part of the oppressive group and oppresses others (BS2 + BO1). His or her prevailing feeling of anger and hatred from being oppressed by others can be transferred and released to those he or she oppresses. In doing so, he or she successfully conceals his good self (GS2) that implies he or she does not deserve oppression by others. This mechanism is different from the first combination. In the first mechanism, the individual unconsciously thinks that he or she is worth being oppressed and that he or she can tolerate or suffer from this oppression. Within this mechanism, the individual's paranoid network becomes bigger and bigger. However, in the second mechanism, the individual's urge to take revenge (BS2) prevails, together with the thinking that he or she does not deserve to be oppressed (GS2), which nurtures the individual's defense mechanism to fight back or deal with all these paranoid attacks and oppression. That means, the stronger BS2 and GS2 are, the more refined and detailed the coping and defense mechanism is.

In the above example, the male adult with schizophrenia, P, in facing the well-developed and organized paranoid network, the combination of BS2 and GS2 enables P to develop different means to cope with this. Under this mechanism, the individual first describes how bad, cunning, and evil his bad colleagues and boss (BO1) are in conspiring with others to hurt him. Then, he may describe how unfairly he is being treated by his bad boss and colleagues. In his mind, he concludes that he had to take revenge. However, he still harbors a strong fear that his bad boss and colleagues are so powerful they can overcome any type of revenge. Thus, it is more secure for him or her to remain isolated and defensive toward their conspired attack and harm. In that way, he or she tries to develop all sorts of odd coping mechanisms. For example, P rigidly avoids saying any words or making any sound related to the words "boss" or "colleagues." He tries to wear a hat and dark glasses so that his boss and colleagues will not recognize him in everyday life. In seeing all these defenses, people around him may label him as insane and crazy. He tries to justify all these means as, in fact, meaningful and necessary. He also attempts to convince others that they have to beware the destructive power of his bad boss and colleagues.

The third combination can be BS1 + BO2 + GS1. The individual internalizes that he or she is bad and deserves punishment (BS1). However, what he or she is afraid of and has internalized is not real. Instead, the bad others are all surrounding the individual (BO2) that are all planning and conspiring together to oppress, to harm, or even to kill the individual. When BS1 and BO2 combine together, the individual harbors a prevailing paranoia that everyone surrounding him or her is conspiring or connected with the paranoid network to harm him or her. The paranoia is greatly intensified by the thinking that he or she is bad and deserves punishment. In doing so, he or she actually conceals their thinking and believes that he or she has special tolerance for, and ability to cope with the all this torture and oppression (GS1). Under this influence, the individual develops psychotic, paranoid delusion and hallucination. In P's situation, his paranoid network gradually becomes a pseudo community in which everyone in his reality is included and connected with his bad boss and colleagues. Even if P is resigned or being sacked from his job, his bad boss and colleagues can still control him. As BO2 developed further, his bad and cunning boss and colleagues may also cooperate with supernatural or unseen powers. In P's case, he may develop a paranoid delusion that his bad boss and colleagues are actually sent by the FBI from the United States. This powerful FBI network penetrates everywhere including restaurants, streets, and even his nearby neighborhood. In his paranoid delusion and hallucination, the FBI cooperates with everyone or inserts tight control on their minds so that they conspire together to hurt or harm him.

The fourth combination is BS2 + BO2 + GS2. The individual harbors an intense anger and a strong urge to take revenge (BS2). However, what he or she identifies is not real. Instead, the BO1 is gradually enlarged to an extent that include unseen supernatural forces or delusive oppressive others. In form psychotic delusions and hallucination, he or she joins with the delusive, oppressive others *(BS2 + BO2).* His or her prevailing anger and hatred feeling from being oppressed by others can be transferred and released onto those he or she defends delusively. In doing so, he or she successfully conceals his good self (GS2) and that he or she does not deserve oppression by others. Within this mechanism, the individual's urge to take revenge (BS2) prevails, together with the thinking that he or she does not deserve to be oppressed (GS2) which nurtures the individual's defense mechanism to fight back or deal with all these delusive paranoid attack and oppression. That means, the stronger BS2 and GS2 are, the more refined and detailed the coping and defense mechanism is. In the above example, the male adult with schizophrenia, P, in facing the well-developed but delusive and well-organized, paranoid FB1 (BO2). The combination of BS2 and GS2 enables P to develop different means to cope with this. First, P describes how bad, cunning, manipulative, and powerful the FBI is in controlling others, especially him. He always warns others to beware of the power of FBI. Even though others may regard him as insane and odd, he still insists on doing so. Secondly, he had to justify why the FBI needs to control and hurt him. It is because he had special talents for knowing about the current situation of the People's Republic of China, which FBI needs to know about so as to build up the economy of the United States. Thirdly, the FBI uses various means to assert cognitive control over him, such as with a computer website and virus, radio electronic waves, and even an invisible satellite. As time goes by, the penetrating and controlling power of the FBI increases drastically.

Fourthly, P uses various means to cope with the controlling and manipulating power of the FBI. For example, P may avoid going to any place or encounter any person connected to the letters F, B, and I. He may also wear a special kind of hat that can protect himself from the detection of the FBI's wireless networks. He tried his best to search for any information about the FBI on its web page and even wrote two thousand words on Facebook about how to prevent being watched by FBI agents from the United States.

In more refined terms, the bad others (BO2) planning and conspiring to impose harm on the individual can be further divided into the following:

BO2a = Bad others in social circles
BO2b = Bad others in and out of social circles
BO2c = Bad others not existing and being delusively constructed by others

In P's case, the FBI did not exist in P's social environment; its conspiracy was delusively constructed by P. Thus, it should be BO2c.

These four combinations, in fact, integrate and reinforce one another forming a comprehensive, well-organized, and delusive, paranoid network.

a. *The first one is BS1 + BO1 + GS1.* The individual internalizes the substantially negative comment from the oppressive others (BO1) admitting that he or she is deserving of being punished and oppressed by the bad others (BS1). In doing so, the individual's good self assumes that the fact that one is tolerable, endurable, and surviving (GS1) within this oppression can be concealed and protected.

(Within this mechanism, the individual's paranoid network becomes bigger and bigger).

b. *The second combination is BS2 + BO1 + GS2*. The individual harbors an intense anger and a strong urge to take revenge (BS2). He or she identifies with the substantially oppressive others (BO1). He or she joins with the oppressive others. He or she becomes part of the oppressive group and oppresses others (BS2 + BO1). His or her prevailing anger and hate over being oppressed by others can be transferred and released to those he or she oppresses. In so doing, he or she successful conceals his or her good self (GS2) that does not deserve oppression by others. (*Within this mechanism, the power of the paranoid network becomes more and more powerful).*

c. *The third combination can be BS1 + BO2 + GS1*. The individual internalizes that he or she is bad and deserves punishment (BS1). However, what he or she fears and has internalized is not real. Instead, the bad others are all surrounding the individual (BO2) who are all planning and conspiring together to oppress, to harm, or even to kill the individual. When BS1 and BO2 combine together, the individual harbors a prevailing paranoia that everyone surrounding him or her is conspiring or connected with the paranoid network to harm him or her. The paranoia is greatly intensified by the thinking that he or she is bad and deserves punishment. In thinking like this, he or she actually conceals the paranoia and believes that he or she has special tolerance and coping with the all the torture and oppression (GS1). (*Within this mechanism, the delusive paranoid network grows larger and larger).*

d. *The fourth combination is BS2 + BO2 + GS2*. The individual harbors an intense anger and a strong urge to take revenge (BS2). However, what he or she identifies is not real. Instead, the BO1 is gradually enlarged to an extent that it includes unseen supernatural forces or delusive oppressive others. In forming psychotic delusions and hallucination, he or she joins with the delusive oppressive others (*BS2 + BO2*). His or her prevailing anger and hate from being oppressed by others can be transferred and released to those he or she defends delusively. In doing this, he or she successful conceals the good self (GS2) that does not deserve oppression by others. (*Within this mechanism, the delusive paranoid network becomes more and more delusive and powerful).*

These four combinations can be integrated as shown in Figure 4.

It is clear that these four combinations integrate closely with one another in the formation of the comprehensive, delusive paranoid network. *The first combination (BS1*

+ BO1 + GS1) integrates with the second combination (BS2 + BO1 + GS2) forming a powerful and enlarging paranoid network. These two mechanisms enable the substantially existing bad others (BO1) to become more and more powerful, and more and more people in actual reality are being included in the paranoid network. Also, the first combination with BS1 and GS1 nurtures intense feelings of inferiority, and the second combination with BS2 and GS2 develops anger toward the growing and powerful and delusive paranoid others. Both of these two combinations harbor intense fearful feelings. The mixture of fear, inferiority, and anger make the individual feel very ambivalent and in pain. In fact, these two mechanisms are in conflict with each other. On one hand, the individual feels he or she is bad and deserves to be punished, and he or she is a suffering hero and can tolerate the external punishment from bad others. On the other hand, he or she thinks that he or she is good and should not be punished, and he or she should take revenge on the bad others. All these inner conflicts, pains, and ambivalence cause the individual to focus all of his or her effort and energy on trying to resolve conflict, clarify ambivalence, and search for the means to ease out of his or her inner pain. However, the more he or she does so, the more he or she is being kept within this self constructed, paranoid network, and the more he or she is distant from actual reality.

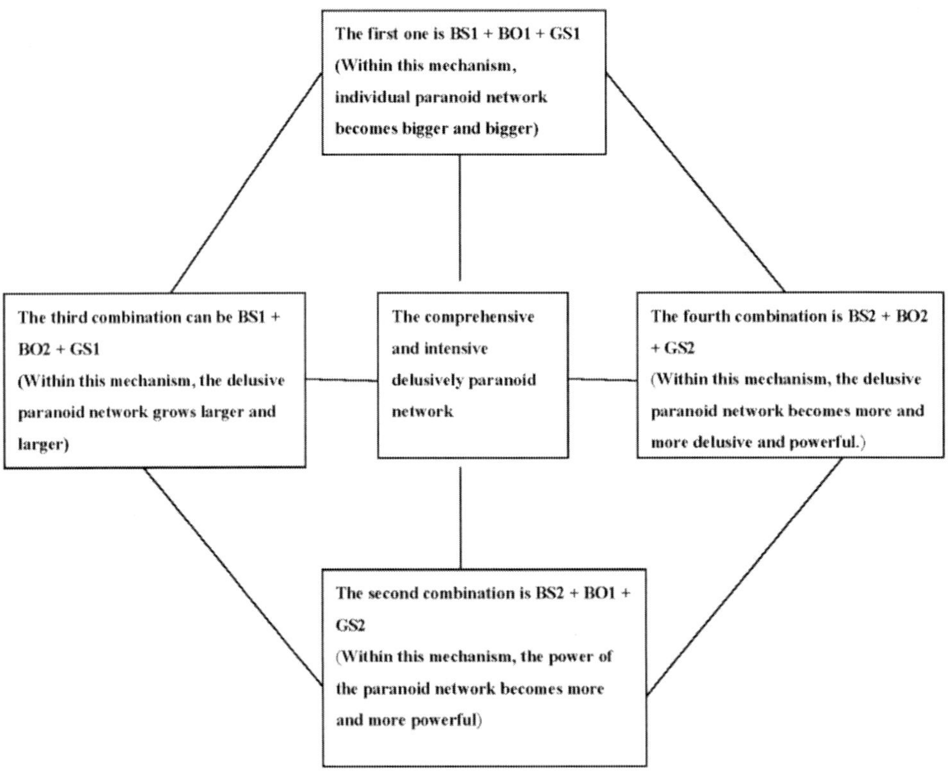

Figure 4. Components and Elements in the Formation of a Comprehensive and Intense delusively Paranoid Network.

The third combination (BS1+ BO2 + GS1) can integrate with the fourth combination (BS2 + BO2 + GS2) nurturing a powerful delusive paranoid network. As the delusive paranoid network grows larger and larger and becomes more and more powerful, BO2 becomes more and more delusive and ambiguous. BO1 implies the bad others is actually existing in related social circles even though they may not be harmful, powerful and over-whelming. However, BO2 simply implies the bad others are not actually existing. They are delusively constructed by the individual. They can be authority but evil figures in the history, supernatural but superstitious evils and demons, secret agents and spies in various countries, forces from outer spaces. Because of delusive and overwhelming power of BO2, individuals harbor both intense and overwhelming senses of inferiority and fear. Also, their internal conflicts between (BS1 + GS1) and (BS2 + GS2) intensify. The more delusive and powerful the bad others are, the more these conflicts prevail. Individuals, at one time, they feel that they are powerful enough to fight back all these delusive bad others. They manifest an intense sense of anger that seems to be quite unreasonable in the eyes of others as all these delusive others are not actually exiting. In extreme cases, such intense anger may even project into those people around that are strangers. At another time, they feel that they are far too weak to fight back in which they manifest an over-whelming sense of fear and inferiority. They may cry for help. They urged to tell people about the delusive paranoid network. They try their best to convince others that they are also under the control of this delusive paranoid network so that other can join them in defending the harm from related objects and persons within the well-organized paranoid network. They hope that people around can be sympathetic with them, understand their pain in being chased and followed by delusive persons and objects in their powerful and delusive paranoid network. They can also attribute recent disasters and bad news happened around the world or in local situation are done by this powerful and delusive network.

The first combination (BS1 + BO1 + GS1) can integrate with the third combination (BS1 + BO2 + GS1). As both combinations consist of the assumption that the individual is worth to be punished (BS1) and he or she is a suffering hero that can tolerate call these suffering and hardship (GS1), there is a strong tendency that the individual tries to build up a strong connection between the bad others that are actually existing within his or her social circle (BO1) with those bad others that are delusively constructed by him or her. For example, if the individual harbors a delusive network of being controlled by FBI in the United States (BO2). Then, he or she assumes that FBI (BO2) not only directly controls him or her but also controls his or her oppressive boss and colleagues (BO1) to exploit him or her. In doing so, his or her delusive but well-organized network becomes bigger and bigger. Gradually, FBI also has a tight connection with people around him or her including his or her relatives, friends, members in the community who reject, exclude, isolate, gossip and criticize him or her.

The second combination (BS2 + BO1 + GS2) can integrate with the fourth combination (BS2 + BO2 + GS2). Similarly with the integration of first combination and third combination, the individual tries to connect BO1 to BO2. However, in the integration of the first and third combinations, in which BS1 is combined with GS1, the well-organized, paranoid network becomes bigger and bigger, and BO1 and BO2 are connected in a way that BO2 becomes larger and larger, from unrelated objects and persons in the individual's own society and finally to unseen ones in other societies or even in religious and superstitious circles or beliefs. In this integration, BO2, the delusive, oppressive others include more and more number of irrelevant persons, events, and objects. However, in the integration of the second and fourth combinations, since it consists of BS2 and GS2, in which his or her urge to take revenge and a sense of perfectionism are projected and combined with BO2, it makes the delusive paranoid network more and more powerful. It can gradually increase from substantially powerful oppressive others, to high supernatural power. For example, the BO1, the oppressive boss of the individual, finally can have connection with the FBI or simply become the FBI, either the FBI is powerful enough to control all people including his boss, or his boss is actually an agent of the FBI. That means, both BO1 and BO2 finally becomes more and more powerful in the well-organized, delusive, paranoid network.

Existential Perspective of Paranoid Delusion in Schizophrenia: The Struggle for Existence and Survival

Existentially speaking, delusive paranoia happens during self splitting, which represents an intense urge for persons with schizophrenia in struggling for existence and survival. According to Laing's (1960) *Divided Self*, it is a struggle for the preservation of one's inner self and identity in the process of self-fragmentation. It is the concealment of the false self embracing the inner self to reach out for other people. Also, the individual's self boundary gets more and more diffused to the extent that the more he or she was urged to reach out for others people, the more he or she felt her being and self being stolen by others. As a consequence, she was continuously and increasingly threatened, hurt, and even diminished by others. The over-whelming fear and urge for existence finally turn into an ontological force for further self splitting and diffusion of the self boundary.

The struggle for existence may be illustrated by the following self narration of a female client with schizophrenia, Rose, as described by Laing (1960).

> My real self is away down—it used to be just at my throat, but now it's gone further down, I am losing myself. It is getter deeper and deeper. I want to tell you two things but

> I am scared. My head is full of thoughts, fears, hates, jealousies. My head can't grasp them. I can't hold to them. (Laing, 1960: 151)

Rose, in this state of self splitting, deeply felt that she was gradually losing her own inner self and identity. She wanted to reach out to other people, but the more she did this, the more she felt she was diminishing and suspicious of others' threats in stealing something from her.

> It was a most significant fact that the more she felt she could reach other people, that other people could not reach her, and the more she felt herself to be in a world of her own, -they can't get in and I can't get out' the more this private and closed world of hers became invaded by psychotic dangers from outside. She becomes more suspicious that of other people and began to hide things in her locker; she had a notion that some person was stealing things from her. She would check her handbag and personal possession frequently to make sure that she had not been robbed of anything. This paradox of being more withdrawn and at the same time more vulnerable found its clearest expression in the statement that she was murdering herself on the one hand, and her fear that self-image be lost or stolen on the other hand, and her self might be lost or stolen on the other, and her fear that her 'self' might be lost or stolen on the other. She had only other people's thought and could think only what other people had said. (Laing, 1960:152)

In Rose's case, the process in the formation of paranoia could be roughly described in the following stages:

1. As being separated by the false self in contacting the outside world so as to preserve the integrity of the inner self.
2. Her inner self became more and more empty and lonely and withered.
3. She harbored a strong urge to reach out to other people. In doing so, she also feared that the wholeness of her inner self would be threatened.
4. She constantly felt that she could not reach out to other people, and other people could not get in.
5. She was kept within a closed ward that was very private and with a constant danger of being invaded by others.
6. The strong urge to reach out to others gradually turned into a high sensitivity to others' ideas, thoughts, and words.
7. The fear of being invaded gradually became a suspicion that part of her inner self would be stolen by others.
8. The stolen part was replaced by others' thoughts, ideas and others' speaking.
9. As time went by, her paranoia was well-developed in a pseudo system that her actual inner self (in terms of identity and image) was in fact being murdered by, or was murdering, others. What was replaced inside were only others' ideas,

identity, and thinking and saying. That meant that she was, in fact, being controlled by others, both mentally and physically.

Within an existential perspective, to protect the inner self from being known, penetrated, and stolen by others, paranoia in persons with schizophrenia can be manifested in many ways:

1. Someone gained control of me, and they put themselves inside me.
2. I murdered myself so that no one can murder me. Now I am immortal.
3. Be aggressive and destructive toward others so that others cannot attack or destroy me when others fail to discover my real inner self. (In the former, the individual wants to keep away those rejecting him or her. In the latter, the individual wants to get protection from supportive others).
4. Play tricks on others or pretend to be someone else so that no one can really understand me.

All these can be shown in the following case illustration described by Laing (1960):

Play tricks on doctors so to avoid being understood and captured by others.

Patients laugh and posture when they see through the doctor who says he will help but really won't or can't. Posturing, for a girl, is seductive, but it also an effort to distract the doctor from all her pelvic functions. The patients try to divert and distract him. (Laing, 1960:165)

Be aggressive toward someone the individual wants to get close to,

Patients' kicks and scream and fight when they are not sure the doctor can see them. It is the most terrifying feeling to realize that the doctor cannot see the real you, that he cannot understand what you feel and that he is just going ahead with his own ideas. (Laing, 1960: 166)

Someone gained control of me: they put themselves on me.

The paranoid has specific persecutors. Someone is against him. There is a plot on foot to steal his brain. A machine is concealed in the wall of his bedroom which emit mind rays to soften his brain or to send an electric shock through him while he is asleep. (Laing, 1960: 60)

I have murdered myself so that no one can harm me, and now I am immortal.

The schizophrenic who says he has committed suicide… . In fact, he makes many statement that of this order, which may be expressly intended as snares for those he regards as idiots and the world… it would probably be a complete non sequitur to attempt to kill his self… . That is his self is virtually unembodied. The self is probably conceived as immortal or make of nearly imperishable non-bodily substance. (Laing, 1960:149)

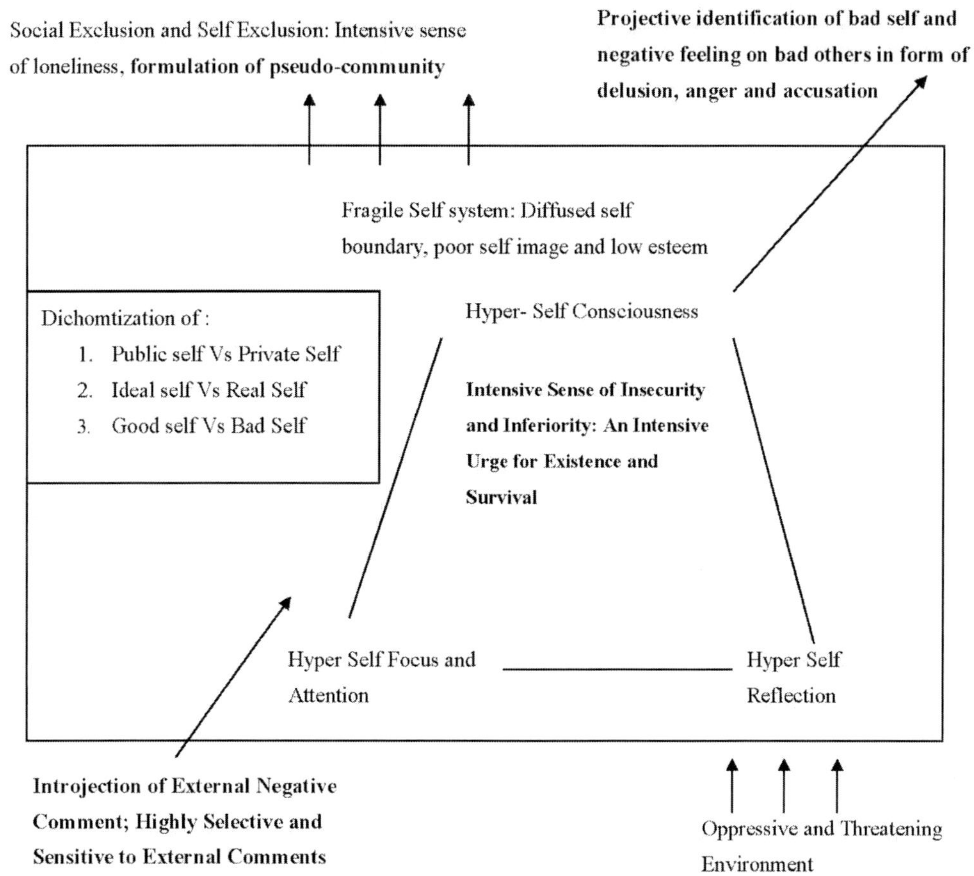

Inter-related mechanisms in **Projective Identification** among bad self (BS1, BS2), good self (GS1, GS2) and good other (BO1, BO2)

The first one is BS1 + BO1 + GS1 (the paranoid network becomes bigger and bigger)

The second one is BS2 + BO1 + GS2 (the power of the paranoid network becomes more and more powerful)

The third one can be BS1 + BO2 + GS1 (the delusive paranoid network grows larger and larger)

The fourth one is BS2 + BO2 + GS2 (the delusive paranoid network becomes more and more delusive and powerful.)

(BS1: worth to be punished by others: BS2: take revenge to bad others: GS1: suffering hero, toleration of others' torture GS2: being perfect should not be criticized: BO1: substantial existing oppression: BO2: Planned but not existing oppression)

Figure 5. Mechanism in Paranoid/Persecutory Delusion

Various mechanisms and theoretical underpinnings of a delusive, well-organized, paranoid network are illustrated in Figure 5.

The Process of Self-Fragmentation and Paranoid Delusions and Hallucinations

In the previous chapter, the process of self-fragmentation was mentioned. This can also appear in the development of paranoid delusions. In the process of self fragmentation, there are seven stages:

Stage 1: Dissociation (dissociation of mind and body, past and present, inner and outer, and self and others).

Stage 2: Splitting occurs when dissociation fails (good and bad self, embodied self and disembodied self, and true and false self).

Stage 3: Molar fragmentation of personality (breaking into more than one partial self system within which may or may not be conflicting with another).

Stage 4: Molecular fragmentation of thoughts within each split/fractured partial self system (confusion of thoughts, perceptions, and interpretation within every fractured sub-self system).

Stage 5: Further fragmentation of all these divided and fractured partial self systems (Each fractured partial self system may have its own delusive identity, boundary, and interpretation of external reality).

Stage 6: There are spontaneous and continuous conflicts and ambiguity within and between these divided and fractured partial self systems (The individual may shift from one delusive identity to another, have a constant manifestation of running tracks of auditory hallucination with one arguing with another, with thought insertion and thought broadcasting).

Stage 7: The fragmentation of all these partial self systems can be continuous until reparation is impossible. (The individual is in a state of severe mental confusion and has a very poor sense of reality that may lead to psychiatric emergency and possible harm to oneself and another).

It is clear that within the development of paranoid delusion and hallucinations, the individual's self-identity is still valid and existing. That means that paranoid delusions and hallucinations only exist in Stage 1: dissociation, Stage 2: splitting, Stage 3: molar fragmentation of personality, and Stage 4: molecular fragment of thoughts within each split/fractured partial self system. In other words, Stage 5 to Stage 7 should not exist in paranoid delusions and hallucination since the individual still has a clear and valid self-identity. It is clear that in stage dissociation, paranoid delusions and hallucinations do not occur. Facing a very oppressive environment and social exclusion, the individual feels very stressed and anxious but only tries to repress these negative feelings of being criticized, oppressed, abused and bullied by others. However, as all these negative comments and the oppression prevail, individuals can no longer tolerate them. As mentioned by Laing (1960), apart from implosion, engulfment, and depersonalization also continuously occur in the oppressive environment.

As a consequence, individuals enter into the *second stage of splitting in which paranoid delusions and hallucinations are formed to cope with the spontaneously oppressive environment.* In this process, the individual's self system is split into a good and bad self, and the perception on others is split into good and bad others (Bion, 1984 & Klein, 1946). It is also split into unembodied self and inner self. The individual begins to feel and perceive that people around are gossiping and intending to hurt him or her.

In Stage 3 there is molar fragmentation of personality in which the split self system further breaks into one partial self system in which both the good self bad self is broken into two partial subsystems. The bad self is broken into BS1 (worth to be punished by others), and BS2 (taking revenge to bad others). The good self is also broken into two partial subsystems. They are GS1 (suffering hero with toleration of others' torture), GS2 (being perfect and should not be criticized). In the same way, the bad others are also broken into two partial sub-systems. They are BO1 (substantially existing oppressive others) and BO2 (those plan to insert oppression). In paranoid delusion, the moral fragmentation of the personality enables partial self system combined together in two forms. The first one is BS1 + BO1 + GS1 in which the paranoid network becomes bigger and bigger. The individual feels more and more people are involved in the paranoid network. For example, an individual has paranoid delusion that her boss is oppressing him or her. Under the influence of this mechanism, first, there may be his boss and his or her colleagues. Later, other people in the building of his or her company are also included in the paranoid pseudo community. Finally, even people in the street may be cooperated or controlled by his boss to oppress him or her. The second one is BS2 + BO1 + GS2 in which the power of the paranoid network becomes more and more powerful. For instance, for the individual with a paranoid delusion that his or her boss is oppressing him or her, at first they can only impose harm on him or her in the company. Under the influence of this mechanism, the boss and their colleagues becomes more and more powerful. They can control other people everywhere to impose oppression on him or her. Within these two combinations, the individual's paranoid delusion and hallucinations grow tremendously. In auditory hallucinations, not only one voice is heard by the individual, but other voices are heard also. The two-self, partial subsystems of good self and bad self as well the two types of combination can result in various kind of voices. These voices (auditory hallucinations) represent various parts of the self system. They can dialogue with one another. In some cases, they can conflict with one another. For example, the individual with an auditory hallucination occurs that his boss and colleagues controlling people around him or her want to impose harm and oppression on him or her, he or she may hear several tracks of voices. One track says that he or she is the bad one who should be punished by other. This voice may resemble his or her boss or colleague or someone who is sent by them. Another track says that he or she is indeed the good one who should not be oppressed, and those who oppress or plan to oppress should be punished and killed. This voice may resemble his or her significant others or someone else who shows support for him or her in his or her life or someone he or she admires.

In Stage 4, molecular fragmentation occurs in which the individual's partial self system is further fractured. The split self system, the bad and good self as well as the split external environment, the good and bad others, also have other combinations, making the split partial self system combine in a very confused ways. In Stage 3, within the two combined mechanisms, BS1 + BO1 + GS1 (I am worth to be punished by others, but I am a suffering hero in facing substantially external oppression), and BS2 + BO1 + GS2 (I am perfect and should not be criticized by others; thus I have to take revenge on those who actually oppressed me), the bad other is actually present or has oppressed the individual. The fear of these bad others grows tremendously, in a way the bad other tries to control unrelated persons around him or her to oppress or abuse the individual. However, in Stage 4, these bad others are not actually existing or they have never done harm to the individual in actual reality. Individuals only perceive that these delusive others have done so. For example, in the above-mentioned case, the individual's paranoid delusion shifts from his or her oppressive boss and colleagues to other delusive and powerful figures. The individual may finally conclude that his boss and the colleagues who are powerful enough to control the people around him to oppress him are not normal persons. They are, in fact, spies sent by the president of the US to invade China. That means, they are agents of the FBI or intelligence agents from the US. In other words, the substantially existing bad others (BO1) turn into imaginative bad others (BO2). Once, this delusive conclusion is anchored and presumed, the third and the fourth mechanisms prevail. They are BS1 + BO2 + GS1 (the delusive paranoid network grows larger and larger) and BS2 + BO2 + GS2 (the delusive paranoid network becomes more and more delusive and powerful). For the third mechanism (BS1 + BO2 + GS1), the individual assumes that the FBI controls his boss and colleagues (or his colleagues and boss are actually FBI) who control him. They try to find out any wrong deeds being committed by him. In that situation, the individual feels fearful and is afraid of the FBI, thinking they are able to find out wrong deeds committed by others. The only thing that can support him or her to survive for the intrusion of bad others are the presumption that he or she is a suffering hero or heroine (GS1) who can tolerate any sufferings imposed by others. Regarding the fourth mechanism (BS2 + BO2 + GS2), the individual simply believes the FBI is everywhere, and he or she is very angry with the FBI who dress or appear as his or her boss and colleagues, and he or she is perfect and does not desert to avoid fault finding by them (GS2). Thus, he or she wants to be take revenge on others (BS2). In doing so, he or she projects his or her anger and urges revenge on the bad others. As the bad others are illusively existing, so is the projection of the bad self. Thus, under the influence of the third and fourth mechanisms, the individual undergoes a molecular fragmentation of his or her thoughts with each split partial self system, in which there is confusion of thought, perception, and interpretation within every fractured self subsystem. In other words, both the bad others and the individual's own good and bad self systems become delusive and unreal with prevailing conflicts. There may be two voices arguing with one another. One voice representing the FBI claiming various shortfalls and deficits in the individual and claiming that the individual needs to be punished. Another voice represents the good self system, claiming that the individual is perfect and needs to be protected. Both voices are far more delusive and confused than those voices induced by the first and second mechanisms.

Dilemmas in Self-Fragmentation and Paranoid Delusion and Hallucinations

In the previous chapters, there are three dynamic forces, self splitting versus self cohesion, self concealment versus self visibility, and self destruction and self preservation.

Within the above-mentioned four mechanisms of paranoid delusions and hallucinations, these three dynamic forces manifest fully.

Self-Splitting versus Self-Cohesion Dynamic Force in Paranoid Delusion and Hallucination

Self-splitting versus self-cohesion exists in the form of pull and push forces. The individual needs to split his or her self system so as to maintain a fragile or even delusive cohesion in facing the extremely oppressive social environment. As mentioned in the foregoing figure, within paranoid delusion there is an intense dichotomization of the public self versus the private self, the ideal self and the real self, as well as the good self and the bad self. In normal circumstance, the individual is sensitive enough to accept that there are differences between actual and real self, private and public self, as well as good and bad self. Within a supportive social environment, he or she is also able to harmonize this dichotomization by trying to be consistent in word and deed, past and present, expectation and actual performance. However, within a very oppressive environment, individuals are spontaneously and continuously attacked by severely negative comments. All these introjected negative comments and threats from the external environment greatly intensify one's negative senses of public self, real self, and bad self. All these negative senses are very intolerable for the individual. They need to bulk up their positive senses of good self, actual self, and private self to overcome them. As a consequence, the dichotomization among good and bad self, public and private self, as well as actual and real self, may be intensified to a degree leading to self splitting. That means the whole self system is split into two contrary partial systems. One represents the negative public self, the bad self, and the unacceptable real self (P1). Another one represents the good private, the ideal and good self (P2). These two partial self systems can no longer be harmonious with one another as individuals' ego-functioning, and the sense of reality deteriorated under the influence of the spontaneously and intensely oppressive social environment. They are antagonistic to one another. Thus, to maintain inner harmony and consolidation of the self system, individuals need to project the partial self system with the negative public self, the bad self, and the real self (P1) outward. The best way to do so is to make P1 identify with external, oppressive others. Unconsciously, instead of admitting P1 as a valid, partial self system, individuals turn P1 into paranoid delusion and hallucination, saying and feeling that external oppressive others are following, chasing, criticizing and/or planning to hurt him or her. That means these individuals are engaged in a self splitting versus self cohesion dynamic force. On the one hand, P1 and P2 are split into two antagonistic, partial self systems. P1 (the negative public self, bad self, and unacceptable, real self) is antagonistic with P2 (the private self, good self, and ideal self). On the other hand, the individual needs to maintain the fragile internal cohesion and solidarity of the internal self system by project P1 outward with identification or merging with the bad and oppressive others. However, the projective identification of P1 made P2 became more and more isolated from external, oppressive reality. In that sense, P2 needs to interact with P1 so as to maintain contact with the reality so to decrease its isolation and exclusion from reality and external environment. In doing so, the splitting and conflicts between P1 and P2 intensified. For individuals who have auditory hallucinations, they may say that they have two voices, one good and one bad arguing with one another. The bad voice is always P1, and the good voice is always P2.

Self-Concealment versus Self-Visibility in Paranoid Delusion and Hallucination

As mentioned in a previous chapter, within the dilemma of self- concealment versus self-visibility, individuals use paranoid delusions and hallucinations as means of concealing their real selves from the very oppressive, social environment. In the delusive, paranoid state, individuals are being obsessively betrayed and followed by others. They are deeply afraid of being visible. They try hard to hide and become invisible so that they will not be hurt by the bad others who exist everywhere. In facing prevailing paranoid delusion, the individual tries every means to escape from oppressive others including avoiding going outside, seeing people, hiding with all sorts of measures to avoid being hurt and harmed by the delusive others. All these concealment measures are continuously modified according the self constructed natures of the oppressive others. For example, if the oppressive others are very powerful in Internet control, the individual may avoid using computers or use some anti-measures to block Internet intrusion. If the oppressive others are present in the neighborhood or in the working environment, the individual may persistently avoid going there. If the individual suddenly discovers the people around in the physical environment are planning or gossiping about him or her. He or she leaves the physical environment immediately despite any ongoing activities and others' response.

In the formation of paranoid delusions and hallucination, projective identification is a form of normal, social camouflage in which individuals identify with their oppressive others. The more individuals identify with their oppressive others, the more individuals conceal themselves from oppressive others. However, in doing so, the more splitting individuals' self system becomes. That means, P1 (the negative public self, bad self and unacceptable real self) in connection with the bad others (BS) in paranoid delusions and hallucinations can serve as an excellent concealment of P2 (the private self, good self and ideal self). P1 tries to be visible in terms of relating to the oppressive and bad others.

Within the projective identification mechanism, as the oppression prevails, it significantly splits the integrity and cohesion of individual's self system. The merging of bad self and bad others with the protection of good self implies that there is a constant splitting of the self system. The opponent projects his bad self BS1 (deserving of punishment by others) or BS2 (taking revenge on others) by merging them with BO1 (substantially oppression) or BO2 (planned but not existing oppression). It is a kind of camouflage concealment of GS1 (the suffering hero) or GS2 (the status of being perfect that should not be criticized), but it is also a prevailing split in the individual's self system. The more the individual leans on camouflage concealment with the merging of the bad others, the more his or her self system is split, and the more diffused his or her self-identity and boundary becomes. In addition, his or her sense of reality and ego functioning to cope with stress and oppression also deteriorate accordingly.

Self-Destruction and Self-Preservation in Paranoid Delusion and Hallucination

The third dilemma is self-destruction and self-preservation. This dilemma starts with the individual's inherent instinct to destruct and to preserve one's own self and others in facing danger and threat in the external environment. Individuals with schizophrenia are heavily involved in a delusive self destruction mechanism in which they try to destruct themselves mentally so that the oppressive others cannot destruct them. It is clear that paranoid delusions and hallucinations provide a powerful mechanism to prevent being destructed by oppressive others by assuming that they are everywhere, they are powerful, and they always intend to impose threat and destruction on the individual. That means, over-whelming paranoid delusion and hallucination are, in fact, a self protective mechanism in which the individual with schizophrenia tries to protect him- or herself from possible threatening others. It is an assumption of the destructive power of bad and oppressive others within the immediate social and physical environment. It can both be BO1(substantially existing bad and oppressive others) or BO2 (planned but not existing oppressive others). However, within these self protective mechanisms, the individual with schizophrenia tends to focus all his or her attention and exhaust his or her psychic and physical energy in assuming the overwhelming presence and destructive power of oppressive others. As a consequence, his or her normal responses, ability, attention, and ego strengths in dealing with events, persons, and objects in actual reality hinder, wither, and deteriorate accordingly. This is an indirect self destruction process. Finally, the individual's inner capacity and strength to harmonize the discrepancies between P1 (negative public self, the bad self, and the unacceptable real self) and P2 (the good private, the ideal, and good self) is deeply hindered and destructed. To maintain the fragile inner balance, the individual may need to minimize all these inner conflicts and dilemmas. Within this fragile inner balance, the easiest way is to destruct one partial self system so as to maintain the stability of the whole self system. Within the mechanism of projective identification, individuals tend to destruct P1 (negative public self, the bad self, and the unacceptable real self) by projecting it outward by merging with the BO1 and BO2. In doing so, individuals can retain P2 (the good private, the ideal, and the good self) within the self system. As a consequence, the fragile balance of the self system can be preservation. However, the projection and destruction of P1 also diminishes the individual's sense of reality (the negative public self and real self). That means individuals, within the prevailing paranoid delusion and hallucination, have their own sense of reality and acceptance of their own deficiency and deteriorate accordingly.

CONCLUSION

In conclusion, this chapter is a full description of the related theoretical underpinnings of paranoia as well as of paranoid schizophrenia. Paranoia can be understood as a self awareness of being watched, a negative self consciousness and self reflection, a self defense against an external threat, a self retreat, an intense manifestation of negative emotions, such as sense of inferiority and fear. In paranoid delusion in people with schizophrenia, paranoia is further developed into a full-blown, persecutory, distorted reality in which the individual feels that he or she is fully threatened by surrounding negative persons or even a network. There are different perspectives in articulating paranoid delusion, namely a cognitive and interpersonal perspective, a psychodynamic perspective in terms of Sullivan's paranoid dynamism, projective identification, and an existential perspective in terms of Laing's divided self. In fact, paranoid delusion in schizophrenia also manifests the dilemma in self-fragmentation and self integration in terms of self concealment versus self visibility, self destruction versus self preservation, and self splitting versus self cohesion. All these have strong implications for the recovery of people with paranoid delusion in schizophrenia.

REFERENCES

Bentall, R. P., Kinderman, P., & Kaney, S. (1994). "The self, attributional processes and abnormal beliefs: Toward a model of persecutory delusion," *Behavior Research and Therapy*, 32:331–341.

Bion, W. R. (1984) *Second Thought: Selected Papers on Psycho-Analysis*, New York: Jason Aronson.

Campbell, M. L. C. & Morrison, A. P. (2007). "The subjective experience of paranoia: Comparing the experiences of patients with psychosis and individuals with no psychiatric history," *Clinical Psychology and Psychotherapy*, 14: 63–77.

Fenigstein, A., & Vanable, P. A. (1992). "Paranoia and self consciousness," *Journal of Personality and Social Psychology*, 62: 129–134.

Freeman, D. (2007). "Suspicious mind: The psychology of persecutory delusion," *Clinical Psychology Review*, 27: 425–457.

Freeman, D. & Gartey, P. A. (2000). "Comments on the contents of persecutory delusions: Does the definition needs clarification?," *British Journal of Clinical Psychology*, 39: 407–414.

Freeman, D., Garety, P. A., Kuipers, E., Fowlers, D. & Bebbington, P. E. (2002). "A cognitive model of persecutory delusions," *British Journal of Clinical Psychology*, 41: 331–347.

Kinderman, P. & Bentall, R. P. (1997). "Casual attributions in paranoia: Internal, personal and situational attributions for negative events," *Journal of Abnormal Psychology*, 106: 341–345.

Kinderman, P. & Bentall, R. P. (2000). "Self-discrepancies and causal attribution: Studies of hypothesized relationship," *British Journal of Clinical Psychology*, 39:255–273.

Klein, M. (1946). "Notes on some schizoid mechanisms," *International Journal of Psychoanalysis,* 27: 99–110.

Laing R. D., (1960). *The Divided Self*, London: Tavistock Publication.

Missinner, W.W. (1978). *The Paranoid Process*, New York: Jason Aronson.

Paranoid Network (2006). *Hearing Voices,* UK: Paranoid Network.

Rethink Mental Illness (2006) *Paranoid Delusion*. New York: Rethink Mental Illness.

Sullivan. H. S. (1956). *Clinical Studies in Psychiatry*, New York: W.W. Norton & Company.

von Gemmingen, M. J. Sullivan, B. F., & Pomerantz, A. M. (2003). "Investigating the relationship between boredom, proneness, paranoia and self consciousness," *Personality and Individual Difference*, 34: 907–919.

Chapter 3

SELF-FRAGMENTATION AND SELF-INTEGRATION IN GRANDIOSE DELUSIONS AND HALLUCINATIONS: INTERPRETATION AND RECOVERY

INTRODUCTION

Grandiose delusion and hallucinations are common among persons with schizophrenia. Very often, a person with schizophrenia may even develop a grandiose identity that he or she is, in fact, a rich man or woman, a hero or heroine, and even god or goddess. Combined with a delusive identity is also active hallucination that he or she is delusively powerful, influential, and competent in many aspects of life. Many persons with schizophrenia, in their actual state of mind, develop a bizarre, grandiose identity. Even after they have recovered from a psychosis, they urge a change in their own names to some bizarre names that are full of power and symbolic meanings. Compared with persecutory delusion and hallucination, grandiose ones are less studied and researched by related scholars and practitioners. In this chapter the writer tries to relate grandiose delusion and hallucination to Kohut's self object relationship and to Laing's (1960) existential orientations.

From Grandiose Self to Grandiosity in Mental Illness

Grandiose Self in Normal Life Development

Kohut, in his self object relationship, affirmed grandiosity, in terms of grandiose self, as an important element in the process of self development

> The term "grandiose self will" be used henceforth in the present work (instead of the previously employed "narcissistic self" to designate the grandiose and exhibitionistic structure which is the counterpart for the idealized parent imago. Since the self is, in general, cathected with narcissistic libido, the term, "narcissistic self" may with some justification be looked upon as a tautology. My preference for the term "grandiose self" is, however, based on the fact that it has greater evocating power than the term "narcissistic self," and I am not discarding the latter primary on theoretic grounds. (Kohut, 1986: 26)

> Kohut's conceptualization of one of the two original attempt to restore the disrupted state of primary narcissistic bliss. Characterized by exhibitionism, expansiveness and a sense of omnipotence, this unconscious configuration changes from in the course of normal development, ultimately fueling the pole ambitions. (Siegel, 1996: 204)

Kohut (1986) affirmed that in the formation of a grandiose self, the child encounters the following stages of development:

1. Infant is able to experience infant's *primary narcissistic bliss,*
2. For various reasons, there are unavoidable disruption due to caretaker's failed ministration.
3. The child engages in attempts to restore lost, happy experiences in primary narcissism
4. The child tries to formulate an *idealized parental imago* (you are perfect, and I am part of you) from his or her significant others (omnipotent others). In doing so, he or she is able to experience idealizing narcissism, internalize it, and create as his or her own *ideal.*
5. At the same time, the child tries to formulate his or her *grandiose self* (I am perfect). In doing so, he or she is able to have exhibitionistic narcissism. It is then modified and integrated into his or her personality as his or her own *ambitions* (Siegel, 1996: 68)

That means, the child needs to mirror and model their idealized parental imago as his or her own ideals. They should internalize these ideals to be his or her own ambitions. In doing so, he or she tries to actualize all these ideals as his or her own attributes. Siegel summarized these two important features as follows:

> In Kohut's schema the grandiose self is the result of the child's second attempt to regain the lost blissful state by creating a sense of perfection within the self. In this effort, all imperfection is assigned to the world outside. These two configurations, the idealized parental imago and the grandiose self, are part of two equally weighted, simultaneously occurring, streams of maturing narcissism . . . omnipotence, grandiosity, and exhibitionistic narcissism are the features of the grandiose self. These features undergo transformation when the child's grandiosity is accepted and enjoyed by the parents. When the demand for an echo to its feelings of expansiveness and unlimited power are responded in a favorable way, the child eventually relinquishes its crude exhibitionistic demands and grandiose fantasies and accepts its limitations. (Siegel, 1996: 87)

That means each individual child needs to model the parental imago to construct his or her grandiose self. Then his or her grandiosity can undergo a proper transformation and becomes an ingredient for him or her to construct a healthy self system. According to Kohut, the transformation of narcissism or grandiosity into an acceptable self system that includes the following features:

1. Creativity: The creative part becomes part of the self. A creative individual embraces the child-like capacity to play imaginatively within his or her surroundings.
2. Empathy: The first perception of the feelings of others comes from the view that the world is an extension of the self. This prepares the self for the recognition of an experience similar to one's own. Empathy, in the recognition of experiences similar to one's own, is the way in which people gather psychological information about each other.
3. Transience: This is the acceptance of one's mortality. It requires one to abandon the insistence upon omnipotence and accept one's impermanence. It is accompanied by a high form of narcissism that contains a quiet pride, even superiority, in having a knowledge unshared with the majority.
4. Humor: This is a transformation of narcissism and not merely an expression of denial; it is also a means to attain transience. It contains a sense of quiet inner triumph, mixed with an undeniable melancholy, that differs from the picture of fragmentary or defensive grandiosity and elation.
5. Wisdom: This is letting go of narcissistic delusions and acceptance of the inevitability of death. In later life, it is an amalgam that includes a stable attitude of the self toward life and toward the world. It includes the ideals of youth with a good maturity in acceptance of transience with humor and the limits of one's power. (Kohut, 1996: 270; Siegel, 1996: 62-3)

In facing the construction of the grandiose self by internalization of the idealized parental imago, individuals may face many discrepancies and conflicts between actual reality and expectation, self perception, and other perceptions, as well as interpretation and experiences. All these discrepancies and conflicts may hinder the internalization of the idealized parental imago in the grandiose self as well as the transformation of the grandiose self into a functional and realistic self system, including a self boundary, self-image, and self-identity. To settle all these discrepancies and conflicts, several tasks need to be accomplished. The first is to set realistic boundary to the grandiose by its own limits. The second should be development of feelings and interpretation of others' needs and presence. The third should be the smooth and constructive acceptance of one's limits and constraints. Finally, there should be continuous constructive and healthy development of the self system. All these mechanisms are shown in Kohut's (1986) five mechanisms. Having creativity and wisdom combine together implies that individual's self becomes more and more mature in including his or her past experiences the idealized parental imago, adjusting his unfulfilled ideals and imaginations on one hand and harboring a continuous urge to actualize his or her ideal and aspiration on the other hand. Within this attunement and continuing of one's aspiration and imagination, the individual is able to accept own capacity and power. Empathy is important; while the individual's grandiose self is nurtured by its primary narcissism, he or she is able to focus on others' needs and rights. That means the individual begins to understand that he or she is not the only focus in the social context. While he or she actualizes his or her own needs and aspirations, he or she also has to understand and fulfill others' needs and right. In doing so, one needs to set boundary and limits. It should be a full articulation of one's own moral responsibility and mandate within one's own family, community, and society. Within this process, the individual's grandiose self is gradually restructured within their own moral responsibilities and others' expectation. Grandiosity creates a sense of superiority in terms of one's self competence and confidence in being a responsible, contributing and disciplined member in his or her family, community, and society. The setting of one's moral limits, being empathic to others; continuous self development; and adjustment of one's aspiration should be a smooth and natural process, within which humor is crucial for the individual to achieve a sense of quiet, inner triumph. That means humor is a means for the individual to dissolve all unhappy feelings and unreachable expectations and the lowering of grandiosity to reality. In fact, humor, empathy, transience, wisdom, creativity all work together in helping the individual to transform his or her grandiose self into a realistic and mature self system. In doing so, his or her former idealized parental imago also decreases from omnipotence to normality and inadequacy. The individual begins to realize more and more the constraints and inadequacy of their significant others. Thus, to enhance upfront their self-image and identity, he or she needs to seek another idealized parental imago and build up another grandiose self. Then, this grandiose self needs another transformation process to transform the grandiosity into a mature and realistic self system. That means the idealized parental imago and the grandiose self and self transformation is an ongoing self development in one's own life. This process is represented Figure 6.

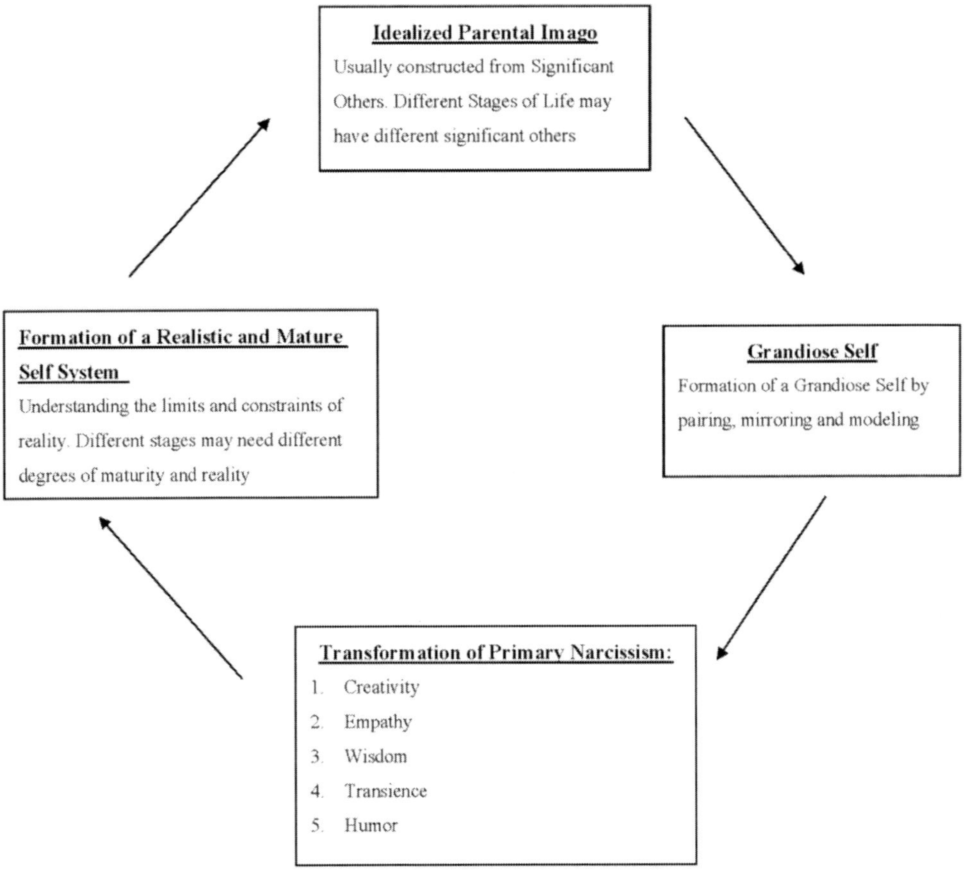

Figure 6. The Developmental Process of the Self System from Primary Narcissism.

Grandiosity: Natures and Components

Grandiosity occurs commonly in many types of mental illness including schizophrenia, mania, and narcissistic personality disorder and also in antisocial personality and histrionic personality disorder. It is defined as:

> It refers to an unrealistic sense of superiority, a sustained view of oneself as better than others that causes the narcissist to view others with disdain or as inferior. It also refers to a sense of uniqueness, the belief that few others have in common with oneself and that one can only be understood by a few or very special people. (Wikipedia, 2007)

The grandiosity section of the Diagnostic Interview for Narcissism (DIN) (Second edition) is as follows:

1. The person exaggerates talents, capacity, and achievements in an unrealistic way.
2. The person believes in her or his invulnerability or does not recognize his or her limitations.
3. The person has grandiose fantasies.
4. The person believes that he or she does not need other people.
5. The person regards him- or herself as unique or special when compared to other people.
6. The person regards him- or herself as generally superior to other people.
7. The person behaves self-centeredly and/or self-referentially.
8. The person appears or behaves in a boastful or pretentious way (Gunderson, Ronningstam & Bodkin, 1990: 670).

That means there are three crucial elements in grandiosity. The first one is *superiority*. The second one is *self-centeredness*. The third one is *related fantasy*. These three crucial elements related to one another form grandiosity. Each of these three elements consists of an unresolved complex. In the sense of *superiority*, the individual actually harbors intense sense of inferiority. He or she may need the sense of superiority to cover up and conceal his or her sense of inferiority. Within the sense of *self-centeredness*, the individual *feels deeply insecure and being threatened*. Thus, he or she is very sensitive to others' comment, criticism, and rejection. The individual is self involved in related fantasy. The *self absorption* in fantasy implies that the individual intends to detach from external reality. That means, the *external reality is fearful, threatening, and oppressive*. The individual needs self constructed fantasy to ensure his or her own values of existence and self integrity. These three elements intermingle and reinforce with one another. The more one indulges in his or her inferior and superior complex, the more the individual becomes self centered and feels insecure, as well as the more one becomes absorbed in his or her self constructed fantasy and detachment from oppressive reality.

Grandiosity in Mania, Narcissistic Personality Disorder, and Other Mental Illness

Within the above-mentioned three complexes are superiority versus inferiority, self centeredness and a sense of insecurity, as well as related fantasy and detachment from reality. These three complexes are fueled by the formation of the grandiose self and the problem in making the transformation of primary narcissism. The complexity (degrees, intensity, duration, stability, and content) of grandiosity can be influenced by the following:

1. Line and Context of Reality
2. Self Control Mechanism
3. Meaning and Function
4. Concerned Self-identity
5. Related Action and Ambition
6. Availability of Idealized Parental Imago and Self-Objects (significant others)

That means the three complexes—inferiority versus superiority, detachment from reality versus related fantasy, and a sense of insecurity versus self centeredness—all influenced by line and a context of reality, self control mechanism, meaning and function of grandiosity, self identity, related action in actualizing ambition, and aspiration as well as the availability of significant others. The relationship between the complexity of grandiosity and the above-mentioned factors can be shown in Figure 7.

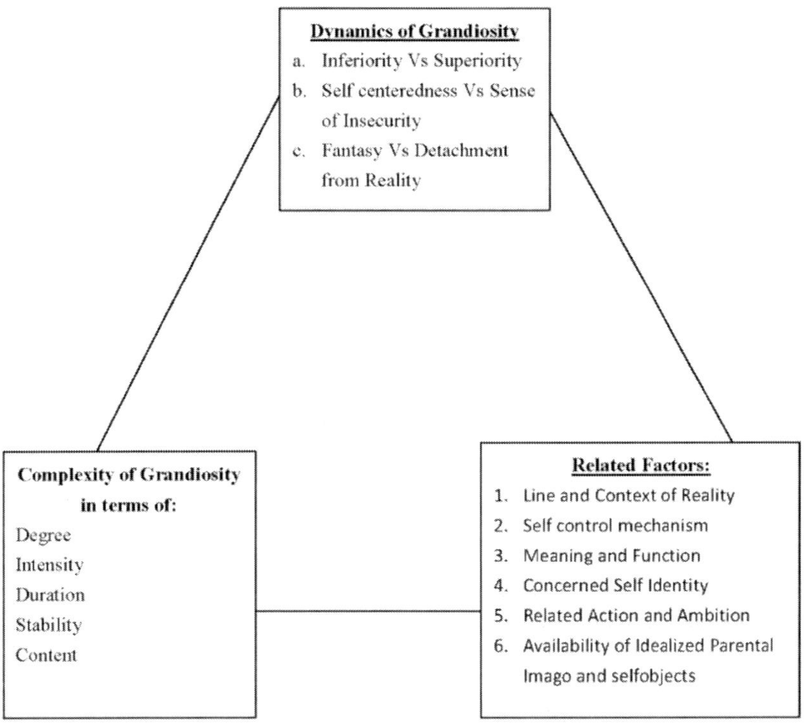

Figure 7. Complexity of Grandiosity and Related Factors

All these factors can be grouped into two main kinds. The first kind is minimizing factors of grandiosity. It can be good sense of reality, good self control mechanism, poor meaning and function of grandiosity, concrete and meaningful ways to actualize one's ambition, and availability of idealized parental imago. All these factors enable the individual to undergo transformation process into maturity. They also enable the individual to resolve dynamics between inferiority versus superiority, self-centeredness versus sense of security, as well as fantasy versus detachment from reality. The second kind is maximizing factors of grandiosity. This include poor self control mechanism, unavailability of idealized parental imago, poor sense of reality, unrealistic, unhealthy or even imaginative ways to actualize one's ambition. All these factors actually maximize the dynamics between inferiority versus superiority, fantasy versus detachment from reality, and self- centeredness versus sense of security. As a consequence, grandiosity tends to increase drastically. Also, individual's ability to undergo transformation mechanism is also difficult.

Within the complexity of grandiosity, the occurrence of mental illness can be due to intensification of three types of dilemmas in grandiosity.

Type A: inferiority versus superiority
Type B: sense of insecurity versus self-centeredness
Type C: detachment from reality versus related fantasy

It seems that mania can be a high intensification of the Type A dilemma of inferiority versus superiority. The individual tends to engage in a state of very high superiority to cover up his or her extremely low sense of inferiority. In the state of mania, the two other dilemmas—a sense of insecurity versus self-centeredness, as well as detachment from reality versus related fantasy—are still present but exist in moderate form. That means the individual with mania still has a certain sense of reality and connection to the external environment. They are still concerned with others' responses, feelings, and related issues happening in the immediate social and physical environment. They are absorbed in their elation, but they still embrace a certain sense of security. They do not need to control others to increase their sense of security. That means for persons with mania, grandiosity is exercised within a clear frame of reality and self-boundary. It performs the following functions in the state of mania:

a. Grandiosity as a way to pull up depressive image and mood.
b. Grandiosity as a way for superiority to deal with intolerable inferiority
c. Grandiosity as a way for recalling previous experiences in resilience of hardship
d. Grandiosity as manifestation of problems in transformation of narcissism
e. Grandiosity with a frame of reality and self boundary

For persons with narcissistic personality disorder, grandiosity is a high intensification of the Type B dilemma of sense of insecurity versus self-centeredness. They experience an intense sense of insecurity, and they try to be self centered so that they feel secure and safe. In doing so, they still have a certain frame of reality with the actual presence of others. Their self-identity is still concrete and integrated. Unlike those persons having a manic episode, they also embrace a certain degree of self-awareness that they are superior but not omnipotent. However, in being self-centered, they also feel lonely. To face the intense feeling of insecurity and loneliness, they intend to regard themselves as far more superior than people around them. That means, others are not good and elegant enough to go together with them. In many ways, intense self centeredness, loneliness, and a sense of insecurity trap persons with narcissistic personality disorder within a self-defensive mechanism by humiliating, controlling, and degrading others so as to pull up their self-image, justifying their sense of loneliness as a form of elegance, and protecting themselves from their prevailing sense of insecurity. In other words, their grandiosity is formed by intense self-centeredness versus a sense of insecurity, moderate superiority versus inferiority, and moderate detachment from reality versus fantasy. Their grandiosity can perform the following functions:

a. Grandiosity as a way to deal with intolerable loneliness and a sense of isolation
b. Grandiosity as a way to catch others' attention
c. Grandiosity as a way to pull up oneself by undermining others
d. Grandiosity as a way to disguise inferiority, avoidance, as well as expectation

Grandiosity, Self Disturbance, and Mental Illness

Within Kohut's (1977) line of thinking, there are two groups of different disturbances: the primary, and the secondary self- (or reactive) disturbances that are due to the problems of transformation of the primary narcissism of the grandiose self. The latter constitutes the acute and chronic reactions of a consolidated self to the vicissitudes of the experience in life. The primary self-disturbance is more crucial and important. It is a problem in the infrastructure of the self and its relationship with the self-object (Kohut, 1971 &1977). He classified five types of primary self-disturbance.

1. *Psychosis* is a permanent or protracted breakup, enfeeblement, or serious distortion of the self. The individual fails to defend this form of breakup and distortion.
2. *Borderline State* is a permanent or protracted breakup, enfeeblement, or serious distortion of self, which is covered by a more or less effective defensive structure.
3. *Schizoid and the Paranoid Personalities* are an intense and spontaneous use of hostility and suspicion to protect the individual from permanent protracted breakup, enfeeblement, and serious distortion of self.

4. *Narcissistic Personality Disorders* are temporary breakup, enfeeblement, or serious distortion of self, manifested predominantly by autoplastic symptoms, such as hypersensitivity to slights, hypochondria, or depression.
5. *Narcissistic Behavior Disorders* are temporary breakup, enfeeblement, or serious distortion of self, manifested predominantly by alloplastic symptoms such as perversion, delinquency, or addiction (Kohut, 1977: 191–193).

Grandiosity in Persons with Schizophrenia

Grandiosity in Extreme Detachment of Reality and Intense Fantasy: A Kohut Interpretation

For persons with schizophrenia, the formation of a grandiose delusion should be the extreme intensification of the dilemma about the detachment of reality versus related fantasy. That means, individuals with grandiose delusions are very detached from reality and are absorbed by a grandiose delusion (fantasy). As a result, his or her self centeredness and sense of insecurity, as well as superiority and inferior dilemmas also increase intensely. The individual may first enter into an initial state of severe mania and then into a first-rank grandiosity (with a change of delusive identity). In the former one, the following characteristics are observed:

Delusive Grandiosity in Persons with Schizophrenia and Severe Mania

a. Parental Imago gradually turns into delusive imago
b. Narcissistic self gradually becomes delusive and out of touch with reality
c. Unavailability of parental imago in reality that can only be obtained by a self constructed parental imago
d. Severe problem in transformation of narcissism
e. Superiority and inferiority complex is intensified and turns into a self-splitting process

First, the parental imago in which the individual tries to identify gradually turns into a delusive imago with unrealistic extreme omnipotence. For example, instead of identifying people in reality, the clients with grandiose delusions may identify with those historic heroic figures or even gods. Secondly, the grandiose self has a severe problem in transformation of narcissism. Thirdly, gradually as there is no availability of a parental imago in reality, all the delusive parental imago can only be self constructed by the individual in forms of delusions. That means the individual become more and more self absorbed in his or her own delusive parental imago. He or she may incline to proclaim that he or she has a close and intimate relationship with all these self constructed, delusive, parental imagos. For example, a person with psychotic grandiose delusion may proclaim that he or she is the disciple of Buddha and the brother of Jesus Christ as well as the girlfriend, boyfriend, or even husband or wife of a very famous movie superstar. Fourthly, as the delusive, parental imago is imaginative and not available in actual reality, it is difficult for the individual to undertake the proper transformation of narcissism. Creativity, wisdom, humor, transience and empathy toward the omnipotent parental imago and grandiose self can only be done within a delusive context. Thus, superiority and inferiority complex can never be regulated and settled within a realistic context and actuality and an integrated ego system. Instead, persons with psychotic and grandiose delusion faced a process of self-splitting.

According to Kohut (1971), there are two types of self-splitting, the vertical splitting and the horizontal splitting.

> The patient will gradually reveal the urge and fantasies of the grandiose self and the slow process is thus initiated which least . . . to the integration of the grandiose self into the structure of reality ego and to an adaptively useful transformation of its energies. . . . the chronic tendency of the reality ego to wall itself off from the unrealistic narcissistic structures by such mechanism as repression, isolation and disavowal. Correlated to the last named mechanism is a specific, chronic structural change to which I would like to refer, in a modification of Freud's terminology as vertical split in the psyche. The ideational and emotional manifestation of a vertical split in the psyche—in contrast to such horizontal splits as those brought about on a deepest level by repression and on a higher level by negation are correlated to the side by side, conscious existence of otherwise incompatible psychological attitudes in depth. (Kohut, 1971: 1776–1777)

Within the above-mentioned description, it is clear that vertical splitting is discrepancies between actual self and the grandiose self that derived from the ominopotent parental imago. Horizontal splitting is the repression of deep seated urge for grandiosity. This two types of splitting is correlated to one another side by side. Successful transformation of primary narcissism and avaiablity of a good, respectable and caring signficiant others means that the individual can construct a good and realistic parental imago and facilitate the proper transformation of the grandiose self to realistic and caring system. However, if the environment is very oppressive and the individual can only search his or her parental imago within his or her delusive world, the vertical splitting and horizontal splitting will be intensified tremendously leading to different types of self-disturbance with a result of different sorts of mental illness.

> The earlier examination invovled the relationship between (1)the vertical split in the psyche which is frequently seen in narcissistic personality disorder; and (2)a horizontal split in the psyche which I believe to be present in all cases of this disturbance, either (less commonly)alone, or in combination with a vertical split is often difficult to ascertain and can be easily overlooked. (Kohut, 1971: 240)

Kohut though that psychopathology is a result of self-disturbance originated from that sort of vertical and horizontal split in psyche structure. The vertical and horizontal splitting can combine together in formulating various types of mental illness. The vertical split is a sector of the personality that is split off from the central sector. It is maintained by the defense of disavowal. It exists in the conscious level. The repression barrier (horizontal splitting) happens in the unconscious level. Together with these two conscious levels is the reality ego that the individual actually experiences his or her own self. Then, in the vertical split, the disavowed grandiosity begins to express in terms of fantasies of greatness, and fears of over-excitation. The horizontal split turns into unconscious depression and archaic narcissistic needs. The reality ego becomes shame, and a humiliation-prone ego, and is deprived of self-esteem (Siegel, 1996: 93). That means, the greater and more frequent is the vertical splitting, the more the individual aspires for superiority, but the more inferior the individual feels in facing his or her reality ego. The more intense is the horizontal splitting, the more the individual's desires is repression. In doing so, individual's ego functioning and ego strengths is also being suppressed accordingly. That means, the reality ego becomes more restricted and confined. In other words, the individual is thus absorbed in his or her related sense of fantasy and detachment from the reality. In no way an inferior and restricted reality ego feels insecure. He or she may try to insert control on others and things in the reality. However, the more he or she tries to control, the more he or she needs to repress his or her desires and restricted his or her involvement in the reality. In fact, the concept of vertical split, horizontal split as well as reality ego mentioned by Kohut in the *Analysis of Self* can also be regarded as an inherent self splitting process in which only transformation of narcissism can glue or integrate this sort of self-splitting. Without proper transformation of narcissism, it can end up with self-fragmentation in schizophrenia. The vertical split is similar to development of positive symptom, the horizontal split can end up very regressive negative symptoms, whereas the residual reality ego can be ended up with a very diffused self-boundary of first rank symptoms. That means, the individual totally absorbs in a severe sense of inferiority and superiority complex and with a gradual intensification of detachment of reality and increase of development of related fantasy.

Putting vertical split, horizontal split and reality ego together may also mean that within psychotic grandiosity, despite it is a positive symptom, it also contributes to the first rank symptoms and negative symptoms for clients with schizophrenia. Relating to first rank symptoms implies that individual's psychotic grandiosity is a total change of one's identity. Individual's identity has been totally merged with his delusive parental imago. He or she is no longer him- or herself, he or she is actually an omnipotent others.

In the process of psychotic self-fragmentation, grandiosity in first rank symptoms may have the following stages of changes:

Stages of Confused First Rank Grandiosity (With change of delusive identity) –

a. From organized to confused Delusive Parental Imago (Omnipotent Others)
b. From organized to confused Delusive Narcissistic Self (Grandiose Self)
c. Delusive Transformation of Narcissism
d. Stability can Change of Delusive Parental Image and Narcissistic Self

In the first stage, the individual's organized parental imago (ominoptent others) begins to change ot confused parental imago. That means, instead of identifying, modeling, mirroring and a superior significant others as the parental imago in well-organized ways in the actual reality, the individual tends to develop his or her delusive parental imago as stated in the non-first rank psychotic grandiosity. The degree of delusion can be ranging from deceased parents, popular but inaccessible stars or figures in the society, historic figures in the history to superstitious gods and even unknown ultra space figures in the univerese. For example, a psychotic male adult with delusive grandiosity may first develop a thought that he or she is actually a very superior power with magic power just like the chief magician in the U.S.A. As the delusive grandiosity develops further, he even change his or her identity that he is actually in fact the chief magician in the U.S.A. or even in the whole world. If all these grandiosity cannot empower himself to deal with the oppressive environment, he even said he is not only a chief magician but rather a almighty fairy from the heaven who in his previous life is a power king Alexander in Greece in ancient time. If this delusive grandiose identity develop further the individual may finally claim that he is a almighty god from another universe coming to this world to save those innocent and punish those sinful in this world. Or he can say that he is an aliented creature in the outer space. The more delusive the grandiose identity is, the more powerful the indivdual feels and the more severe his psychotic self-fragmentation becomes.

Before the total replacement of the actual identity by the delusive grandiose identity, individual can also establish different type of linkage with the delusive parental imago. The first relationship is direct relationship in terms of subordinates of the delusive parental imago. For example, a female with grandiose delusion may delude that she is the girlfriend, sister, mother or even wife of a popular star or a famous intentational figure. A male with grandiose delusion may delude that he is the boyfriend, brother or even husband of an authority figure in the society or in other countries. The second type of relationship is indirect relationship is terms of distant or secret relationship such as the secret agent of FBI, the spy of certain country, and decendants of the certain gods in the history such as the chief disciple of Buddha, the eldest child of the god in the history. For the client with grandiose delusions, all these secret relationships should be concealed and unknown by others. Once, it is disclosed or discovered by others, the whole secret relationship will be ruined.

Finally, the more developed the grandiose delusion, the more extreme and delusive the grandiose becomes ranging. *According to relationship with the parental imago as well as shifting of grandiose identity from accessible admirable figures to inaccessible figures in the history and in superstitious gods*, *degree of severity of grandiose delusion* can be listed as follows:

1. Indirect relationship with admirable figure in the society
2. Direct and intimate relationship with admirable figure in the society
3. Indirect relationship with admirable figure in the world
4. Direct relationship with admirable figure in the world
5. Indirect relationship with historical hero
6. Direct and intimate relationship with historical hero
7. Indirect relationship with god
8. Direct and intimate relationship with God
9. Shifting of self-identity to admirable figure in the society
10. Shifting of self-identity to admirable figure in the world
11. Shifting of self-identity to historical hero
12. Shifting of self-identity to God
13. Shifting of self-identity from different admirable figures, historical heroes, or gods

Grandiosity and Existentialism: Delusive Autonomy, Freedom and Creativity

Apart from Kohut's interpretation, grandiose delusion can also be interpreted by existential orientation, in particular those suggested by Laing (1960) in his book, Divided Self.

Loss of Autonomy, Freedom and Creativity in Actual and Substantially Reality

In facing the oppressive reality that creates sense of ontological insecurity to the individual, the development of the false self, on the one hand separates the inner self from the oppressive environment. On the other hand, it seems to allow the inner self to be free to dream and imagine anything.

'The self, as long as it is uncommitted to the objective element, is free to dream and imagine anything. Without reference to the objective element it can be all things to itself --- it has unconditioned freedom, power and creativity. But its freedom and its omnipotence are exercised in a vacuum and its creativity is only the capacity to produce phantoms. The inner honesty, freedom, omnipotence and creativity, which the inner self cherishes as its ideals, are cancelled, therefore, by a coexisting tortured sense of self duplicity, of the lack of any real freedom, of utter impotence and sterility.' (Laing, 1960:89)

Paradoxically, all these freedom, creativity, and omnipotence need to manifest in the substantial reality. Thus, the separation of the inner self from the oppressive reality on the one hand protect the inner self from being intruded and hurt by oppressive others. However, it also implies all these freedom, creativity and omnipotence fail to be stretched in the reality.

'It has no freedom in reality. Moreover, even in its own enclave, in its detachment it is constantly subject to the threat of an implosive or engulfing reality and whereas it is preoccupied by itself and its own object, it is still hyper-acutely aware of itself as on object in the eyes of other.' (Laing, 1960: 90)

Formation of Grandiose and Delusive Identity

Facing the inner emptiness and the risk to loss one's identity, the individual engages on the following tactics.

To Shift from One Identity to Another Identity

In being afraid of losing one's own identity because of external threats and inner emptiness, one of the tactic can be used is to change one's identity so that he or she can use this new identity to protect his or her own identity. In doing so, the individual can use any signs or symbols from the environment, familiar or popular persons or figures, unfulfilled wish and expectation as ingredients in formation of temporary or disguising identity. As the new identity comes out, the inner but fragile self hides or camouflages under this disguising identity. The more the individual does so, the more the inner self feels being isolated and vacated by the camouflaged identity. The only way he or she can do is shift from one identity to another identity. In Laing (1960), he encountered the following case.

'He attempts to assert his identity by eccentricity of ideas. He was a pacifist, a theosophist, an astrologer, a spiritualist, as occultist, a vegetarian. It seems that the fact her could share with others at least his odd ideas was perhaps the most important single factor in preserving his sanity. For in those limited areas he was sometimes able to be with others with whom he shared his ideas and peculiar experiences. Such ideas and

> experiences tend to isolate a man from his fellows in our present Western culture and unless they serve at the same time to draw him into a small group of similar eccentrics, his isolation is greatly in danger of passing over into psychotic alienation … . (Laing, 1960:140)

That means, the shifting of eccentric identity, is in fact a way to hide or to separate the inner self so that it can be protected and preserved. However, it also means a prolonged self alienation with a continuous splitting from one identity to another identity. It is a kind of combination of psychotic fragmentation and self alienation. To avoid his or her inner self being isolated by the thickening of false self systems, the individual shift his or her identities by relating inner self to external object. However, the relating of external object means threatening to the safety of the individual so the individual needs to separate him- or herself to preserve his or her inner self. Thus, he or she needs to stay away from this established but ambivalent identity. However, as he or she stays longer and longer in his or her inner self, intolerable sense of loneliness and emptiness make him or her come out and change to another identify by projective identification of external object. It is a kind of vicious cycle. As the individual becomes more and more insecure and the shifting of identity is quicker and quicker and the process of self-splitting turns faster and faster. *Within this process, it is a kind of dilemma of self visibility and self concealment* in which the individual urges to be visible by connecting with the external object in establishing a new identity on one hand. On the other hand, it creates threats and ontological insecurity to the inner self that the individual tries to avoid by concealing inner self to the increasing false self system. He or she also disregards the formed identity into the false self system. The longer his or her inner self is being concealed, the more lonely and empty he or she becomes and the more urgent for the inner self to be visible again. Thus the dilemma of visibility and concealment moves on and on.

To Engage in a Grandiose or Manic State of Self

The escape from oppressive reality and concealment by the thickening of the false self system implies the loss of creativity, freedom and autonomy in substantially reality. To avoid being dead inside, the individual shift from identity to identity by projective identification with external objects as well as turning formed identity to the false self system. Within this process, the individual also allows himself or herself to absorb in delusive inner space in which he or she can free to imagine anything, to create any object, to project any omnipotent identity. In many cases, it intermingles with the individual's religious and superstitious beliefs as well as life aspiration. Laing (1960) had a refined description about that sort of delusive grandiosity.

> 'Another patient oscillated between moment when he felt as though he was bursting with power, and moment when he felt he had nothing inside was lifeless. However, even his manic feeling of himself was that he was a container full of air under tremendous

pressure, in fact, nothing but hot air, and his sense of deflation came with this thought.' (Laing, 1960: 90)

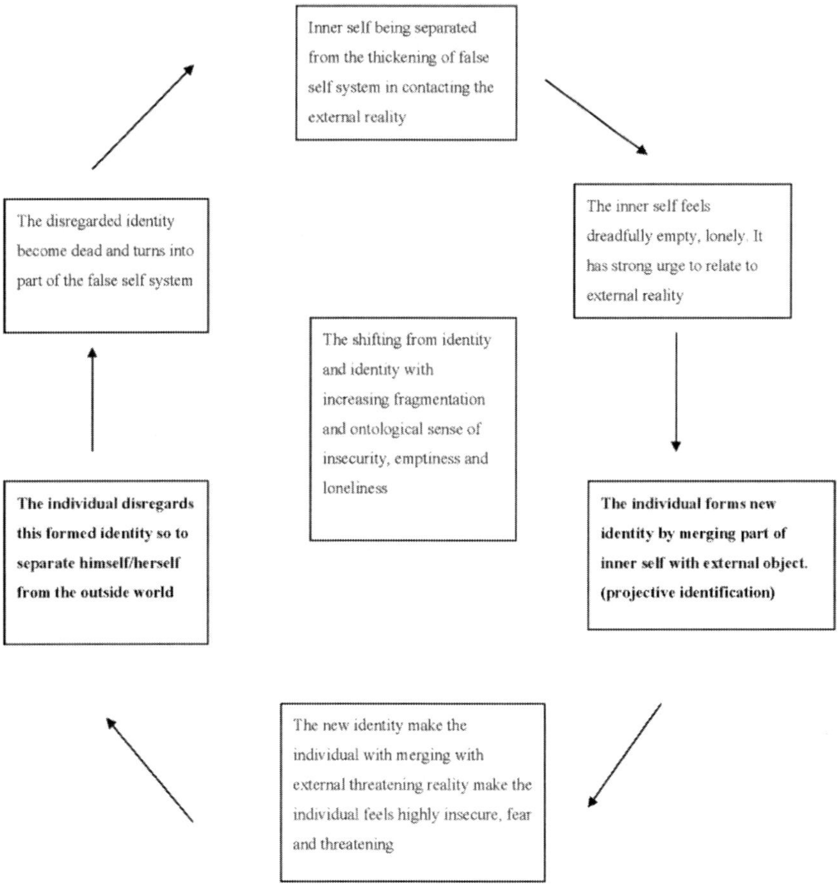

Figure 8. The vicious cycle in continuous formation and shifting from identity to identity in self-fragmentation.

Laing (1960) affirmed that sort of grandiosity is not a stable state. Instead it is an oscillation between powerfulness and nothingness. In terms of nothingness, he or she is lifeless and empty. In terms of powerfulness, the individual is full of power. However, this sort of powerfulness is not a substantiality of power and realistic actualization. Instead, it is a kind of delusive state of mania in which the individual is merely a container full of air under tremendous pressure. That means, it is full and it is powerful but easily bursts out and finally becomes empty and nothing. Within the manic but delusive powerfulness, it is only an outrageous manifestation of phantasy and imagination in which the inner self relates itself to itself through magical relationship.

'The object of phantasy or imagination obey magical laws, they have magical relationships, not real relationships, when the self becomes more and more in phantasy relationships, less and less a direct relationship a direct participant in real relationships, in doing so it loses its own reality. It becomes, like the objects to which it is related, a magical phantom. One implication of this is that, for such a self, everything and anything become possible… . In imagination the conviction was growing and gathering of having fantastic powers (occult, magical, mysterical)… of someone very special, with extraordinary mission, a reincarnation perhaps of the Buddha or Christ.' (Laing 1960:141)

Within that sort of imaginative relationship, the individual is full of delusive power, he or she can be anything or anyone as long as he or she can imagine. He or she can be Buddha or Christ. He or she can be powerful spy and famous movie star. He or she can owe magical powerful to understand others or control others. He or she can have special mission to save the whole world or actualize his or her religious and omnipotent duties. In doing so, the super power, talents, missions and identities can shift from time to time as well as at one time, it is powerful and one time it is not. In some cases, the individual may even regard his or her super power, talents, missions and identities are top secretes and confidential that should only be disclosed to those he or she is very familiar with.

Process of Self-Fragmentation in Grandiose Hallucination and Delusion

Within the above-mentioned stages in the development of self-fragmentation, paranoid delusion and hallucination tend to proceed in stage 1 to stage 4, grandiose delusion and hallucination tend to occur from stage 5 to stage 7.

Stage 5: Further fragmentation of all these divided and fractured partial self systems (Each fractured partial self system may have its own delusive identity, boundary and interpretation of external reality)

Stage 6: There are spontaneous and continuous conflicts and ambiguity within and between these divided and fractured partial self systems (The individual may shift from one delusive identity to another one, has constant manifestation of running tracks of auditory hallucination with one arguing with one another, with thought insertion and thought broadcasting).

Stage 7: The self fragmentation of all these partial self systems can be continuous until reparation is impossible. (The individual is in a state of severe mental confusion and has a very poor sense of reality that may lead to psychiatric emergency and possible harm to oneself and another).

The writer tries to describe these three stages in grandiose delusion and hallucination in details.

Stage 5: Formation of Grandiose Delusive Self-Identity by Transformation of Delusive Parental Imago

As mentioned above, within the development of grandiosity, there are three dynamic forces, superiority versus inferiority, self-centeredness and sense of insecurity, as well as related fantasy and detachment from reality. For persons with schizophrenia, the formation of grandiose delusion should be the extreme intensification of the dilemma about the detachment of reality versus related fantasy. That means, individuals with grandiose delusion are very detached from reality and is absorption of grandiose delusion (fantasy). In doing so, his or her self centeredness and sense of insecurity, as well as superiority and inferior dilemmas also increase intensely. The individual may first enter into an initial state of severe mania and then into a first rank grandiosity (with change of delusive identity) with the following characteristics:

- Parental imago gradually turns into delusive imago
- Narcissistic self gradually becomes delusive and out teach of reality
- Unavailability of parental imago in reality: It can only be obtained by self - constructed parental imago
- Severe problem in transformation of narcissism
- Superiority and Inferiority complex is intensified and turns into a self -splitting process

The self-splitting of superiority and inferior complex will finally end up with two parts of partial self system. One represents the superiority but delusive parental imago. One represents the inferiority in which the individual is fearful to expose to others. In terms of projective identification, the partial self system of inferiority is in terms of bad self (BS) and the partial self system of superiority is in terms of good self (GS). In the process of paranoid delusion and hallucination, the partial self system of inferiority (BS), in facing the oppressive others (BO) is projected outwards in the following mechanisms

a. The first one is BS1 + BO1 + GS1 (the paranoid network becomes bigger and bigger)
b. The second one is BS2 + BO1 + GS2 (the power of the paranoid network becomes more and more powerful)
c. The third one can be BS1 + BO2 + GS1 (the delusive paranoid network grows larger and larger)
d. The fourth one is BS2 + BO2 + GS2 (the delusive paranoid network becomes more and more delusive and powerful).

(BS1: worth to be punished by others: BS2: take revenge to bad others: GS1: suffering hero, toleration of others' torture: GS2: being perfect should not be criticized: BO1: substantially existing oppression: BO2: Planned but not existing oppression)

1. In all these four mechanisms of paranoid delusion, the fragile and split self system becomes more and more fragile and has the following changes from paranoid delusion and hallucination to grandiose delusion and hallucination.
2. The individual becomes more and more isolated from the actual reality.
3. The individual projects his or her bad self and good self outwards with connection with bad others, that means, the inner true self becomes weaker and weaker.
4. As the prevailing bad others (BO) becomes more and more intensified in the formation of paranoid delusion and hallucination, the individuals' own self identity and boundary becomes weaker and weaker.
5. In the spontaneous absence of good others, facing the need of parental imago, the individual needs to create his or her delusive parental imago (delusive good others (DelGO) so as to maintain the stability of inner self system.
6. However as the parental imago is delusive, individuals fail to have proper transformation of narcissism Instead, a delusive good self (DelGS) is formed and becomes his or her new grandiose self identity.

That means, in stage 5, individual's self system not only split into two sub-systems, good and bad self. The individual's actual self-identity is disguised and transformed into a delusive self-identity. In terms of mechanism described in the formation of paranoid delusion and hallucination, the transformation process can be further described into the following sub-stages

Stage 5A: GS2 + BS2 + BO2 Begins to Cover Up GS1 + BS1 + BO2

As the non-existing oppressive others prevail because of the intensification of paranoid delusions and hallucination, the individual needs to intensify his or her GS2 (I am perfect and I should not be criticized) and BS2 (I need to take revenge), and suppress his or her GS1 (I am a suffering hero) and BS1 (I am worth to be punished and criticized). The suppression does not imply that GS1 and BS1 are vanished. Instead, it become the deep sense of inferiority behind the development of grandiose delusion and hallucination. The suppression of GS1 and BS1 also implies that the individual's actual sense of identity and image are gradually repressed. That means, in suppressing individual's own sense of inferiority, his or her own identity is also deteriorated.

Stage 5B: GS2 Is Gradually Transformed to Form DelGS as BO2 is Gradually Transformed to DelGO

Because of the overwhelming of GS2 and BS2 and the suppression of GS1 and BS1, GS2 (I am perfect and should not be criticized) and BS2 (taking revenge on bad others) would gradually transform to delusive grandiose self (DelGS). The transformation process gradually involves three components. The first component is the transformation of BO2 (non-existing bad others) into delusive good other (DelGO). That means, instead of lettering the non-existing bad others doing bad thing, there should be the occurrence of a powerful good others to defend or to punish this delusive bad others. That means, the power of BS2 and GS2 is not powerful enough to deal with the BS2 so it dreadfully needs the support of a powerful good other. But it does not exist in the reality. Thus, the only alternative is to create one's delusive good other. The evolvement of the delusive good other also implies the urgent need for the individual to seek external but delusive support proving that the prevailing non-existing bad other (BO2) is worth to be punished.

The second component in the transformation of GS2 to DelGS is that the delusive good other (DelGO) gradually become a delusive omnipotent other in the formation of the delusive parental imago the individual. Then, the individual tries hard to pair up, mirror with and idealize with the delusive parental imago. First, he or she tries to tell other or think that he or she has very close relationship with that parental imago. Secondly, he or she also attempts to exhibit to others that he or she becomes more and more alike to this delusive parental imago. He or she becomes a mirroring imago of his or her delusive parental imago. Thirdly, he or she regards the delusive parental imago as an idealize figure in which he or she wants to learn, copy and model from this figure. In doing so, he or she becomes more and more powerful in a way he or she can deal with or even diminish the bad others personally.

Stage 5C: Transformation of Delusive Narcissism

Within the change from DelGO to DelGS, there is the transformation of Delusive Narcissism. In the transformation of primary narcissism, according to Kohut (1996) there are five important elements, creativity, empathy, wisdom, transience and humor. These five mechanisms also work in change from DelGO to DelGS. Within the change from DelGO to DelGS, these five mechanisms also occur. Creativity in transformation of delusive narcissism means the delusive parental imago is creatively shaped, modified and even maximized by the individual according to his or her own fulfilled needs as well as his or her cultural and social background and experiences. The creative shaping may be done in building up a delusive relationship between the parental imago and the individual. For example, a male adult, A first harbors a paranoid delusion that his life is being controlled and condemned by an evil spirit causing her every bad luck and traumas in life. Then, to rid of this prevailing bad others, A may gradually develop a delusive parental imago that a powerful fairy is helping him to deal with their evil spirit. In transformation of delusive narcissism, A may creatively shape and modified the fairy. He may proclaim that this powerful fairy may actually be an angel but dressed in a Buddhist monk with omnipotent power to detect evil spirit within human being. Also, this powerful fairy is very fond of him. Actually knows A well in his previous life. In this life, the powerful fairy comes and helps the individual to be his chief disciple in diminishing all evil spirit. Certainly, all the content of grandiose delusion is creatively shaped by A to fulfill his own needs and within his own cultural and religious background. As his mother is a Buddhist and his father is a Christian that is why he creatively combines the angels and Buddhist together in his grandiose delusion.

Empathy means that the individual tries to make the delusive parental imago as part and extension of him- or herself. That means, the individual not only develops close and intimate relationship with the delusive parental imago, he or she also assertively affirms that him or her has similar natures, ingredients and characteristics as the delusive parental imago. For example, A firmly believes that the powerful fairy comes and helps him and invites him to be his Chief disciple. The reasons behind are that he shares many similarities with this powerful fairy. First, he was born in the same month as the powerful fairy. Secondly, in A's previous life, he was actually the son of the powerful fairy. Thirdly, A does not like to eat meat. It means that A harbors an inherent nature to be a monk. Fourthly, A's mother always says that A is handsome and smart and appears like a lovely angel. For A, all these seem to be convincing evidence, that he and the powerful angel have close and intimate relationship.

Transience is the acceptance of one's mortality, impermanence as well as constraints and limitation in relation to one's omnipotence others. In the transformation of delusive parental imago, transience implies that the individual clearly admits his or her own limitations, constraints and deficiencies. The more one's admits his or her shortfalls, the more he or she regards the importance of the delusive parental imago to his or her own existence. Also, in terms of delusive narcissism, transience can be interpreted as unique and stylish personal features that are distinctive from others. For example, in the case A, transience is also important in developing his grandiose identity. As far as he recognizes that he is not competent enough or very limited in dealing with the delusive bad others, thus, it is better for him to rely on the power of the powerful fairy. The closer he relates to the powerful fairy, the more he can compensate all these shortfalls. Finally, he may even transform himself to become the powerful fairy.

Wisdom is acceptance of variation and a stable attitude toward life and world. In transformation of delusive parental imago, the individual may gradually regard the existence and presence of the delusive parental imago is constant and stable in life. He or she also slowly transforms his or her own delusive identity as the delusive imago. In doing so, he or she may not only create refined details about the delusive parental imago according to his or her own needs. He or she may even feel that he or she has special wisdom in knowing about his or her life. He or she feels that with the togetherness of delusive parental imago or transforms into his or her new delusive and grandiose identity, he or she is specially insightful, wise and always has wisdom in many things. Some may even say that they are wisest men/women with special gift to look through one's mind. Some may have interest in reading and digesting philosophical readings. In other words, wisdom is a both a cause as well as product in the transformation of delusive narcissism. For example, in the case A, he certainly thinks that once he is the follower or the chief disciples of the powerful fairy, he becomes wise and clever. He has special insight in knowing the myth of the nature. When he walks around in the community, he knows who are bad by listening into their voice in their mind. He recites and read Buddhism bible and think related messages consist of special messages. He is insightful and wise with everlasting wisdom to work through difficulties in life. He becomes clever and clever until one day he becomes the powerful fairy and destroys all bad others in the society.

Humor is kind of attitude of being at ease or laughing at one's own difficulties, constraints and morality. It works to achieve transience in an enlightening way. It is an inner symbol that one not only accepts his or her own limitation and difficulties but also harbors an inner drive to look down all related difficulties to work through them and to integrate them in the process of personal development. In the process in shifting his or her delusive parental imago into his or her own delusive grandiose self-identity, the individual may even invent interesting and humorous stories, signs and rituals symbolizing the transformation is smooth, reasonable and manageable. For example, in the case A, he invents an interesting and humorous story in transforming himself into a powerful fairy. As mentioned above, as he born in the same month as the powerful fairy; he was the son of the powerful fairy; and he did not like to meat, he actually possesses the inherent quality of being a powerful fairy. Then, one day, in his dream, the powerful fairy clearly told him that the powerful fairy injected all his mighty power to him through his hand. When he woke up, he immediately got an insight that if he did push up seven hundred times a day for seven hundred days, he can learn the power hidden in his body being injected by the powerful fairy. Thus, from that day onward, he forced himself to do push up seven hundred times every day. He even affirms that if one day, he fails to do so. He needs to compensate this in the next day. Being a powerful fairy is a difficult or even impossible for others, however, for him, he can attain it in an easy and humorous way. That means, for clients with grandiose schizophrenia, the use of humor, creativity and wisdom makes the transformation of delusive narcissism attainable.

Thus, in the stage 5, individuals gradually shift from paranoid delusion to develop grandiose delusion. The self-fragmentation is deep and profound with the development of delusively grandiose identity. The formation of delusive and grandiose identity (DelGS) can be represented by the following:

a. DelGS = BO2 (Non-Existing Bad others) changes to DelGO (Delusive Good Other) + GS2 (Grandiose Good self: I am perfect) + BS2 (diminish or punish the bad other) + Transformation of Delusive Parental Imago (TDelPI) by using of Wisdom, Transience, Creativity, Humor and Empathy. (DelGS = BO2 -DelGO + GS2 + BS2+ TDelPI).

b. Within the formation of delusively grandiose self-identity, the individual's own bad and good self is disguised and distorted. The bad self and the bad others are totally suppressed and repressed. The good self and good others are totally combined and transformed into a new delusively grandiose identity.
c. This delusively grandiose identity has own self-image, boundary and core natures. All these are vastly different from the original self- image, boundary and core natures of the individual. For example, a timid and passive male in the delusive grandiose identity becomes a powerful, active and mighty god or superman. In some cases, the individual's gender may even shift from to counter sex.

Stage 6: Shifting from One Delusively Grandiose Self-Identity to Another One

Apart from the manifested delusively grandiose self, the individual still embraces the suppressed and repressed self system of the individual. It consists of the following:

BS2 (the unseen bad others) + GS1 (good self: suffering hero and worth to be punished) + BS1 (bad self: deserving of punishment). This suppressed but still existing partial self system becomes in conflict with the newly formed delusively grandiose self-identity. All these conflicts become a good breeding bed for further self-fragmentation in stage 6.

Stage 6A: Delusive Voices Arguing with One Another

The newly formed delusively grandiose self identity (DelGS) is in conflict of the repressed partial self system (BS1 + GS1 + BO2). The conflict is aroused because of several reasons. First, by nature, they are opposite to one another. While delusively grandiose self-identity representing an actualized and manifested but delusive urge to empower oneself with new mighty power to diminish the bad others in the world, the repressed partial self system remains an introjected sense of guilt that the individual is worth to be punished by bad others. Secondly, the development of the delusively grandiose self identity implies that the actual but partial self-identity such as BS1 and GS1 have to be repression. Spontaneous repression of this partial self implies that the individual is going to lose his/her self-identity. The total loss of one's self-identity also implies a loss of one's past experiences and memories. That is unacceptable and intolerable for the individual. Thirdly, the individual still needs the partial but genuine self-identity to survive within daily activities.

Thus, the partial self system (BS1 + GS1 + BO2) rebounces frequently in the development of the delusively grandiose self-identity. It appears as in a form auditory hallucination with two voices arguing with one another. In active paranoid delusion, the two voices, one representing BS2 + GS2 + BO2 (the voice saying that the individual is worth to be punished), another one representing BS1 + GS1 + BO1 (the voice saying that the individual is good and perfect), argues with one another. However, the development of delusively grandiose self-identity, the voice representing the BS1 + GS1 + BO2 (the individual is bad and worth to be punished) begin to dim down. However, the voice representing the original BS2 + GS2 + BO2 (the individual is good and the bad others should be diminished) begins to grows louder and louder and finally change to many delusive good others (DelGO) claiming the badness of the delusive bad others. However in the process of transformation of delusive good others to delusively grandiose self-identity (DelGS), the residual partial self system re-bounce occasionally still saying that the individual is worth to be punished and pointing out the badness/fault/guilt of the individual. Even with the final transformation to the delusively grandiose self identity, the voice representing the bad self still occasionally rebounces because of being triggers by various clues in the environment. Thus, there should be a confusing of different voices (delusive good others, the partial self system as well as the self-talks of the delusively grandiose self) arguing with one other. In other words, the formation of DelGS should not be a stable stage. Instead it is a state of unstable mental condition with high potential for further changes.

Stage 6B: Creating Another Delusively Grandiose Self-identity

As the newly formed delusively grandiose self-identity (DelGS) is based on the transformation of narcissism of delusive parental imago, it is not stable and powerful enough to face the continuous appearance of oppressive bad others in the actual reality. Also, as stated above, there is also an occasional re-bounce of the repressed partial self system (BS1 + GS1 + BO2) as threatening and persecutory delusion and hallucination. That means, DelGS should be in constant changing and unstable. The most preferable change is to increase the grandiosity and power of the DelGS. However, individual's grandiose self-identity may be limited in its grandiosity and power. For example, if an individual develops a grandiose delusion that he is a governor in Hong Kong but he still feels that FBI from the United States is still following him or her everywhere, he needs a more grandiose and powerful identity to rid of the bad influence and control of FBI. In that sense, probably, he would shift his grandiose identity to become a president in the United States. In the process of shifting from one less powerful delusively grandiose self-identity to a more power one, there is also corresponding changes in BO2, DelGO, GS2 and BS2. There is also another process of the transformation of the new delusive parental imago. Within this process, the residual partial self system (BS1 + GS1 + BO2) re-bounces constantly reminding the individual about his or her own original but weak self-identity that need to be punished by others. He or she is thus trapped within an intense superiority (delusive grandiose self-identity) and suppressed inferiority (frequent reminder about his or her own weak and depowered self-identity by the re-bounce of residual partial self system) complex. The struggle within this superior and inferior complex is a vicious circle. The more inferior the individual feels, the more he or she urges to pull up his or her self-image to delusive sense of superiority. However, the more he or she feels delusively superior, the more he or she needs to cover up his or her sense of inferiority by powerful grandiose delusion. In other words, the individual is inclined to develop more and more powerful and delusive grandiose identity. In doing so, his or her mental state becomes more and more unstable. As mentioned above, before the full establishment of the new delusively grandiose self-identity, the grandiosity of the individual is increased by having more and more close relationship with the grandiose figure (the parental imago). After the establishment of new delusively grandiose self-identity, the grandiosity should be increased by changing to another more delusive and more powerful self-identity. It can be a shift from a fairy to an almighty God, a hero to a superman, and a man with noble blood to a king.

Stage 6C: Shifting from One Delusive Self-Identity to Another

In the creation of second delusive and grandiose self-identity, the mental state of the individual becomes more and more volatile. Also, as every delusively grandiose self-identity is transformed from the delusive parental imago with actual contact of the substantially objects and persons in reality, thus, its structure, content, boundary and strengths are subjected to change according to the inner psychic needs of the individual. The second delusively grandiose self-identity, as mentioned above, is more powerful and grandiose but more delusive than the first one. Also, after the formation of the second delusively grandiose self-identity, the self system of the individual is actually dived into three partial self systems:

The residual but very repressed partial self system originated from paranoid delusion (BS1 + GS1 + BO2) = RepDelParanoia

1. The first delusively grandiose self-identity (DelGS1 = BO2 + GS2 +BS2 + TDelPIa).
2. The second delusively grandiose self-identity (DelGS2 = DelGS1 + TDelPIb).

These three partial self systems are interacting with one another in various ways. First, the more partial self systems are split, the more diversified the individual's mental and physical energy and the more fragmented and fractured the individual's self system is. Secondly, they may also reinforce or oppose with one another. For example, RepDelParanoia is opposite with DelGS1 as well as DelGS2. Also DelGS2 is a transcendent form from DelGS1. That means, DelGS2 is an exaggerated form of DelGS1. In doing so, DelGS2 is actually satisfying the unfulfilled needs of DelGS1 and RepDelParanoia. Thirdly, the interaction and intermingling among three partial self systems means that individual is shifting his or her own self-identity making him- or herself feels very confusing and puzzling. For example, the individual harbors a repressed self-identity that his previous boss is still assigning secret agents from the U.S.A. to search for his mistakes in his everyday life (RepDelParanoia). However, at the same time, he is also the head of all secret agents assigned by the government of the People's Republic of China (DelGS1). By means of manifestation of this self-identity, the individual feels he is powerful enough to identify, to deal with and even to get rid of all these secret agents from the U.S.A. As he lives in China, he properly concludes that, within China, local secret agents, of course should be much more powerful than those secret agents from the U.S. A. If the secret agents from the U.S.A. are too much well equipped with modern high technologies and hidden powerful weapons from the U.S.A., it seems that his self-identity as the head of secret agent in China may not powerful enough to deal with secret agent from the U.S. A. (RepDelParanoia > DelGS1). Thus, the individual has to engage in new but more delusive and more grandiose self-identity as a 'superman from the outer space' (DelGS2) in which he is far more powerful than any secret agents in this world (DelGS2 > DelGS1 > RepDelParanoia). However, the more delusive and grandiose the new self-identity is, the more vulnerable and the more unstable it is. That means, even though the delusive self-identity as a 'superman from the outer space' is far more powerful than 'secret agents in China' and 'secret agents in the U.S.A.', it is also very delusive, grandiose and far more out touched of reality. In other words, its substantiality and interaction with related persons, issues and events in the immediate social and physical environment is slim and insufficient. In other word, the transformation of narcissism of the very delusive parental imago is very insufficient and incomplete. Thus, its stability, substantiality and cohesiveness of the newly form delusively grandiose self-identity is far more inadequate than the partial self system of DelGS1 and RepDelParanoia. In other word, the powerfulness and the substantiality of three partial self systems can be represented in the following:

- *In terms of powerfulness and grandiosity:* DelGS2 > DelGS1> RepDelParanoia
- *In terms of substantiality and cohesiveness:* DelGS2 < DelGS1< RepDelParanoia

In terms of powerfulness and grandiosity, DelGS2 can fulfill the duty in getting rid the prevailing but delusive oppressive others. However, in terms of substantiality, it is the most fragile and vulnerable. Thus, the individual has to shift him- or herself among these three partial self systems. The re-bounce of the RepDelParanoia can help the individual to consolidate the cohesiveness of the individual. But it also arouses the overwhelming fear toward the delusive oppressive others in which the individual needs to shift back to DelGS2. The fluctuation and shift between DelGS2 and RepDelParanoia needs DelGS1 to maintain the balance of the three partial self systems. In other words, the individual needs shift among two different delusively grandiose self identities plus the re-bounce of original self-identity with fear of the delusive oppressive others. In that sense, individual's mental state is very unstable.

Stage 7: Further Fragmentation and Confusions of Partial Self Systems

The continuous shifting of DelGS1, DelGS2 and RepDelParanoia is unstable. If the external oppressive from immediate physical and social context continues and prevails, further self-fragmentation can go on making the individual becomes very confused and in a state of psychiatric emergency that require immediate treatment and even hospitalization to avoid possible harm to oneself and another. The state of further confusion and fragmentation can be occurred in several ways. First, apart from the occurrence of DelGS1 and DelGS2, new grandiose self identities can also occur. That means, there is a possibility of a further occurrence of DelGS3, DelGS4 and DelGS5 or even other grandiose identity. Nevertheless, the more new grandiose and delusive identities occur, the more fragmented the self system becomes. Secondly, together with the occurrence of more new self identities, the shifting among various grandiose self identities also becomes quicker and quicker as well as more and more diffused. That means, in facing different triggers or internal psychic conditions, the individual can shift his or her self-identity among DelGS1, DelGS2, DelGS3, DelGS4, DelGS5 and RepDelParanoia. Thirdly, as every split partial self system may have its unique identity, character and function to the ontological existence for the individual, there may be inconsistencies and even conflicts among these partial self systems. In other words, inner voices (hallucinations) speaking to the individuals can be very confusing and conflicting with one another making the individual feels dreadfully painful and intolerable. Fourthly, as the individual engages more and more in developing new delusively grandiose self-identity, and shifting among these split partial self system and tolerating inconsistencies among them, he or she is very alienated and excluded from the actual reality. He or she becomes more and more out of controlled, irritated and absorbed in the deeply confused state of mind with unpredictable outburst of violence, persistent odd and bizarre behaviors or very intense and insensible response to selective triggers in the external environment.

Dilemmas in Self Fragmentation and Grandiose Delusion and Hallucination

The three types of dilemmas in self fragmentation: self splitting versus self cohesion, self concealment versus self visibility as well as self destruction versus self preservation also occur in grandiose delusion and hallucination. These three dynamic forces can be fully described in terms of the above mentioned three partial self systems as well as the powerfulness of and substantiality of grandiose delusions and hallucinations

1. DelGS1 = BO2 (Non-Existing Bad others) changes to DelGO (Delusive Good Other) + GS2 (Grandiose Good self: I am perfect) + BS2 (diminish or punish the bad other) + Transformation of Delusive Parental Imago (TDelPIa) by using of Wisdom, Transience, Creativity, Humor and Empathy. (DelGS1 = BO2-DelGO + GS2+ BS2 + TDelPIa).
2. The residual but very repressed partial self system originated from paranoid delusion (BS1 + GS1 + BO2) = RepDelParanoia.
3. The first delusively grandiose self-identity (DelGS1 = BO2 + GS2 +BS2 + TDelPIa).
4. The second delusively grandiose self-identity (DelGS2 = DelGS1 + TDelPIb)
5. In terms of powerfulness and grandiosity: DelGS2 > DelGS1> RepDelParanoia.
6. In terms of substantiality and cohesiveness: DelGS2 < DelGS1< RepDelParanoia.

Dilemma in Self-Splitting versus Self-Cohesion

In terms of self-splitting versus self-cohesion dynamic forces, individuals with grandiose delusions and hallucinations gradually split into the above mentioned three partial self systems, RepDelParanoia, DelGS1 and DelGS2. As mentioned above, the formation of the RepDeluParanoia *(BS1 + GS1 + BO2)* to protect the self system from potentially oppressive others. It represents the potential fear and self internalization that he or she is worth to be punished by others and the oppressive others are actually everywhere. The formation of DelGS1 is intensification of the good self (I am perfect), and bad self (I have to diminish the bad others) with the transformation of delusive parental imago so that the individual thinks that he or she can have delusive power to diminish the potentially oppressive others. DelGS2 is the further intensification of DelGS1. The coexistence of the three partial self systems implies a continuous message that:

1. There is a continuous risk and threat in the environment that is out of control of the individual and always proves that the individual is worth to be punished.
2. The individual has to equip himself so that he or she can protect him- or herself from all these potential risks and threat.
3. Rooted from the sense of superiority, the individual also thinks that he or she possesses power to diminish all potential enemies and oppressive others.
4. He or she can obtain prevailing power by being changed into another delusively grandiose figure.
5. If this grandiose figure cannot obtain enough power, he or she can change to another delusively grandiose figure.

There is a continuous message representing individuals' fear and insecurity as well as his or her own urge for protection and fight out. This is also a cohesive message demonstrating individual's urge to have a secure social environment so that he or she can feel secure and integrated. While the three partial self systems represent a self splitting, the coexistence of these three partial self systems imply individuals' urge and sense of cohesion in facing the prevailing threat and risks in his or her immediate social and physical environment. These three partial self systems have different degree of powerfulness and grandiosity (DelGS2 > DelGS1> RepDelParanoia) and substantiality and cohesiveness (DelGS2 < DelGS1< RepDelParanoia), When the splitting is too much influencing the overall integrity and cohesiveness of the self system, the individual will incline more to the RepDelParanoia with a decrease of adherence to DelGS2 and DelGS1. However, when the external environment becomes threatening, the individual may need to shift back to those partial self system with high grandiosity and powerfulness such DelGS2. Thus, the shifting among DelGS2, DelGS1 and RepDelParanoia fully demonstrates the needs and dilemmas of self splitting (to increase grandiosity and powerfulness of delusive self-identity) and self cohesion (to increase self awareness and original self-identity).

Dilemma in Self-Concealment versus Self-Visibility

Within grandiose delusion and hallucination, self-concealment versus self-visibility appears in several ways:

1. concealment of paranoid delusion by visibility of grandiose delusion.
2. concealment of less powerful grandiose delusion by visibility of more powerful grandiose delusion.
3. concealment of sense of inferiority by being delusively superior in facing the prevailing oppressive others.
4. concealment of sense of powerlessness and impotence by being delusively powerful and omnipotent.

In the concealment of paranoid delusion by visibility of grandiose delusion, RepDelParanoia (BS2 + GS2 + BO2) is repressed, the individual is no longer afraid of delusively oppressive figures in the immediate social and physical environment. Instead, his or her delusively grandiose identity (DelGS1) become visible giving him or her new courage, strength and power to diminish all potential oppressive figures in the immediate social and physical environment. If DelGS1 is not powerful enough, then DelGS2, DelGS3 or even DelGS4 would appear. When a new delusively grandiose identity becomes visible, the previous ones do not disappear. Instead, they are concealed. There are many ways in the manifestation of concealment and visibility dilemmas in delusively grandiose identity. They can be listed out as follows:

1. RepDelParanoia (Concealed) + DelGS1 (Visible)
2. RepDelParanoia (Concealed) + DelGS1 (Concealed) + DelGS2 (Visible)
3. RepDelParanoia (Concealed) + DelGS1 (Concealed) + DelGS2 (Concealed) + DelGS3 (Visible)
4. RepDelParanoia (Concealed) + DelGS1 (Concealed) + DelGS2 (Concealed) + DelGS3 (Concealed) + DelGS4 (Visible)

In all these possible forms of manifestation of grandiose delusion and hallucination, the individual can only have one delusively grandiose self-identity all at one time so that he or she can interact with others and respond to stimuli in immediate social and physical environment. The more partial self systems are being concealed, the more the individual's mental and physical energy as well as the more unstable and vulnerable the visible partial self system is. That means, despite DelGS5 is more powerful than DelGS4, DelGS3, DelGS2 and DelGS1, its stability and duration in visibility is the weakest as it needs to conceal and repress of DelGS4, DelGS3, DelGS2, DelGS1 and RepDelParanoia. When DelGS5 is unstable, it may shift back to DelGS4, DelGS3, DelGS2 or even RepDelParanoia.

Within the concealment and visibility dilemma among DelGS5, DelGS4, DelGS3, DelGS2, DelGS1 and RepDelParanoia, there is also the concealment of sense of inferiority by being delusively superior in facing the prevailing oppressive but delusive oppressive others. Underlying the deep seated RepDelParanoia, there are senses of fear and inferiority. In the generation of delusive grandiose self-identity, these senses of fear and inferiority are carefully covered and concealed. The individual, no longer be afraid of the delusive oppressive others, he or she has to face them squarely. He or she has to blow up his or her self confidence and competence so that he or she believes that he or she can diminish them. However, the sense of superiority is not generated by enhancing ego strength within an actual reality. Instead, it is enhanced by being adherent or transformed into a grandiose delusive figure. That means, the sense of superiority is not substantially or long last, it is fragile and unable to face the testing of the oppressive reality. It can easily shift back to the sense of inferiority. The dilemma of superiority versus inferiority is parallel to the dilemma of visibility and concealment. The more one conceals his inferiority and the more fragile the visibility of superiority is. That means, on one hand, the individual feels superior consciously within his or her delusive grandiose self-identity. On the other hand, his or her sense of inferiority within repressed delusive paranoia still prevails unconsciously.

Together with the concealment of sense of inferiority and the visibility of sense of superiority, there is also the concealment of sense of powerlessness and the visibility of sense of powerfulness. Facing the prevailing of the delusive oppressive others, individuals feel dreadfully powerless in his or her paranoid delusions and hallucination. In RepDelParanoia, this sense of powerlessness is well concealed. Instead, it visualizes in forms of delusive powerfulness in grandiose delusions and self-identity, DelGS1, DelGS2, DelGS3, DelGS4 and even DelGS5. In the process of formation of a new and more grandiose delusive self-identity, the weakness and inadequacies of previous delusive grandiose self-identity is properly concealed. Instead, the sense of delusive powerfulness increases until the individual feels that his or her sense of powerfulness turns into a state of delusive omnipotence in which he or she exercise in almighty power to threat or even diminish all his or her delusive enemies. The more he or she visualizes his or her omnipotent power, the more he or she can conceal his or her sense of powerlessness. However, the visualization of the newly formed delusive grandiose self-identity is very vulnerable and unstable. The more visible and powerful it is the more vulnerable and unstable it becomes. Thus, the individual may need shift to less powerful and less visible form in delusive grandiose self-identity. As a consequence, individuals with grandiose delusions and hallucinations in psychotic self-fragmentation tend to shift among different forms of delusive grandiose self-identity in concealment and visibility dilemma.

Dilemma of Self-Destruction versus Self-Preservation

As mentioned above, the third dilemma is self destruction and self preservation. This dilemma starts with individual's inherent instinct to destruct and to preserve one's own self and others in facing danger and threat in external environment. Individuals with schizophrenia, involve heavily in a delusive self destruction mechanism in which they try to destruct themselves mentally so that the oppressive others cannot destruct them. Within the formation of grandiose delusive self-identity, the original and inherent self-identity of the individual is destroyed. Within the formation of a new and more powerful grandiose self-identity, the former less powerful grandiose self-identity is destroyed. The process of self destruction versus self preservation go together. The self destruction of RepDelParanoia goes together with the birth of DelGS1 so to preserve the ontological but delusive security and preservation of the whole self system. Similar process occurs in self destruction of DelGS1 to the evolvement of DelGS2, from DelGS2 to DelGS3 and from DelGS3 to DelGS4. In doing so, the process of self destruction versus self preservation becomes more and more vulnerable and unstable with a potential threat of extreme confusion and very fractured self-fragmentation This a real threat for the ontological existence of the whole self system and the individual. As a consequence, when the perceived delusive potential oppressive others are under controlled or with less power than the newly formed delusive and grandiose self-identity, the self destruction versus self preservation mechanism ceases. The newly formed delusive and grandiose self-identity becomes relatively stable. When the oppressive others becomes less and less threatening, the individual may incline to regress back to the previously formed delusive grandiose self-identity so as to preserve self system from further splitting and self-fragmentation Thus, there tend to a spontaneous shifting forward and backward among RepDelParanoia, DelGS1, DelGS2, DelGS2, DelGS3, DelGS4, andDelGS5.

In terms of powerfulness and grandiosity, DelGSn is more powerful than DelGSn-1. Then, the formation of DelGSn is a self destruction of DelGSn-1so that to preserve the whole self system against the increasing of power of delusive oppressive others. In terms of stability of self system, DelGSn-1 is more stable than DelGSn. Thus, the re-bounce to DelGSn-1 when the delusive oppressive others is less powerful is to preserve the stability of the whole self system.

CONCLUSION: IMPLICATIONS TO INTERVENTION AND RECOVERY

As a conclusion, this chapter is a comprehensive description of grandiose delusion and hallucination in people with schizophrenia. According to Kohut's self object relationship, grandiose self and omnipotent others is a spontaneous process in normal self development. Within grandiosity, there are three important components including superiority, self centeredness and related fantasies. Degree of grandiosity are dependent on six factors, line and context of reality, self control mechanism, concerned self-identity, meaning and function, related action and ambition, as well as availability of idealized parental imago and self objects.

In fact, grandiosity in mental illness. Within the complexity of grandiosity, the occurrence of mental illness can be due to intensification of three types of dilemmas in grandiosity. Type A dilemma is inferiority versus superiority. Type B dilemma is sense of insecurity versus self centeredness. Type C dilemma is detachment from reality versus related fantasy. It seems that mania can be a high intensification of type A dilemma inferiority versus superiority. Individual tends to involve in a state of very high superiority to cover up his or her extremely low sense of inferiority. For persons with narcissistic personality disorder, grandiosity is a high intensification of type B dilemma of sense of insecurity versus self centeredness. They experience an intense sense of insecurity and they try to be self centered so that to feel secure and safe.

For persons with grandiose delusion in schizophrenia, all three types of dilemmas are being intensified, in particular type C in terms of extreme detachment of reality and absorption in delusive fantasies.

Delusive grandiosity in people with schizophrenia occurs when parental imago gradually turns into delusive imago; narcissistic self gradually becomes delusive and out teach of reality; unavailability of parental imago in reality; self constructed parental imago; severe problem in transformation of narcissism; as well as superiority and inferiority complex being intensified and turning into a self splitting process. In severe grandiose schizophrenia, there are confused first rank grandiosity in which the individual replaces his or her actual self-identity into delusive grandiose identity. It can change from organized to confused delusive parental imago (omnipotent others), and from organized to confused delusive narcissistic self (grandiose self). It can be a delusive transformation of narcissism. Finally it can be from stability from rapid changes of delusive parental image and narcissistic self.

All these have important implications to recovery and treatment. It is important to dissolve all these unresolved complexes in terms of superiority and inferiority, insecurity and self centeredness, detachment from reality and absorption in fantasies. Among all these three unresolved complexes, for people with grandiose schizophrenia, the most important complex is detachment from reality and absorption in fantasies. That means, people with grandiose delusion should be encouraged to have substantially contact of reality. It implies regular and healthy daily living, meaningful activities as well as spontaneous and constructive interaction and relationship with others. Only by substantially contact with reality, individuals can be less and gradually come out from their absorption in their grandiose identity, delusion as well as hallucination. Regarding the second complex, superiority and inferiority, individual with grandiose schizophrenia should be encouraged to reshape and rebuild a positive, constructive and substantially sense of self-identity. They should be encouraged to develop their potentials, talents and ability in a gradual, consistent and substantially training and recognition so that they do not have to rely on formation, manifestation and absorption in their grandiose identity and delusion to pull up or conceal their intense sense of inferiority. Finally, to resolve the third complex of self centeredness and insecurity, it is important that people with grandiose schizophrenia should be given a secure and supportive social and physical environment so that they do not need to lock up in self constructed grandiose identity to empower and to convince themselves delusively in facing their prolonged threat, humiliation, abuse and victimization in their former insecure and oppressive social environment.

Apart from Kohut's orientation, Laing's (1960) existential and phenomenological orientation is also important in understanding grandiose delusion in schizophrenia.

Laing (1960) affirmed that sort of grandiosity is not a stable state. Instead it is an oscillation between powerfulness and nothingness. In facing the very oppressive environment, individuals loss their autonomy and enter into a stage of ontological insecurity that is a stage of nothingness. Grandiose delusion is a mean used by the individual to obtain inner autonomy, creativity and control. It is a state of delusive powerfulness without substantially contact of reality. It is merely a container full of air under tremendous pressure. That means, it is full and it is powerful but easily bursts out and finally becomes empty and nothing. It finally becomes a vicious circle of the more delusively powerful one feels, the more easy one enters into a stage of nothingness. That means in the recovery of people with grandiose schizophrenia, it is crucial that that sort of vicious circle and the oscillation between powerfulness and nothingness can be resolved. Practically speaking, it occurs only when the individual ontological insecurity can be changed into a state of ontological security and substantially. In Laing's terms, ontological insecurity comes from prolonged implosion, engulfment and petrification. Ontological security and substantially existence should be nurtured by a very autonomous, respectful, supportive and encouraging social environment. The sense of powerfulness should be exercised and manifested in forms of substantially self actualization within actual reality.

In terms of self fragmentation, grandiose delusion is formed by the following natures:

- Parental Imago gradually turns into delusive imago
- Narcissistic self gradually becomes delusive and out teach of reality
- Unavailability of parental imago in reality: It can only be obtained by self constructed parental imago
- Severe problem in transformation of narcissism
- Superiority and inferiority complex is intensified and turns into a self splitting process

In terms of projective identification, grandiose delusion is a further development of paranoid delusion in which the individual no longer needs to defend or be afraid of the threatening other. Instead, grandiose delusion implies transformation of good self into delusive good self and transformation of bad others into delusive good others. In severe and confused grandiose schizophrenia, individuals can shift from one grandiose delusive identity to another one, or having two delusive identity, one good and one bad arguing with one another. In actual clinical practice, the more consistent and stable the delusive grandiose identity is, the less confused the individual is. In the process of recovery, it is better to accept the client's delusive grandiose identity and gradually channel it into meaningful, constructive and substantially activities and interaction with others so that the client can develop a healthy self-identity within the actual reality. The following is a case illustration in helping a client with grandiose schizophrenia in building up a realistic and healthy self-identity. Client's consensus in using his story for academic purpose was sought. For the sake of confidentiality, personal information and identity was properly disguised.

'John was a client with grandiose schizophrenia. He harbored an intense grandiose delusion that he was a heroic god 'the King of Kwan' (a famous god who was a righteous hero and excellent general in Three Kingdom Dynasty around 200 AD). Occasionally, he believed that he was also a descendent of famous British General in the Second World War. These two grandiose delusion always argued with one another. In acute state of psychosis, he yelled in the name of these two heroes and ran into a police station saying he ordered policemen to join in his own army. He was then hospitalized. After some constant intake of psychotic medication, John's mental state seemed to stable and related social functioning was improved after joining occupational therapy in the hospitals. He was then discharged six months later and was admitted into a psychiatric half way house for rehabilitation and recovery.

Under the clinical supervision of the writer, related social workers in this half way house tried to induce the following psychosocial intervention for John.

1. Accept John's delusive and grandiose identity as King of Kwan and British General.
2. Facilitate John to ventilate his superior and inferior complex, self centeredness and insecurity, as well as detachment from reality and absorption in fantasies.
3. Increase John's sense of reality by encouraging him to work daily in sheltered workshop. He was responsible to lead a crew of mobile cleaning team. As King of Kwan and British General, he really enjoyed being a leader.
4. After several months regular daily work, John gradually enjoyed the self-identity as a team leader of his crew more than being British General. He tried to call his crew in terms of related heroic figures in the Three Kingdom Dynasty.
5. As all these heroic figures were well known by most Chinese, his crew enjoyed all these. They teased one another in a humorous way.
6. By means of all these meaningful, interesting and constructive day to day interaction, John was gradually regarded by his crew as an interesting leader. They gave John a new identity as 'big brother'.
7. John really enjoyed this new realistic self-identity. He loved meaningful activities in performing the mobile cleaning crew. He also enjoyed happy encounter and interaction with all his crew.
8. Gradually, John's grandiose delusion as King of Kwan decreased. He enjoyed being the big brother and leader of his crew rather than being a historic hero. He regarded this only as a nickname rather than his actual identity.

References

Gunderson J., Ronningstam E., Bodkin A. (1990) "The diagnostic interview for narcissistic patients," *Archives of General Psychiatry*, 47, 676-680

Kohut, H. (1971). *The Analysis of the Self*, New York: International University Press.

Kohut, H., (1977). *The Restoration of the Self,* New York: International Universities Press.

Kohut, H. (1985). *The Analysis of Self: A Systematic Approach to the Psychoanalysis Treatment of Narcissistic Personality Disorder*, New York: International University Press.

Laing R. D. (1960). *The Divided Self*, London: Tavistock Publication.

Siegel, A. M. (1996). *Heinz Kohut and the Psychology of the Self,* New York: Routledge.

Chapter 4

CATATONIC STUPOR AND FIXATION IN PEOPLE WITH SCHIZOPHRENIA: A DILEMMA OF EXISTENCE AND NON-EXISTENCE FROM EXTERNAL THREAT

INTRODUCTION

Within positive symptoms of schizophrenia, apart from grandiose and paranoid delusions and hallucination, there are also catatonic features. People with catatonic features do not engage in hyperactive thoughts, emotions, and action as those with paranoid and grandiose delusion and hallucinations do. Instead, they are inert and stagnant. They are stagnant but not withdrawn. They are inert but not detached from the external environment. Catatonia exists in a state of extreme intension and urgency with a very sensitivity to the external environment. In this chapter, the writer explores natures and features of catatonia and its relations with various types of mental illness. Various perspectives of catatonic delusion and hallucination are fully discussed. Its implications to recovery and intervention are also mentioned.

NATURES AND DEFINITIONS OF CATATONIA

History of Catatonia

Fink and Taylor (2003) asserted that catatonia is a "cluster of motor features that appears in many recognized psychiatric illnesses. The classical sign are mutism, a rigid postures, fixed staring, stereotyped movement and stupor." (Fink & Taylor, 2003:6). Fink et al. (2010) affirmed that it originated with Karl Kahlbaum in 1874. Its relationship with persons with schizophrenia started with Emil Kraeplin in his concept of dementia praecox and was later further endorsed by Eugen Bleuler. Gradually, it was also discovered in other forms of mental illness, such as mania and depression by American authors. They regarded it as a toxic response in general medical and neurologic illnesses, around only 10 percent of acute psychiatric admissions (Fink et al., 2010). Regarding diagnosis and treatment, it is described as follows:

> When looked for, catatonia is found in 10 percent or more *of* acute psychiatric admissions. It is readily diagnosable, verifiable by a lorazepam challenge test, and rapidly treatable. Even in its most lethal forms, it responds to high doses *of* lorazepam or to electroconvulsive therapy. These treatments are not accepted for patients with schizophrenia. Prompt recognition and treatment saves lives. It is time to place catatonia into its own home in the psychiatric classification. (Fink et al., 2010: 314)

Definitions of Catatonia

According to Medical-Library (2007), catatonia has the following features:

1. change in muscle tone or activity
2. association with serious mental illness and physical illness
3. catatonic stupor in which individual experiences a deficit of motor activity that can render him or her motionless
4. catatonic excitement or excessive movement that is associated with violent behavior toward oneself or others

That means catatonia is a muscle tone with either catatonic stupor or catatonic excitement that associated with mental illness or physical illness, including schizophrenia. In a catatonic stupor, the individual's motor activity may be greatly reduced to a degree of immobility or even poor physical hygiene.

> In catatonic stupor, motor activity may be reduced to zero. Individuals avoid bathing and grooming, make little or no eye contact with others, may be mute and rigid, and initiate no social behaviors. In catatonic excitement the individual is extremely hyperactive although the activity seems to have no purpose. Violence toward him - or herself or others may also be seen. (Fink et al., 2010: 315

That means individuals with catatonia and mental illness are kept in an intense mental and physical tension that he or she is fully alert, he or she is always very sensitive, and he or she is always prepared to fight back and respond to all external threats and negative physical stimulation. In doing so, he or she may even stop all kinds of normal, social functioning and physical and mental activities.

Also, catatonia can be found in the neuroleptic malignant syndrome in which patients with schizophrenia, after taking anti-psychotic medication may be vulnerable to symptoms of catatonia.

> Features of catatonia may also be seen in Neuroleptic Malignant Syndrome (NMS) which is an uncommon (but potentially lethal) reaction to some medications used to treat major mental illnesses. NMS is considered a medical emergency since 25 percent of untreated cases result in *death*. Catatonia can also be present in individuals suffering from a number of other physical and emotional conditions such as drug intoxication, depression, and *schizophrenia*. It is most commonly associated with *mood disorders*. (*Medical-Library*, 2007:1)

Catatonia and Mental Illness

Prevalence of Catatonia in Mental Illness

Related studies showed that various degrees of catatonia is found in various types of mental illness. In particular, it accompanies schizophrenia, mood disorders, autism, and others due to general medical conditions.

> It is found between 5 percent and 9 percent of all psychiatric inpatients show some catatonic symptoms. Of these, 25 percent–50 percent are associated with mood disorders, 10 percent–15 percent are associated with schizophrenia, and the remainder are associated with other mental disorders. Catatonic symptoms can also occur in a wide variety of general medical conditions, including infectious, metabolic and neurological disorders. They may also appear as side effects of various medications, including several drugs of abuse. (*Encyclopedia of Mental Disorders*, 2007: 5)

Around 5 percent to 9 percent of psychiatric inpatients have catatonic symptoms. Of them, between one-fourth and one-half are mood disorders, and one-tenth are schizophrenic. For mood disorders with catatonia, the most common features are depressive disorders. Persons with major depressive disorders may feel inert, withdrawn, and passive. Many of them may even be stagnant, lying on their own beds and refusing to eat, drink, or do anything. In doing so, they remain in a state of catatonic stupor. On one hand, the individual experiences a deficit of motor activity that can render him or her motionless. On the other hand, the individual is excited inside, feeling deeply angry with him- or herself and others continuously.

People who are severely depressed may show disturbances of motor behavior resembling those of patients diagnosed with catatonic schizophrenia. These depressed persons may remain virtually motionless, or move around in an extremely vigorous but apparently random fashion. Extreme negativism, elective mutism (choosing not to speak), peculiar movements, and imitating someone else's words or phrases (echolalia) or movements (echopraxia) may also be part of the symptomatic picture. These behaviors may require caregivers to supervise the patient, to insure that he or she does not hurt him- or herself or others. . . . A severely depressed person may experience intense emotional pain from simply moving a finger. Even getting up out of a chair can be a painful chore that may take hours for the severely depressed individual. As the depression begins to lift, the catatonic symptoms diminish. (*Encyclopedia of Mental Disorders,* 2007: 5)

Catatonic Behaviors in Adult and Childhood Mental Problems

Catatonic behaviors also happen in clients with bipolar disorders. Within a heightened state of mania, individual may exhibit immobility or agitated behaviors similar to catatonic behaviors. Catatonia may also occur in autistic disorders. Individuals with autistic disorders, apart from mutism and repeated odd behaviors, occasionally may also exercise stupor and fixation on certain postures and gestures. Dhossche, Wilson, and Wachtel's (2010) research showed that catatonia occurs in following:

- developmental disorders such as autistic disorders, childhood disintegrative disorder, mental retardation, Prader-Willi syndrome
- mood disorder
- psychotic disorders such as schizophrenia and schizoaffective disorders
- Substance abuse disorder
- Tourette's syndrome
- Mental disorders due to a general medical conditions
- Medication induced movement disorder (neuroleptic malignant syndrome)

Table 4. Common Catatonic Symptoms in Children and Adults (Dhossche, Wilson & Wachtel, 2010: 35

	Children (%)	Adults (%)
Mutism	87	78
Posturing	52	66
Stupor	80	66
Staring	49	57
Waxy flexibility	62	35
Incontinence	45	-

Regarding the prevalence of catatonia in various forms in children and adults, Dhossche, Wilson and Wachtel's (2010) described Table 4.

Catatonia in Schizophrenia

Natures and Diagnosis of Catatonic Schizophrenia

Catatonic schizophrenia is a typical type of schizophrenia in which the individual is totally occupied by stupor of stagnancy or excitement. Catatonia within schizophrenia is characterized by the following natures (Mayo Clinic, 2010):

1. *Physical immobility.* You may be completely unable to move or speak, or you may stare, hold your body in a rigid position and seem to be unaware of your surroundings (catatonic stupor). You also may have a form of immobility known as waxy flexibility. For example, if your arm is moved into a certain position, it will stay in that position for hours.
2. *Excessive mobility.* Rather than being unable to move, you may move in an excited manner that appears to have no purpose. You may pace in a frenzy, turn in circles, flail your arms or make loud noises.
3. *Extreme resistance.* You may not respond to instructions, may resist any attempt to be moved or may not speak at all.
4. *Peculiar movements.* You may have inappropriate or unusual postures, grimace for long periods or adopt unusual mannerisms. You may also have habits known as stereotyped behaviors, which can include repeating words, obsessively following a routine, or always arranging objects exactly the same way.
5. *Mimicking speech or movement.* You may repeatedly say a word just spoken by someone else (echolalia) or repeatedly copy a gesture or movement made by someone else (echopraxia). (Mayo Clinic, 2010: 3)

Wikipedia (2004) tended to a very vivid and refined about catatonia in schizophrenia in particular related stupors.

> 'It is characterized by severe disturbances in motor behavior. Individuals with catatonic schizophrenia often show extreme immobility. They may stay in the same position for hours, days, weeks, or longer. The position they assume may be unusual and appear uncomfortable to the observer; for example, the person may stand on one leg like a stork, or hold one arm outstretched for a long time. If an observer moves a hand or limb of the catatonic person's body, he or she may maintain the new position. This condition is known as waxy flexibility. In other situations, a person with catatonic schizophrenia may

> be extremely active, but the activity appears bizarre, purposeless, and unconnected to the situation or surroundings. The patient may, for example, run up and down a flight of stairs repeatedly. Catatonic stupor is characterized by extremely slowed motor activity, often to the point of being motionless and appearing unaware of surroundings. The patient may exhibit negativism, which means that he or she resists all attempts to be moved, or all instructions or requests to move, without any apparent motivation.'

From the above description, it is clear that individuals experiencing catatonic schizophrenia are on a stage of separating his or her boy to response to the spontaneous reality. Instead of using our bodies to respond to external stimuli, individuals try using his or her to separate his or her mind to the connection of the oppressive and threatening immediate physical and social environment. Stupors in forms of resistance, peculiar movements, immobility all serve the important function that the body used as a defensive measure to protect the individual from external threats and insecurity. The mind of the individual actually detaches from the body, he or she is observing or manipulating the body as a foreign object to shelter him- or herself from external threats. Interestingly within the self constructed stupors, individuals tend to regard time and space as frozen and immobile. Even though related objects in external environments are kept moving and changes, individuals regard themselves as stagnant with internal power to hold up any movements from external objects. In doing so, they can defend against any attack or oppression from external objects.

Sense of Insecurity and Urgency in Catatonic Schizophrenia

Within manifestation of symptoms of catatonia in schizophrenia, the stupor in forms of stupor of immobility and extreme excitement, the alienation of body from the mind, the urge to freeze the time and space in externality can be interpreted as sense of intense insecurity and urgency in facing the very oppressive environment. Sullivan (1956) described this internal mechanism with the following characteristics:

1. *Severe need of sense of security and free of anxiety* to a degree that deteriorate one's sense of consciousness and awareness on oneself and environment.
2. *A loss of boundary between Self system and related environment* (the boundary between the individual and the universe, particularly the personal universe, undergo the same diffusion).
3. *A notion of getting what happens* and being able to tell another person about it, continued to be a present of the schizophrenia episode.
4. *There is a strong feeling of urgency* that the clients feel that something need to be done or to be insisted immediately without delay (panic to get away from

something, or panic to do something immediately. Or resolve some difficulties urgently, or think through something immediately).
5. *The state of an observable mind* (The client think that he or she is closely observing the surrounding world or the something in the world he or she is closely attending to). There is a constantly fixation of the sense of space and sense of time.
6. *A State of Stupor, Excitement and Tension* (It is a state of power, some great cosmic force, tied up the muscles and prevents action.
7. *A State of Meaningfulness* (The tense inactivity is not enough; the urgency calls for something more than that, so instead of feeling that a power has hypnotized him, or however he might to try to describe it as a meaningful act with a clear focus and urgency) (Sullivan, 1956: 311-323).

These seven characteristics, coupled with the seven characteristics of catatonia described by Mayo Clinic (2010), can be divided into three groups. The first group of characteristics is internal state of mind of people with catatonic schizophrenia. It includes the following:

A1: Severe need of sense of security and free of anxiety
A2: A notion of getting what happens
A3: A strong feeling of urgency
A4: A state of meaningfulness

The state of mind of individuals with catatonic schizophrenia implies that they are in a great internal tension. They may feel very anxious and insecure about external environment. They have serious doubt what is happening within the external environment. They embrace a fear that they are in a great urgency to find out what is happening within the environment so that they can defend from external threat effectively and efficiently. They just like soldiers preparing themselves to fight against related enemies in a threatening environment. However, before they fight back, they have to make sure who are enemies and where as well as how they attack them. Psychologically, they feel anxious, tense and in an urgency to clarify all these doubts to be fully prepared for the possible fighting.

The second group of characteristics is external manifestation of catatonic behaviors. It includes the following:

B1: Physical immobility or excessive mobility
B2: Extreme resistance or peculiar movement
B3: A state of stupor and excitement

The second group of characteristics meaning facing the hidden external threats, individuals with catatonic schizophrenia is also physically prepared for the fighting. They are two different ways to be physically prepared. The first way is to keep in a state of stupor. The second way is to be a state of excitement. In the state of stupor, individuals with catatonic schizophrenia assume that others are going to attack them. As the attack and threat is unclear and may be hidden, any movement may make their enemies embrace chance to launch such attack. Thus, it is better to remain in a state of stupor with full mental and physical energy as well as full and powerful observation so that they can defend themselves from any attack. For those with prevailing paranoid delusion, they may presume others control their own body in a way they can move even a bit. In the second way, there is a state of excitement. That means, the individuals are trying every means to defend themselves and attack the invisible or hidden enemies. The state of excitement may be together with all sorts of peculiar and excessive movements, all these movements occur in a regular and repeated manner as a sign representing their power in defending themselves and fighting back the invisible enemies. For those with grandiose delusion, they may even presume that they are powerful gods, heroes and famous persons and these catatonic peculiar movements are signs of these gods, heroes and persons.

The third group characteristics are a diffusion of self boundary. It includes the followings:

C1: The state of an observable mind

C2: A loss of self boundary of self system and related environment

Within a catatonic schizophrenia, the individual is very diffused in self- boundary in a way that he or she is unable to distinguish self and his or her related environment. Without a sufficient and clear self-boundary, individual feels very threatened that related persons, objects and issues within the external environment easily insert and intermingle into the self system to an extent he or she feels that he or she is incomplete and his or her self system is wither. Also, the individual is a state of an observable mind, he or she tries to dissociate his or her body and mind. His or her mind watches over his or her own body in a way that he or she regards him- or herself as a foreign body. This is a process of self-fragmentation with splitting of mind and body as well as a diffusion of self-boundary. That means the whole self system is weakening with a deteriorating ego functioning, diffusing self-boundary and confused self-identity. That means, the individual being absorbed in the catatonic delusion and hallucination, his or her ability to engage in the actual reality decreases and his or her sense of reality reduced. His or her senses of insecurity and anxiety increase drastically. He or she spontaneous feels being threatened by related objects, persons and issues in external reality. These three groups of characteristics, state of mind, external behaviors and self boundaries are all intermingle together that can be presented in the figure on the next page.

These three characteristics in individuals with catatonic schizophrenia combine with one another. Catatonic behaviors are in fact are fuelled by a catatonic state of mind. Individuals feel very insecure, anxious, urgent, doubtful and suspicious in a way they try every mean to make sure they are secure, safe and free from external threat. Catatonic behaviors are only ways to guarantee security, safety and make meaning of hidden threat. The diffusion of self boundary and observable mind is a representation of psychotic self-fragmentation. With that sort of diffused self-boundary, individuals' of insecurity, anxiety and worries increase drastically. Their sense of reality is blurred and confused. They cannot distinguish whether or not these external objects or persons are threatening them. Thus, it greatly intensifies their catatonic behaviors as defensive means from prevailing external threats. In doing so, individuals' self system into two parts, one represents a well-concealed but basically secure state of mind to observe things happening in external environment. Another part represents individuals' insecure state of mind interacting and defending him- or herself from insecure environment by engaging in catatonic behaviors. The self splitting gradually contributes to a vigorous process of self-fragmentation with contribution of catatonic related psychotic symptoms. Some clients full believe that they are no longer human being but transform into a powerful but catatonic objects such as "tree," "penguin," "umbrella," or even "outer universe monster" with mighty power to defend themselves from any external threat or attack as well as saving other similar victims in this world.

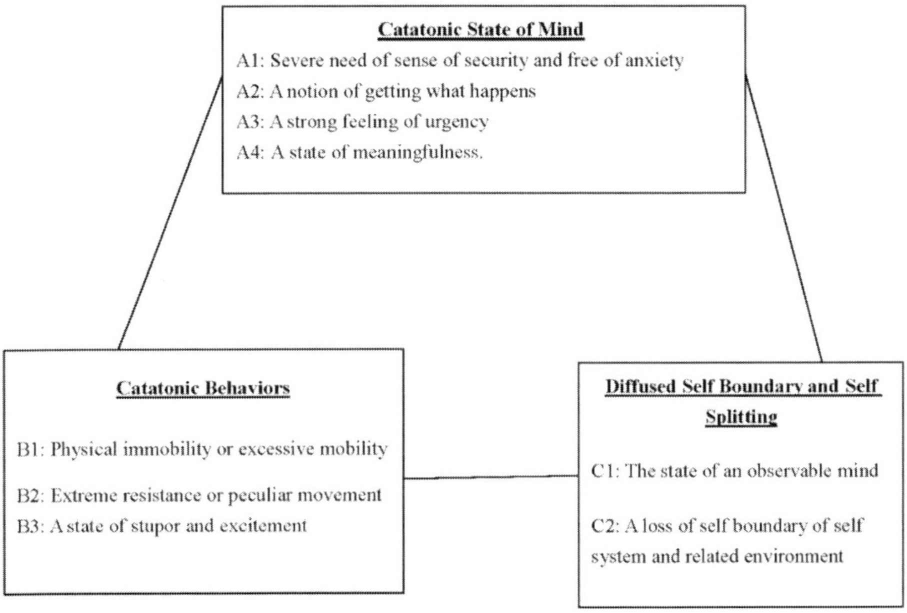

Figure 9. The Three Characteristics of Catatonic Schizophrenia

DEVELOPMENT OF VOLITION IN CATATONIA

Arieti (1974) had a full description about the developmental process of catatonic schizophrenia. This process involves several stages of development.

Strict and Demanding Parents and Prevailing Guilt

In the childhood of persons with catatonic schizophrenia, they have to struggle within their parents' choice and actions. In many cases, their parents are very strict and punitive. That means, individuals embrace overwhelming fear in doing wrong thing. Thus, the best coping is avoiding doing anything wrong. In extreme situation, the panic can be very generalized to a degree that individuals should do nothing including drinking and eating.

> 'Thus, in catatonic, the typical schizophrenic childhood struggle with the significant adults is connected particularly with the patient's actions and choices, The fear of action become panic. *The catatonic state is a way of remove action in order to remove the panic connected with the willed action.* Sometimes the panic is very generalized... . The overwhelming fear of doing the wrong thing, which would either hurt or disappoint him, possess him to an increasing degree (from avoiding doing anything wrong... to do nothing including eating, drinking and finally become motionlessness). (Arieti, 1974: 317–318)

Blind Acceptance and Inertia

> In order to avoid anxiety and guilt, the patient cannot will any act, but he may passively follow orders given by others, because the responsibility will not be his. This blind acceptance is due to the complete substitution of someone else's will for his own. Waxy flexibility, of retention of uncomfortable body positions in which the patient is passively put, can also be explained in this way. When the patient is passively put, can also be explained in the way. When the patient is put in a given position, the will or responsibility of someone else is involved. If he wants to change positions, he has to will the change, and the will engender anxiety or guilt. (Arieti, 1974: 320)

Facing the prevailing guilt and anxiety, the best coping in facing very critical, demanding, and strict parents is to follow their orders blindly. In doing so, individuals actually involve in a self splitting process of their mind and body. The individual's body works strictly according to the autocratic figure's instruction. However, his or her mind is paralyzed. He or she does not have any feeling or emotion. He or she does not have any thinking toward his or her actions. His or her will is substituted by the others' will and instruction. That means, psychologically and cognitively, he or she is a vacuum. He or she becomes a "machine of others." This is similar to those clients with catatonic schizophrenia. Their waxy flexibility and retention of certain position is being controlled by an "imaginative other." His or her mind or his or her self system, within psychotic splitting, is broken into two partial systems. One represents his or her own. The other represents the oppressive others. In addition to that, his or her own body is also separated from his or her own mind. Thus, if he or she wanted to have any movement, he or she has to undergo the following process:

1. The delusive, oppressive, but hidden. Others send an instruction for him or her to move.
2. His or her own, but split, self receives the instruction from the delusive and oppressive others.
3. He or she has to follow the instruction of this delusive but oppressive others. If he or she fails to do that, he or she may then harbor intense guilt and anxiety.
4. His or her body then follow the instruction to move until he or she receives further instruction from the delusive but oppressive other.

Negativism and Resistance

> Quite often the reverse seems to occur. The patient will resist the order or will do the opposite. This is the phenomenon of negativism. The resistance is due to the fact that often the patient feels the responsibility for an act, even when it is ordered by somebody else. It is true that he is ordered to act, but he himself must will to move. Therefore he resists . . . the patient absorb into his fantasies, which makes every influence acting from without a comparatively intolerable interruption. According to this interpretation, the patient wants to be left alone or wants to be unaware of all stimuli emanating from the outside world because of they are unpleasant. (Arieti, 1974: 320)

Strict and blind acceptance of others' comment is very unpleasant and uncomfortable. Prolonged separation of the body and mind, as well as the splitting of the self system is very intolerable for the individual. The only way to stop that is to resist the hidden control of others. Thus, the more one involves oneself in blind acceptance, the more one is reluctant to do it again. That means individuals engage in a state of inertia in catatonic schizophrenia. They simply refuse to do anything or engage in any activities. In this stupor, they try to shut themselves from any outside physical stimuli. The state of inertia is further enriched by psychotic fantasy that they are engaging in an intense, defensive action toward hidden, oppressive others who try to control them.

Retreat versus Attention to External Environment

As the negativism and resistance develop further, the client enters into a state of dilemma. On the one hand, the client appears to have an intense retreat from the oppressive, external environment as he or she regards this as the most effective way in defending themselves from the control of the hidden, oppressive others. On the other hand, he or she is still attending to stimuli in the external environment. He or she is still very observant so that he or she can be fully aware of any possible or hidden threat in the related environment.

> The patient who comes out from the stupor is able to give an accurate account of the events that occurred or of the words which were spoken in his presence when he could not move or talk. This indicates that, in spite of appearances, the attention toward the external world is preserved and that only actions are blocked because only actions are willed. (Arieti, 1974: 321)

Delusive and Unrealistic Interpretation of the External Environment

Within this dilemma, the client may try to link up this trap by an unrealistic and even delusive interpretation.

> It is true, however, that in several instances, the attention of the patient is withdrawn from his surroundings because the patient cannot will to pay attention. In numerous other cases the catatonic pays attention to his surroundings, but his interpretation of the external world is unrealistic and paleologic. This is particular true in cases that present mixtures of catatonic and hebephrenic features. On the other hand, in the typical catatonic, the perception of the external world is well-preserved. Arieti, 1974: 321–322)

This sort of delusive interpretation enables the individual to strike a balance between his or her need to retreat from the oppressive environment as well as his or her need to be very attentive to hidden threats in the environment. For example, an individual with catatonic schizophrenia may come to a delusive conclusion that there is an overwhelming, but hidden, secret agent from the Central Intelligence Agency (CIA) in the United States that controls everybody's minds to do evil things. The only way to prevent it is to remain immobile so to counteract the control of the CIA. In doing so, he or she keeps a keen eye on everybody in the environment so that he or she can at least know about the hidden influence of the CIA secret agent. In his or her mind, he or she is actually removed from the environment as he or she refuses to join in any activities within the immediate psychosocial environment. However, he or she is still observing the environment and preserving his or her keen perception of his or her environment.

Residual Sense of Reality and Response

Despite all these dilemmas and delusive interpretations of the external environment, individuals with catatonic schizophrenia do in fact, still harbor a residual sense of reality causing them to have sensible responses to risks and crises in the social environment.

> Psychiatrists who have worked in institutions for many years know of several examples providing this to be so. We know that in case of fire in hospitals, catatonics suddenly move, start to run, or even help others. It is equally true that some preserve their catatonic state and perish in the flames. In many psychiatric hospitals, we hear anecdotes about unpredictable and very appropriate behavior and actions of catatonic patients. (Arieti, 1974: 322)

Not only they have a good awareness of fires and emergencies in mental hospitals, they can also lend a helping hand to others who are in desperate need of help. For example, Arieti (1974) described an interesting case. Once, he was talking in a psychiatric ward with another psychiatrist. At that moment, both of them were absorbed in their talk, and they began to criticize their superintendent in the mental hospital. At that moment, a male catatonic schizophrenic patient was standing in front of them. His eyes were staring through the glass window and looking at the external environment. While they were totally absorbed in their talk and criticism of the superintendent, they did not notice that their superintendent was coming into the ward quickly. Suddenly, the catatonic patient, who had been in his catatonic stupor for many hours without speaking a word, spoke in a loud voice saying that the superintendent was coming. With such warning, they stopped their criticism immediately and greeted the approaching superintendent. Interestingly, after the warning, the catatonic patient returned back to his catatonic stupor, in the same posture again. It was the first and last time in the ward that he murmured or spoke any word in such a large voice (Arieti, 1974: 322-3)

Sense of Existence in Catatonic Schizophrenia

Catatonic State as a Manipulation of False Self by Inner Self

In Laing's terms, catatonia is self manipulation of the false self by the inner self. That means the individual is fully aware of the existence and stagnancy of the false self and unembodied self. His or her true inner self is actually watching the movement and stupor of the body within a very, or potentially, threatening external environment. As mentioned above, in Pamwagg's (2004) subjective experiences, catatonic schizophrenia implies a distant feeling from one's own body, a detachment from related persons and things in the immediate environment, and an immobility of the body, allowing one to observe mobility in reality clearly and independently. That means, the individual can choose his or her right time, the right way, the right pace to respond to the environment. He or she can be autonomous and independent in choosing his or her own ways of responding without being influenced by the environment. In line of Laing's concept of self splitting, catatonia is the manipulation of the false self (the dead and unembodied self) by the inner self. According to Laing (1960), the false self is a split part from the self system with a total deadness and totally submissive to the external oppressive others.

> False self system's compliance with the will of others reaches its most extreme form in the automatic obedience, echolalia, and flexibilities **cerea of the catatonic.** Here obedience, imitation, copying are carried to such excess that the grotesque parody produced becomes a concealed indictment of the manipulating examiner. (Laing, 1960: 102)

That means the catatonic stage is a defense shield for the protection of the inner self. It is not the false self. It is the manipulation of the false self by the inner self or inner true self. By doing it, the inner true self can be shielded from the external environment. The relationship of the inner self or the inner true self with the unembodied self, or the false self, can be complicated and exists in several forms.

1. Manipulation of the unembodied self by the inner self (primary self splitting).
2. Manipulation of the false self by the inner true self (secondary self splitting).
3. Manipulation of the false self and the unembodied self by the inner true self (complicated secondary self splitting).
4. Within each type of manipulation, there can also be two ways:
   A. Excessive excitement in terms of movements, explorations, and responses to potential threats in the oppressive environment;
   B. Intense and prolonged stagnancy and stupor in terms of posture, observation, and body tension to avoid control by foreseeable threats in the oppressive environment.

In the first type of manipulation, the split unembodied self is used by the inner self to shield from potential or existing threat from the oppressive, external environment. For example, in facing external blaming and intense criticism, the individual's split, unembodied self appears inert or with a quick, but very simple, apathetic and ritualistic admission of one's faults. In the individual's inner self shield it from self blaming and criticism. In the secondary self splitting, the self system is further split into three components: the unembodied self, the false self, and the inner self. The unembodied self seems to tackle with the external threat in a regressive and apathetic way, the false self tends to presume the environment is full of potential threats, the inner self tends to interpret and manipulate both the false self and the unembodied self in a catatonic stupor. In manipulating the unembodied self, the inner self sustains the body to remain in a stage of stagnation regardless of external stimulations or have excessive movements to search or respond to potential external threats and stimulation. In manipulation of the false self, the inner self facilitates the formation of a catatonic mind in a heightened mental stage with a full consciousness and keen observation to all possible threats and stimulations in the oppressive, external environment. In a full, psychotic catatonia, the inner self manipulates both the unembodied self and the false self together. In that situation, individuals, who are under a severe process of self fragmentation, feel their inner self overwhelmed by unforeseeable threats from various dimensions of the external environment. Thus, they tend to need the unembodied self to absorb and respond to all external threats squarely and let the false self have a keen observation of all possible threats and stimulation. With the protective shield from the unembodied self and the defensive observation from the false self, the inner self is able to maintain a withdrawn but powerful interpretation and passive response to any possible and potential external threat. In this full state of catatonia, the individual also harbors a grandiose idea that he or she is powerful enough to protect and shield him- or herself from any possible threat and oppression.

Catatonic Delusion as a Form of Self Paced Autonomy

Laing (1960) affirmed this as a form of withdrawal so that the secret self (inner self) can be caricaturing from external reality.

> If all the individual's behavior comes to be compulsively alienated from the secret self so that it is given over entirely to compulsive mimicry, impersonating, caricaturing and to such transitory behavioral foreign bodies are well, he may then try to strip himself of all his behaviors. *This is one form of catatonic withdrawal.* (Laing, 1960: 105)

In comparison to Pamwagg's (2004) subjective experience in catatonia, Laing's (1960) articulation of the catatonic stage as false self in self-fragmentation tended to neglect two important aspects:

1. In a catatonic stage, the individual is not in a state of passive inertness. Instead, the individual chooses to be inert so as to detach from external demands.
2. In a catatonic stage, the individual, being detached and inert from the external environment, he or she can use his or her own pace to interact with the reality.

That means, instead of being controlled by external reality, the individual tries to regain the autonomy to control and to intervene in reality.

In other words, catatonia in psychotic self-fragmentation is not part of the false self, where the individual loses control or is completely obedient and submissive to the external environment. Instead, *it is a part of the inner self, where it shields itself with the false self in order to observe the outside and to intervene anytime.* In fact, while the self can be totally manipulated by others, it can also be manipulated by the inner self. The inner self also projects his or her anger toward the false self.

> The inner secret self hates the characteristics of the false self. It also fears that, because of the assumption of an alien identity is always experienced as a threat to his own. The self fears being engulfed by the spread of the identification. To some extent, the false self system would seem to act analogously to the body's reticulo-endothelial system, which walls off the encapsulated dangerous intruding foreign matter and thus prevents these alien intruders from spreading more diffused throughout the body. But if such is its defensive function it must be judged as failure. The inner self is not truer than the outer. David's inner secret self turned into a most controlling manipulating agency which used his false self very much like the puppet he felt he had been for his mother. That is, the shadow of his mother had fallen across his inner self as well as his outer self. (Laing, 1960: 103)

Catatonic State in Self-Fragmentation: A Case Illustration

Thus, catatonic state in self-fragmentation should be understood as follows:

a. It is a manipulation of both the un-embodied self and the false self to serve the need of the inner self.
b. It is a detachment of the externality by inner self.
c. It is an immobility of the inner self so that it can focus all its energy to observe and interpret externality continuously.
d. It is a full but passive and inert defense by the inner self from external threat.
e. It is a store up of inner energy so that the inner self can empower itself to face external threat.

All these may be illustrated in the following case illustration. Related parties' consensus in using their stories for academic purpose was sought. For the sake of confidentiality, their personal identity and information were properly disguised.

C was a client with catatonic schizophrenia. He was born in a single parent family in which his father died when he was only a small boy. His mother took care of him, his elder sister and his younger sister. The whole family depended on public assistance, and they had to live hand to mouth. As the only son in the family, C was always reminded by his mother C to be independent and assume a male role to protect the female figures in his family. Physically, C was quite well-built and comparatively stronger and taller than his schoolmates in his class. Academically, C's performance was poor; he had problems in keeping up with his studies in English and Chinese. C also had problems in expressing his feelings and ideas. He appeared a bit inert and silent in front of others. However, if any classmates tried to bully or molest him, C might burst out in anger and physically attack them. C's irrational response made his situation even worse. He was thus severely bullied, isolated, and excluded by his peers and classmates. Many of them tried to stir up his anger and went away leaving C trapped within his overwhelming rage. They enjoyed this "hit and run game" very much. At home, C's mother was very enmeshed with C and required him to follow her in every refined detail. All these did make C's mental state quite unstable with a habitual catatonic stupor of standing still or sitting tightly in his own chair for an hour. Within this gesture, he appeared angry and furious and would curse anyone who came close to him. C's academic performance was poor, and he finished his secondary school with a very poor result in his public examination. C became a manual worker in a transport company. Gradually, he fell in love with a sales girl in a wine company.

Unfortunately, his courtship did not last long. His girlfriend left him and fell in love with his supervisor at his transport company. At the same time, his supervisor sacked him from his job. He was furious, he stood still in the middle of the car park entrance, with his hand stretch widely and tried to deter any lorry from leaving the car park. No one, including his colleagues, supervisor, and company guard could persuade him to move or change his posture. Finally, they called the police and C was taken to a mental hospital. He was diagnosed as having catatonic schizophrenia.

In the mental hospital, whenever he felt anxious or bullied or criticized by others, he would remain in this catatonic stupor for hours. In doing so, he made some strange sounds just like an eagle flying in the sky. He only finished his catatonic stupor when he felt tired or others fully acknowledged that he was a powerful, mythical, righteous eagle to come the world to save the powerless victims who were oppressed by others. Fortunately, he encountered a very empathic and genuine psychiatric nurse and kindhearted psychiatrist. They did not impose electric shock treatment to his catatonic stupor. Instead they tried to understand his feelings and needs behind his psychotic catatonia. They called him "eagle of righteousness". They started to share his feelings underlying his psychotic, catatonic manifestation. At first, he refused to say anything. Under the care of them, he gradually elaborated the strange feelings behind his catatonic manifestation, especially after hours of "tired eagle manifestation." What follows was his self narration about that:

> *C: "For sure, I am a righteous eagle. I need to defend myself from all sorts of attack in the world. In the world, there are many bad guys. They hide everywhere. They wait for the right time to attack me. In my life, I had to face many attacks, my bullying classmates, my oppressive boss, and many others. Only by keen observation and prompt defense, can I save myself from any unnecessary attack and oppression. My enemies are hidden. I told you the best way is to remain silent, appear to be inert and stagnant so that your enemies are not aware that you are observing and even defending yourself. In doing so, I am also able to clearly discover who are my enemies. On the surface, I am inert and even stagnant in facing others' criticism. In doing so, people around are not aware that I am observing them, noticing and screening any potential danger occurring in the environment. With all the latent and continuous observation, deep down in my heart, I am preparing to defend myself, to protect both myself and others. Also, I am spontaneously interpreting what sort of strategies I should use to defend and to protect myself. In times of deep frustration and within a very insecure environment, I can obtain extra physical and mental energy to counteract the unseen control of my enemies. They use some strange machines to control the electric waves from my brain. However, turning myself into a righteous eagle can fully deter all these electric waves from controlling my brain."*

From C's description, it is clear that C's psychotic catatonia implied a serious self-fragmentation C's self system was split into three sections: the unembodied self, the false self, and the true self. In fact, under the influence of psychotic delusions, C had already shifted his identity to become a "righteous eagle" to defend potential bad buys in his social environment again. His embodied self, that was his own body reminded stagnant and inert in responding to external stimuli, including others' criticism, rejection, and ignorance. His false self, that was his very tensed and anxious mind that tried to observe clearly about any potential risky and threatening movements or related stimuli in his social environment. His true self was his actual, deep mind that was continuously assessing, interpreting, and articulating what was exactly happening and how he would respond to related threats and risks in the immediate social environment. His inner self felt safe and secure as his mind was concealed under the stagnant, but tense, body and very alert mind. He believed that no one, including his enemies, could detect his keen observation since he was stagnant and inert in the surface. In times of frustration and insecurity, his catatonic stupor of being a righteous eagle can also defend him from attack and threats by his enemies.

CONCLUSION: IMPLICATIONS FOR CLINICAL PRACTICE

In conclusion, this chapter is a comprehensive discussion of the related theoretical underpinnings of catatonia, catatonia in different mental illnesses, as well as catatonic delusion in schizophrenia.

Catatonia is a change in muscle tone or activity, associated with serious mental illness, catatonic stupor, excitement, or excessive movement. In catatonic schizophrenia, there are catatonic states of mind (a state of urgency, security, and meaningfulness), catatonic behaviors (physical immobility, resistance, stupor and excitement) and diffused self boundary (state of observable mind, loss of self boundary in the self system).

Arieti (1974) describes the development of catatonic volition in terms of strict and demanding parents and prevailing guilt, blind acceptance and inertia, negativism and resistance, retreat versus attention to the external environment, delusion and unrealistic interpretation of external environment, as well as a residual sense of reality and responsibility. It implies that the individual in facing very demanding and guilt-provoking parents, on one hand, is accustomed to accepting and following. On the other hand, unresolved tension, anger and resistance are bottled up in the form of a catatonic stupor and the dilemma of retreat versus over-attention and sensitivity to the external environment. In doing so, the individual can only have a residual sense of reality but a diffused sense of self boundary in catatonic delusion. All these have strong implications to clinical practice and recovery of people with catatonic schizophrenia. That means, people with catatonic schizophrenia harbor a strong superego and sense of morality and righteousness. He or she also bottle up an intense sense of anger, resistance and tension. Related professionals need to facilitate clients airing out all these tensions, anger, and resistance. They also need to channel clients' intense sense of morality and righteousness in meaningful activities, volunteer work as well as contribution to family, community, and society.

In Laing's existential and phenomenological terms, catatonic delusion is a manipulation of the false self by the inner self in regaining control and automony from a very abusive and oppressive external environment. The catatonic state in self-fragmentation in schizophrenia is a manipulation of both the un-embodied self and the false self to serve the needs of the inner self. It is a detachment from externality by inner self. It is also an immobility of the inner self so that it can focus all its energy on observing and interpreting externality continuously. In many ways, it is a full, but passive and inert, defense by the inner self from external threat. Finally, it is a storing up of inner energy so that the inner self can empower itself to face an external threat. In the above-mentioned case illustration, it is clear that the client "eagle of righteousness" needed to manifest his sense of righteousness and morality in a constructive and realistic ways. When he was discharged from the hospital and admitted to a psychiatric halfway house, related social workers, under the supervision of the writer, tried to actualize his sense of morality in a meaningful way within the actual reality. The client was facilitated to serve as a volunteer for those child victims in families with domestic violence. He was also given responsibility for helping those vulnerable and new residents adapt a new and fair treatment in the halfway house.

REFERENCES

Arieti, S. (1974). *Interpretation of Schizophrenia (2nd edition)*: Completely Revised and Expanded, London: Crosby Lockwood Staples.

Dhossche, D. M., Wilson, C. & Wachtel, L. E. (2010). "Catatonia in childhood and adolescence: Implications to DSM5," *Primary Psychiatry*, 17(4): 35-39.

Encyclopedia of Mental Disorders (2007). http://www.minddisorders. com/Br-Del/Catatonic-disorders.html.

Fink, M., Shorter, E., & Taylor, M.A. (2010). "Catatonia is not schizophrenia: Kraepelin's error and the need to recognize catatonia as an independent syndrome in medical nomenclature," *Schizophrenia Bulletin, 36(2):* 314-320.

Fink, M. & Taylor, M. A. (2003). *Catatonia: A Clinicians Guide to Diagnosis and Treatment,* New York; Cambridge University Press.

Mayo Clinic (2010). *Catatonic Schizophrenia.*

Medical Library (2007). *Catatonia in Mental illness*

Sullivan. H. J. (1954). *Clinical Studies in Psychiatric*, New York: W.W. Norton & Company.

Wikipedia (2004). "Catatonia." *Wikipedia.* https://en.wikipedia.org/wiki/Catatonia.

Chapter 5

INTERCHANGE AND SHIFTING AMONG PARANOID, GRANDIOSE, AND CATATONIC DELUSIONS AND HALLUCINATIONS: INTERPRETATION AND RECOVERY

INTRODUCTION

In previous chapters, the writer described quite comprehensively the various theoretical underpinnings of paranoid delusion, grandiose delusion, and catatonic delusion. Within a cognitive and diagnostic dimension, clinicians easily regard paranoid, grandiose, and catatonic delusions as separated from one another. However, in actual clinical practice, different types of delusions and hallucination are interchangeable with one another. Many clients with schizophrenia manifest a shift from paranoid delusion to grandiose delusion. Some experience a change from catatonic delusion to grandiose delusion. Many have a combination of both catatonic and grandiose delusion together.

There is quite a lot of literature that describes and compares the features and natures of paranoid and grandiose delusion. Lake (2008) asserted that paranoid delusion in schizophrenia is caused by grandiosity and guilt. As grandiose delusion occurs when the individual has a poor self esteem. However, the more grandiosity is engaged, the more the individual's self esteem is threatened. As the individual's concealed sense of inferiority increases drastically, he or she is easily to form paranoid delusion in which he or she is being persecuted by others. Kitamina (et al., 1998) study on 429 psychiatric patients with psychotic symptoms showed that 33 percent of clients had catatonic excitement, 71.8 percent harbored persecutory delusion, and 18.6 percent had grandiose delusion. There were six most common dimensions in positive symptoms. They were paranoia, loose ego boundaries, catatonia, hypochondriacal, grandiose, and visual hallucination. Knowles (et al., 2011) formulated that grandiose delusion is closely related to paranoid delusion in which both of them are related to poor self esteem and loose self boundaries. All these showed that paranoid, grandiose, and catatonic excitement are closely related to one another. In this chapter, based on the theoretical underpinnings mentioned in previous chapters, the writer tries to figure out the shifting of paranoid, grandiose, and catatonic delusion and hallucination in people with schizophrenia.

A Case Illustration: Transformation among Paranoid, Grandiose, and Catatonic Delusion and Hallucination

Related Negative Emotions

Apparently, paranoid delusions and hallucinations are persecutory in that the individual feels inferior, insecure, anxious, and lonely. Grandiose delusions and hallucination seems to be the opposite, in that the individual feels omnipotent, powerful, and mighty. In catatonic delusions and hallucinations, the individual feels both threatened and powerful as he or she tries to defend him- or herself from external threats. He or she remains in an excited stupor so that he or she can manipulate the situation in full energy.

Case Illustration: John, the Righteousness Protector (Flying Fox in Snow Mountain)

In an actual case, these three types of delusions and hallucinations mix together and intermingle with one another. All these can be demonstrated in the following case illustration: Related parties' consensus to use their personal stories for academic purposes was sought. For the sake of confidentiality, their personal identities and information was properly disguised.

John was a male Chinese who suffered from schizophrenia for quite a number of years. He was born in a Chinese family. His parents worked very hard to live a hand to mouth life. Every day they went out to work leaving John and his elder sister to take care of themselves. John, although he was still a small child, had to do all household chores and go to school with his younger sister. As a consequence, his school academic performance was far from satisfactory. He also appeared as pale, weak, and a bit malnourished. He thus felt inferior and ashamed in comparison with his classmates. They bullied him as if he were a weak, sick doggie. They also bullied his younger sister as if she were a small chick. John felt terribly angry. Once he tried to protect his younger sister fought from his bullying classmates. He was thus beaten by them. John reported this to the discipline master in his school, but he pointed out that it was John's own fault for provoking fighting with others. Both John and his classmates were punished. John felt it was very unfair. From that time onward, John did not go to school. Instead he strolled around and joined a delinquent gang.

He participated actively in all sorts of the criminal activities of the delinquent gangs including drug trafficking, gang fighting, and breaking in commercial property. His delinquent peers told him that he was too young to be punished by the police. Even though he was caught by the police, he would only be sent to detention center for several months. Once, he was involved in a gang fight with other delinquent groups. His close friend, who was his classmate, was chopped to death by others. Despite tremendous fear, he managed to escape from being killed but was seriously hurt in his arm and leg, He dared not return home. One member of the delinquent gang also disclosed that the police was chasing after him. For several months, John hid everywhere to escape from other delinquent groups as well as from the police. Day and night, John was totally absorbed in intense anxiety and fear of being killed or caught by the police. Gradually, he developed a prevailing paranoid delusion feeling that no matter where he went, the bad guys and police joined together and used satellite measures to locate him and read his mind through electronic measures. John had nowhere to hide himself from all these horrible, paranoid delusions. He attempted suicide by jumping down from a high rise building. Fortunately, he was saved by the security guard there. John was taken to a nearby mental hospital. He was diagnosed as having paranoid schizophrenia.

John was hospitalized for six months in the mental hospital, and he was then transferred to a psychiatric halfway house. Despite constant intake of psychiatric medication, John's paranoid delusion of being followed by police and bad guys still continued. Sometimes, he needed to hide in his dormitory and refused to go out to work and to go to a sheltered workshop for vocational rehabilitation. He engaged in a street fighting and Internet games as well as reading a lot of Chinese martial art fiction to fill up his profound sense of boredom and emptiness in life. Gradually, John developed a grandiose delusion that he was in fact a hero from marital arts fiction. His name was the Flying Fox in Snow Mountain (a famous hero in Chinese marital art fiction).

He was able to fight off any enemies, including the police and bad guys in delinquent peers. He told the halfway house wardens that he, in fact, possessed omnipotent power to detect and read the mind of others especially their hidden, evil ideas. From that time onward, John was no longer afraid of being followed by the police and delinquent gangs. He claimed that he could actually engage in fighting or defending himself from bad guys and delinquents. In extreme situations, he said that he possessed the power and magic ability to identify and change the evil thoughts of others. In doing so, his grandiose delusion nurtured a catatonic stupor and fixation. Whenever he exercised his power to detect evil thought from others, he needed to stand still with a finger pointing to his own brain and focused all his mental energy for hours. He said it was the only way to focus all his mental energy on his brain. By doing so, he could radiate energy to detect and control evil thoughts of others.

MENTAL ENERGY, SELF CONSCIOUSNESS, SENSE OF REALITY, SOCIAL FUNCTIONING IN PARANOID, GRANDIOSE, AND CATATONIC DELUSION AND HALLUCINATION

Self Esteem and Mental Energy

In John's case, it was very clear that his paranoid delusion and hallucination was closely related and intermingled with his grandiose and catatonic delusion and hallucination. Their interaction and relationship can be described in several ways. First, the development and growth of paranoid delusion and hallucination implies the budding of a grandiose delusion hallucination. While John was occupied by prevailing paranoid delusion and hallucination that he was followed by bad guys and the police, his self importance grew accordingly. That meant the more he felt he was important, the more the police and bad guys needed to follow him or even diminish him. Underlying a prevailing fear from paranoia was actually a hidden or subtle need for self importance and an increase of self esteem from confidence. In other words, grandiosity in terms of a delusive, omnipotent self tended to be the only way to resolve fear from prevailing persecutory delusion and hallucination.

Secondly, under normal conditions, the manifestation of grandiose delusions and hallucinations require a high level of mental energy and physical energy. In prevailing paranoid delusion and hallucination, individuals usually tend to isolate or restrict themselves from being exposed to the external environment so as to preserve their mental and physical energy. A transformation from paranoia to grandiosity implies a need to increase mental and physical energy levels that may be out of individuals' affordability. Under that condition, fixated catatonic stupor within very focused activities and thought can be the only workable strategy to keep mental and physical energy in proper usage. In John's case, the prevailing paranoid delusion that he was continuously enclosed by bad guys and the police was very threatening. He needed to be very sensitive and suspicious to any stimuli and/or persons within external environment. Underlying over-sensitivity and over-suspiciousness was an intense use of mental and physical energy. This was why John tended to reserve his physical and mental energy by avoiding going outside frequently. In extreme situations, John might even refuse to go out as there were numerous policemen and bad guys chasing around him everywhere. His inner urge to defend from all these fearful, paranoid delusion transformed him to a grandiose delusion that he was capable to defeat all these bad guys and policemen by supernatural power. However, the demonstration of all these grandiose delusion and hallucination might need a lot of mental and physical energy. To make the energy affordable, John tended to focus his mental and physical energy through catatonic stupor. In standing still and pointing his finger on his brain, he could preserve his mental energy and physical energy for effective use.

Sense of Reality

Apart from mental energy, paranoid, grandiose and catatonic delusions and hallucinations also have different degree of sense of reality. In John case, in his childhood and adolescence, his sense of reality was full of being oppressed, bullied by his classmates as well as betrayed by his peers or captured by the police. That means, in his adolescence and adulthood, his sense of reality became more and more focus on threatening objects, issues, and persons in the immediate social environment. Gradually, his sense of reality was full of paranoid delusions in which he was spontaneously chased by bad guys and police everywhere. Despite his paranoid delusions and hallucinations, his sense of reality was still strong. Apart from being burdened by self perceived delusions and hallucinations, he was able to engage in most daily activities and interaction. He spontaneously told others that bad guys and policemen were everywhere. As his paranoid delusion grew, his social and daily activities would gradually decrease as he avoided being discovered by the bad guys and policemen. When he was seriously isolated from external reality, he began to develop a grandiose delusion that he was transformed into a mighty hero that could identify, detect, and fight off any bad guys and bad policemen in the world. In fact, his self-identity, John's identity, was changed into that of The Flying Fox of the Snow Mountain. This new, grandiose identity was constructed in isolation from reality. John simply isolated the external environment and locked himself in at home. He was totally absorbed in reading Chinese, marital arts fiction. All this fiction gave John important ingredients for constructing his new, delusive, grandiose self-identity. On the one hand, he escaped from the threatening, paranoid-related, external reality. On the other hand, the isolation of this delusively paranoid, external environment/reality gave him space to construct his own delusive, grandiose self-identity. Once the grandiose, delusive identity was constructed, his sense of reality was totally changed from a high sensitivity to a paranoid environment with a keen observation of all related objects, issues, and persons. It became very diffused and egocentric. John turned into the Flying Fox of the Snow Mountain who was not afraid of anything. He felt safe, secure, and powerful. He did not need to be very alert to possible threats. Instead, he looked for a chance to defeat his enemies. His very negative, but sensitive, sense of reality turned into an omnipotent but diffused and selective sense of reality. Compared with a paranoid sense of reality, a grandiose sense of reality is far more diffused, narrow, selective, and inert. John was simply absorbed by his own delusion and hallucination that he was powerful and almighty without fear of anything. He could go everywhere but without engaging in any meaningful activities. This diffused and confused sense of reality tended to further narrow down related stimuli in the external environment so that John could manage them well. John was unable to regard everyone in the environment as his enemies and fight back. He could only identify a few of them. Thus, as his grandiose delusion grew, his activity level would become more and more inert, selective, and restricted so that his omnipotent thought, actions, and identity could be fully manifested. This was a process of nurturing his delusively catatonic stupor. In John's case, he became more and more absorbed in his new self-identity, Flying Fox of Snow Mountain. Gradually, he dressed in white clothes and asked other to call him Flying Fox of Snow Mountain rather than John. He even changed his name to it on his identity card. To make sure he was in a good enough physical and mental condition to perform his anti-oppressive duties in fighting against the bad boys in this world, he learned and practiced Chinese marital art frequently. Also, he meditated two to three hours a day so that he could have enough "internal air." In doing so, he took himself into a catatonic stupor. His sense of reality decreased, became restricted, and narrowed to actions, internal meditation, and power strictly related to his grandiose identity.

Sense of Self Consciousness

Apart from the sense of reality, the sense of self consciousness is also different among paranoid, grandiose, and catatonic delusions and hallucinations. Individuals tend to have the highest self consciousness in paranoid delusion. The more serious the paranoid delusion is, the more conscious the individual becomes. He or she has to be very conscious about him- or herself as well as hidden foes and threats in the external environment. Individuals with severe paranoid delusion tend to shift their consciousness to the external environment and their own frequently. In John's situation, he kept himself very alert to policemen and bad guys who came to get and caught him in all sorts of external environments. However, the more he frequently shifted his awareness from himself and others, the more tired and fearful he became to extent beyond his tolerance and attention limits. Thus, he had to convince himself that he no longer need be afraid of these threats and turned himself into a martial arts hero. Once the new self-identity was formed, his self consciousness of his new identity increased but consciousness on threatening external environment decreased accordingly. He was no longer afraid of external threats as he was a new martial arts hero who could fight back. Strictly speaking, his self consciousness was concealed and changed into consciousness of a new, martial arts hero. He did not need to shift his consciousness from self to others; he simply focused his attention as a new, powerful, marital arts hero that could diminish or fight back any external threats. His delusive self consciousness was very egocentric. He tended to perceive everything in terms of his own grandiose and delusive identity. However, this new, grandiose self-identity was no longer his own self-identity. That meant he intended to hide his self-identity within this new grandiose one. In other words, he was not conscious about his own weak and inferior identity. Instead, he was only conscious about an externalized, delusive new identity. Actually, his actual self conscious was dim and decreasing. For John, the decreasing self consciousness was uncomfortable and intolerable. Thus, he needed to focus his weak self consciousness by developing catatonic delusion and hallucination in which he focused his attention on himself in forms of a catatonic stupor. John justified this by saying that the catatonic stupor helped him to concentrate all his inner, mental energy to fight back potential enemies. In fact, it was a re-orientation of his diffusing and weakening self consciousness. Within this catatonic stupor, John did not need to overtly manifest his inferior and fragile self-image; he just needed to recollect his own consciousness and self-identity covertly behind his grandiose self-identity. In other words, within catatonic delusions, the individual's self consciousness became more focused and restricted than this in grandiose delusion.

Social Functioning

Regarding social functioning, it is clear that within psychotic, positive symptoms, the individual's social functioning is restricted in comparison to those persons without psychotic symptoms. In paranoid delusion, social functioning is limited and confined by paranoid delusion. Individual focuses his or her attention to related delusive paranoia. Nevertheless, he or she is able to a certain level of social functioning in normal life. In grandiose delusion, social functioning is filtered and shaped by related grandiose and delusive self-identity and hallucination. For example, a male with a grandiose delusion as a superman may dress like a superman and act like a superman in daily life. He may perceive himself to save the whole world and fight with all sorts of criminals. In doing so, he feels powerful and omnipotent. In catatonic delusion, individuals' social functioning is mostly frozen and fixated to a state that is inert and very passive toward the external environment; basic, individual self care may even be neglected or ignored. The above can be summarized in the following Table 5.

Table 5. A Summary of Related Difference among Paranoid, Grandiose and Catatonic Delusions and Hallucination

	Sense of Reality	Self Consciousness, Self-identity and Self Boundary	Usage of Mental and Physical Energy	Social Functioning
Paranoid Delusion and Hallucination	A strong sense of reality as the individual is very alert to possible threat (paranoia) in a related external environment.	Very self conscious as the individual tries his or her best to avoid possible hurt and harm by related persons, objects, and issues in the external environment (Frequent shifting of consciousness and awareness toward oneself and others)	Intense use of mental and physical energy as the individual needs to focus all her energy to beware, identify, and defend themselves from related paranoid objects, persons, and issues	Social functioning is limited and confined by paranoid delusion. The individual focuses his or her attention on related delusive paranoia. Nevertheless, he or she is able to reach a certain level of social functioning in normal life.
Grandiose Delusion and Hallucination	Weak sense of reality as the individual only alert to how powerful and omnipotent he or she is in controlling related issues, persons, and objects in the external environment	Very weak self consciousness as the individual has already changed his or her self-identity to a delusive, grandiose identity so that he or she can have omnipotent power to diminish external threats and challenges	Grandiose delusions and hallucinations absorb mental and physical energy in a more diffused and confused way. To preserve the exhaustion of mental and physical energy, the individual exhausts mental and physical energy by manifesting his or her grandiose delusion and hallucination without regarding the response of external issues, objects, and events.	Social functioning is filtered and shaped by related grandiose and delusive self-identity and hallucination. For example, a male with a grandiose delusion as a superman may dress like a superman and acts like a superman in daily life. He may perceive himself to save the whole world and fight with all sorts of criminals. In doing so, he feels powerful and omnipotent.
Catatonic Delusion and Hallucination	Moderate sense of reality as the individual only be sensitive to narrow focus within his or her catatonic stupor and activities	Catatonic self-identity is far more fixated than those induced by paranoid and grandiose delusion. Individual needs to focus all his or her consciousness within the catatonic stupor and excitement so to ensure his or her own ontological existence.	Catatonic delusion and hallucination try to focus and fixate the individual's mental and physical energy on a catatonic stupor and excitement. On the one hand, the individual is very tense; on the other hand, they are very detached from those issues and persons that are unrelated to catatonic stupors.	Apart from catatonic hallucination, delusion, and behaviors, individuals' social functioning is mostly frozen and fixated to a state that is inert and very passive toward the external environment; individual basic self care may even be neglected or ignored.

Theoretical Assumptions about Transformation among Paranoid, Grandiose, and Catatonic Delusion and Hallucination

Five Different Assumptions of Catatonic Delusion in Relation to Paranoid and Grandiose Delusion

Schizophrenia is a process of self-fragmentation Related symptoms including positive, negative, and first-rank symptoms can be described as the product of the process of self-fragmentation Underlying this self-fragmentation process are three unresolved dilemmas: self splitting versus self cohesion, self concealment versus self visibility, and self destruction versus self preservation. Within the process of psychotic self fragmentation, there are several possible theoretical assumptions among paranoid, grandiose, and catatonic delusions, hallucinations, and behaviors.

1. Assumption 1: Catatonic schizophrenia is a further development of paranoid schizophrenia and grandiose schizophrenia.
2. Assumption 2: Catatonic schizophrenia is a shifting between the change from paranoid schizophrenia and grandiose schizophrenia.
3. Assumption 3: Catatonic schizophrenia is a mental state for the restoration of mental and physical energy in paranoid schizophrenia.
4. Assumption 4: Catatonic schizophrenia is a mental state for the restoration of mental and physical energy in grandiose schizophrenia.
5. Assumption 5: Catatonic schizophrenia is a unique types of schizophrenia that is different from paranoid and grandiose schizophrenia.

All these assumptions should be tested within related concepts of catatonic schizophrenia. As mentioned above, for persons with catatonic schizophrenia, schizophrenia has three major components: a catatonic state of mind (including a severe need for security and freedom from anxiety, a notion of knowing what happens, a strong feeling of urgency, and a state of meaningfulness); catatonic behavior (physical immobility or excessive mobility, extreme resistance or peculiar movement and a sense of stupor and excitement); and diffused self boundaries and self splitting (the state of an observable mind, a loss of boundary between the self system and the related environment) (Sullivan, 1956). It is also a representation of the deep dilemma and paradox of blind acceptance to others versus extreme inertia but full attention to very selective external stimuli (Arieti, 1974). It is also manipulation of unembodied self and false self by the inner true self in the process of self-fragmentation (Laing, 1960),

From all these related theories, it is clear that catatonic schizophrenia has the following natures that are closely related to paranoid schizophrenia:

1. A severe need for security and freedom from anxiety
2. The state of an observable mind
3. A state of urgency
4. A state of meaningfulness

Within paranoid delusions and hallucinations, the individual also harbors an intense sense of insecurity and fear that he or she is closely monitored, followed, watched, and manipulated by hidden or unseen oppressive others. To avoid being controlled or hurt by them, the individual tries to keep a keen eye on every person, thing, and event in the immediate physical and social environment. He or she tries to make meaning of what he or she observes, listens, smells, and touches. He or she interprets all these in terms his or her bizarre delusions. As the paranoid delusions and hallucinations grow tremendously, individuals feel very insecure, fearful, and uncomfortable. They may harbor a sense of intense urgency in which they want to get rid of all these potential enemies and foes immediately. All these showed that catatonic schizophrenia has similarities with paranoid schizophrenia.

Interestingly, grandiose delusions and hallucinations also have similarities with catatonic schizophrenia. These similarities are listed as follows:

1. A sense of stupor and excitement
2. Manipulation of the false self and unembodied self
3. Absorption in self fantasy and delusion
4. A loss of self boundary and related environment

In grandiose delusion and hallucination, individuals feel very excited within their own new, grandiose and delusive self-identity. They are self absorbed within their own sense of power and omnipotence. In doing so, their real self-identity (inner true self is well-concealed within the split, inner, false self with a new, grandiose and delusive self-identity. The more the individual becomes absorbed in this new delusive and grandiose false self, the more excited he or she becomes. As a consequence, the loss of self boundary and related environment becomes more and more serious and diffused.

As mentioned above, in John's case, his catatonic delusions and hallucinations are a further development of paranoid and grandiose delusions and hallucinations in terms of the following:

1. The development and growth of paranoid delusion and hallucination implies the emergence of grandiose delusions and hallucinations and also a need for a lot of mental and physical energy.
2. To make mental and physical energy affordable, catatonic stupor is a mechanism to save mental and physical energy with a very selective focus on catatonic stupor and excitement.
3. Within delusive catatonic stupor and excitement, the sense of reality is very restricted and confined.
4. Prolonged and continuous consciousness of the delusive, grandiose self-identity is very intolerable. Catatonic stupor provides a mental and physical space to recollect original or previous Self consciousness and identity. Within catatonic delusions, the individual's self consciousness becomes more focused and restricted than this in grandiose delusion.
5. In catatonic delusion, the individual's social functioning is mostly frozen and fixated to a state in which it is inert and very passive toward the external environment, and individual basic self care may even be neglected or ignored.

Assumptions, 1, 3 and 4 Should Put Together

Putting all these together, it is clear that catatonic stupor and excitement in schizophrenia possess natures very similar to paranoid and grandiose delusions and hallucinations. *That means, assumption 5 is invalid since it is not in the nature of paranoid and grandiose schizophrenia. It also means that assumptions 3 and 4 are doubtful as catatonic schizophrenia not only contains either paranoid or grandiose schizophrenic natures. Instead assumption 3 and 4 should be put together.*

Assumption 1: Catatonic schizophrenia is a further development of paranoid schizophrenia and grandiose schizophrenia.

Assumption 2: Catatonic schizophrenia reflects a shift between the change from paranoid schizophrenia to grandiose schizophrenia.

Assumption 3 + 4: Catatonic schizophrenia is a mental state for the restoration of mental and physical energy both in paranoid and grandiose schizophrenia.

Different Types of Combinations of Catatonic, Grandiose, and Paranoid Delusion

Combining these assumptions, it is clear that catatonic stupor and excitement should commonly exist within both paranoid and grandiose delusions and hallucinations. It is state in which mental energy and physical energy are purposely restored so that further change in paranoid and grandiose delusions and hallucinations are possible. In that sense, there should be several different types of catatonic stupor and excitement in the process of psychotic self-fragmentation:

- Type 1: Catatonic stupor and excitement in paranoid delusions and hallucination (CatParDel).
- Type 2: Catatonic stupor and excitement facilitating the change from paranoid to grandiose delusions and hallucinations (CatParGranDel).
- Type 3: Catatonic stupor and excitement in grandiose delusions and hallucinations (CatGranDel).
- Type 4: Catatonic stupor and excitement facilitating the change from grandiose delusions and hallucinations to paranoid delusion and hallucinations (CatGranParDel).

Type 1: Catatonic Stupor and Excitement in Paranoid Delusions and Hallucination (CatParDel)

All these four types of catatonic stupor and excitement can be described in terms of the combinations of bad self (BS), good self (GS), bad others (BO), and good others (GO), as mentioned in paranoid and grandiose delusions and hallucinations.

In the first type, catatonic stupor and excitement occurs in paranoid delusions, and delusion can both exist in full manifested form (ManifestDelParanoia) and in repressed form (RepDelParanoia). As mentioned above, in manifested paranoid delusion, there are two types of combinations. The first combination is BS1 (I am bad and deserve to be punished by others) + BO2 (Non-existing bad others) + GS1 (I am a suffering hero). The second combination is BS2 (I would diminish anyone who do bad thing to me) + BO2 (Non-existing bad others) + GS2 (I am perfect). The first combination enables the delusive, paranoid network to grow larger and larger. The second combination enables the delusive paranoid network to grow more and more powerful. Catatonic stupor and excitement in paranoid delusion tends to exist during the shifting between these two combinations.

For example, a female client harbored a strong, paranoid delusion that she was closely followed by an evil spirit. In BS1 + BO2 + GS1, the client felt that she was bad and deserved to be followed by the evil spirit. She was strong and tough enough to tolerate any punishment or maltreatment imposed by the evil spirit. In BS2 + BO2 + GS2, the female client thought that she was pure, sacred, and kind; that was why the evil spirit was so jealous of her and tried to seduce and harm her. In this situation, she also employed special talents, abilities, and measures to deter the bad influences of the evil spirit. The female client embraced different types of self-image. In type 1, she felt inferior and guilty. In type 2, she felt superior and noble.

In normal situations, both types of paranoid delusion and hallucination exist together. Coexistence of type 1 and type 2 paranoid delusion are very conflicting and antagonistic to one another. Thus, the individual needs to shift between type 1 and type 2 paranoid delusion and hallucination. That means, when type 1 is manifested, type 2 is latent. Similarly, when type 2 is manifested, type 1 is latent. The shifting from one type to another type needs a re-orientation of the individual's mental and physical energy, attention, and sense of reality.

For the female client, there was a need to shift her inferior self-image to a superior self-image. She shifted her thinking that she is pure, kind, and noble to a sense that she is guilty and inferior. She changed her perception toward the delusive, evil spirit that it was so jealous of her it would impose punishment on her misdeeds. The shift was so painful that she needed to maintain a temporary sense of catatonic stupor and excitement in which she could fully consider whether or not she should have such shifting. Within this catatonic stupor, she paid full attention to her immediate social and physical environment in which she tended to find any clues that he or she needed to shift his orientation from inferiority to superiority, from superiority to inferiority, or swinging/combining superiority and inferiority. When she encountered someone in reality who oppressed, rejected, isolated, and criticized her in which she could not fight back, she might engage in type 1 paranoid delusion and hallucination. The oppression and unfair treatment was imposed by the evil spirit to punish her misdeeds in this life or previous life. (In Buddhism, everyone has three lives: the current life, the previous life and the next life. What one did in the previous life would be rewarded or punished in this life). She was powerful and could tolerate any suffering and hardships in this life so that she could have a better life in the next. In that sort of thinking, her paranoid delusions and hallucinations grew larger and larger. More and more persons were involved in the paranoid delusions and hallucinations. As a consequence, she tended to feel more and more insecure and inferior to an intolerable extent. Prevailing fear and overwhelming inferiority turned her into a paranoid led catatonic stupor and excitement. She needed to recollect all her inner psychic, mental, and physical energy to fight back. In that recollection, she was in a stage of catatonic stupor and excitement in which she turns herself from type 1 paranoid hallucination and delusion to type 2 paranoid delusion and hallucination. It is drastic shift from fear and inferiority to superiority and confidence, from suffering heroine to brave fighter with the prevailing but delusive oppressive others. That means catatonic stupor and excitement facilitate change from type 1 to type 2 paranoid delusion and hallucination. She gradually recognized that, instead of being inferior and threatened by endless torture and by unseen oppressive others, it was better for her to fight back as she was also powerful and good.

The prolonged existence of type 2 paranoid delusion and hallucination (BS2 + BO2 + GS2) demands a high level of courage as well as mental and physical energy. It understandable one needs to use much more energy to avoid rather than fighting with his or her enemies rather than fighting back. It is much easier to avoid and escape from oppressive others than to face oppression squarely and bravely. Thus, spontaneous involvement in type 2 paranoid delusion and hallucination (BS2 + BO2 + GS2) may finally exhaust the individual's mental and physical energy.

For example, after the catatonic stupor, the female client changed her perception that the delusive, evil spirit was too bad and too oppressive. Indeed, she had had enough of the delusive, evil spirit; she needed to protect her own purity and own being. Thus, she ought to engage in certain measures to protect own self, and she went to nearby temples in which there were indigenous gods and goddess from Buddhism and Taoism. From there, after worshipping these gods and goddesses, she obtained some magic power and magic spells to counteract the power of the evil spirit. At that moment, she might continuously engage in reciting magic spells and words from Buddhism such "Nan Mao All Li Tau Fu" (There is no true Buddha in the south). At first, it seemed that the magic Buddhist spells tended to function well. The delusive, evil spirit seemed to decrease in power and influence and control of her. It gave her hope and power to face the oppressive reality thinking this magic spell might finally help her to diminish the evil spirit completely. However, once she got back into the frustrating reality in life, difficulties, oppression, and stress in life came back. Instead of coping with them squarely, she attributed all these to the hidden power of the evil spirit. Then she properly became more and more engaged in reciting the magic spells and worshipping the Buddha. Finally, the sense of urgency and immediacy in dealing the evil influence of the evil spirit became stronger and stronger. She might need to focus most of her psychic, mental and physical energy reciting these words and spells. The more she did so, the more she performed it in a catatonic way. In terms of catatonic stupor and sense of urgency and excitement, she might do this for days and nights without stopping so that she could gain enough Buddhist power to fight against the power of the evil spirit. In doing so, the connection of her good self (GS2: being perfect) to her bad self (BS2; to diminish her enemies) to fight against the delusive evil spirit (BO2) was fully exercised and developed. However, prolonged engagement in such catatonic-based, paranoid defense might use up her mental, physical, and mental energy. When she felt dreadfully tired, her concentration deteriorated making her feel that she did not have enough power and energy to face the dreadful, evil spirit. She might attribute this to the increase of power of the evil spirit as well as to her inherent weaknesses and fate in life to be controlled by the evil spirit. At that moment, she might then shift her type 2 paranoid delusion and hallucination (BS2 + GS2 + BO2) back to type 1 (BS1 + GS1 + BO2). That means, in the whole process of shifting, her engagement in the state of catatonic stupor and excitement was deeper and deeper. Parallel to this is an ongoing re-assessment of the power of the evil spirit as well as continuous reciting the magical Buddhist spells with a consequence of losing her physical, mental, and psychic energy. Finally, she needed to change her coping mechanism back to avoidance of the evil spirit by shifting back her paranoid action from type 2 to type 1.

Type 2: Catatonic Stupor and Excitement from Paranoid to Grandiose Delusions and Hallucinations (CatParGranDel)

The shifting from paranoid to grandiose delusion and hallucinations should be an extension of type 2 paranoid delusion and hallucination (BS2 + BO2 + GS2) with a full repression of type 1 paranoid delusion and hallucination (RepDelParanoia = BS1 +BO2 + GS1). As mentioned above, prolonged existence of type 2 paranoid delusion and hallucination (BS2 + BO2 + GS2) demands a high level of courage as well as mental and physical energy. Facing the exhaustion of mental and physical energy, the individual has only two choices: either shifting back to type 1 paranoid delusion and hallucination or changing to grandiose delusion and hallucination. If he or she shifts back to type 1 paranoid delusion, he or she can save enough mental and physical energy by avoiding the delusive, bad others. However, he or she takes a risk that the delusive bad others are actually everywhere. If there is no supportive others within his or her social environment in which he or she can ask for help or ventilate his or her intense sense of fear and insecurity, the only alternative is that he or she has to develop his or her grandiose delusion and hallucination in which he or she is no longer him- or herself. Instead he or she becomes a powerful figure with omnipotent power to control and even diminish the delusive bad others. In doing so, as mentioned above, he or she has to undergo several mechanisms:

1. Shifting his or her attention toward delusive bad others (BO2) to delusive good others (DelGO).
2. Constructing the delusive good others into delusive parental imago (TDelP1).
3. Transforming the delusive parental imago (TDelP1) into grandiose and delusive self-identity (DelGS).

All these require the individual to have full attention and focus his or her mental, psychic, and physical energy. Thus, a stage of catatonic stupor and excitement may help the individual to go through all these. The catatonic state in the construction and maintenance of grandiose delusions and hallucinations (type 2) is far more durable, persistent, and powerful than this in paranoid delusion, as it has to undergo these five important functions and processes.

Type 3: Catatonic Stupor and Excitement in Grandiose Delusions and Hallucinations (CatGranDel)

Also, as mentioned above, the maintenance of grandiose delusion, hallucination, and new, delusive self-identity requires immense physical and mental energy. Thus, the individual needs to reengage into the catatonic state (Type 3A) to recharge his or her mental and physical energy so that he or she can sustain his or her state of delusive grandiosity. Comparing with Type 2, Type 3A catatonic state should be much shorter, but very repetitive. In some cases, the individual needs to perform the catatonic ritual everyday so that he or she can gather enough mental and psychic energy to sustain his or her grandiose delusion, hallucination, and identity.

As mentioned above, when the external environment is very threatening, one in which the delusive grandiose self-identity is not powerful enough to diminish or counteract the delusive enemies, the individual may need to develop a more powerful but more delusive self-identity to deal with the delusive, external threat. In the process of transformation, he or she needs to recall his or her old, significant others or symbolic worshipping images to construct his or her delusive, parental imago so as to construct his or her new, delusive self-identity. In doing so, he or she needs to engage in a new, catatonic state (type 3B) to facilitate that sort of transformation. In many ways, the type 3B catatonic state resembles Type 2. The difference is that type 3B is more bizarre and symbolic. In many ways, it may need some supernatural type of rituals to convince the individual that he or she is being transformed into a more powerful, but more delusive, self-identity. For example, after a type 2 catatonic state emerges, a male adult is transformed from fearing the gossip of others saying that he is thin and sexually impotent to becoming a very attractive and sexy man. The individual needs type 3A catatonic state to preserve his or her attractive but delusive self-image by engaging in repetitive bodily and facial massage to sustain his handsome and attractive appearance. If the individual is still being dumped away by his girlfriend or being bullied or excluded by women, the individual needs to transform his delusive self-identity to a more powerful but more delusive one—James Bond. Within this transformation, he needs to undergo a type 3B catatonic state. By nature, type 3B should resemble type 2, the only difference is that it should be shorter and less durable. In type 2 catatonic state, the individual needs a longer period of time to recognize that he is actually handsome and sexy. He might be repetitive and catatonic in reading beauty magazines or being obsessive in using male cosmetics. After weeks or even months of catatonic rituals and stupors, the individual is able to transform to a handsome man with his name change from James Wong to Handsome Wong. However, in a type 3B catatonic state, he may watch James Bond movie tapes or fiction for two days and then be transformed from Mr. Handsome Wong to Mr. James Bond. The process of type 3B catatonic state should be much shorter than Type 2. However, as the new delusive self-identity is far more powerful and delusive than old one. Thus, the individual needs to engage in a longer time in a Type 2A catatonic state to sustain his new delusive self-identity as Mr. James Bond. In doing so, he may do a lot of repetitive rituals or being on catatonic stupor to ensure his new James Bond's identity can be ensured. He then may need to read the James Bond fiction or putting the book on his head for hours to ensure that he can obtain enough psychic and mental energy to sustain his or her grandiose and delusive identity and delusion.

In many situations, the changed new, delusive self-identity may not powerful enough to deal with the changing delusive but threatening social and physical environment. Under that condition, the individual needs to shift and transform to another new, delusive self-identity. As mentioned above, the more powerful the delusive self-identity is, the less cohesive the self system becomes. Thus, the individual needs to shift from different types of grandiose and delusive self-identity. It can be a shifting from the less powerful to more powerful and delusive ones or vice versa. In both directions, the individual needs to go through a state of catatonia (Type 3C) in this shifting and transformation so that the individual can focus his or her physical, mental, and psychic energy to facilitate the change. The quicker the shifting and transformation, the shorter is the state of catatonia.

Table 6. Natures and Functions of Sub-types of Catatonic States

Sub-types of catatonic state	Functions	Natures
Type 2B	Facilitates the change from paranoid to grandiose delusions and hallucination as well as the formation of the delusive self-identity	A durable and long need to have a long period of time to focus the mental and psychic energy to recall former supportive human relationships, to select supportive others as delusive good others, to change delusive other to delusive parental imago, and to transform delusive parental imago to delusive grandiose self-identity
Type 3 A	Sustain the appearance of grandiose delusive, and delusive identity. It is a recharge of psychic and mental energy	It appears in a form of repeated or daily rituals.
Type 3 B	Facilitate the individual to transform from one delusive self-identity to a more powerful but also more delusive self-identity	It resembles Type 2 but its duration is much shorter. The more delusive the new self-identity is, the shorter the duration requires and the more fragmented the individual's self-identity and self system is.
Type 3 C	Facilitate the individual to shift among different types of delusive self identities.	The quicker is the shifting, the shorter is the catatonic state and the more delusive the individual becomes.

Four Subtypes of Catatonic State in Relation to Paranoid and Grandiose Delusion

As a summary, there are four sub-types of catatonia in the grandiose and delusive hallucination and self-identity. They can be listed as follow:

As a summary, there are altogether four sub-types of catatonic state within grandiose delusion and hallucination and self-identity. Each of them has its own functions and natures. They are listed in Table 6.

Type 4: Catatonic Stupor and Excitement Facilitating the Change from Grandiose Delusions and Hallucinations to Paranoid Delusion and Hallucinations (CatGranParDel)

The change and maintenance of grandiose and delusive self-identity requires and demands a high amount of physical and mental energy. It also confuses and fractures the individual's self system making him or her more and more isolated from external reality. With the frequent shifting of delusive self identities, the individual faces a risk of severe fragmentation and confusion of his or her self system. At that moment, the individual may need to face three choices:

1. Sustain the shifting of delusive and grandiose identity and delusion with a risk of very fragmented and confused self system.
2. Shift back to a more realistic but inferior, self-identity in facing the threat from the external environment.
3. Search for substantially good others in the external environment so that he or she can rely on facing the threatening social environment.

If the perceived threat in the social environment continues and increases, the individual tends to sustain his or her shifting in various forms of grandiose delusion, hallucination, and self-identity. However, if the perceived threat in the social environment decreases, and there is some supportive others to preserve his or her mental and physical energy and increase the solidarity and cohesiveness of the self system, he or she may shift the grandiose delusions and hallucination back to the paranoid delusion and hallucination. In many ways, this process can be interpreted as a self-healing process for the individual. In doing so, his or her sense of reality increases accordingly. Within this process, the individual needs to undergo the following mechanism:

1. Changing his or her grandiose delusive self-identity back to his or her own realistic, but inferior and weak self-identity.
2. Recognizing the delusive parental imago is unrealistic or too distant for the individual to face the threatening social environment.
3. Building trust and enhancing social interaction with supportive or potentially supportive others in the social environment.

That means, within the grandiose delusions and hallucinations, the residual, but very repressed, partial self system originated from paranoid delusion (BS1 + GS1 + BO2 = RepDelParanoia) begins to re-activated. The inferiority-oriented bad self (BS1 = I am bad, and I should accept or even internalize others' criticism) and good self (GS1 = I am patient and tolerant to others' negative comments) gradually come into place. The reactivation of the inferiority orientation certainly comes for the encounter of some supportive good others in actual reality, making the individual believe that others' comments and advice are doing good for him or her. Inferiority with RepDelParanoia greatly neutralizes the superiority within grandiose delusions, hallucinations, and self-identity and facilitates the individual shifting to paranoid delusion and hallucination. Apparently, the individual first engages in Type 2 paranoid delusions and hallucinations (GS2 + BS2 + BO2) to replace the grandiose delusions and hallucination.

During the process of reactivation of RepDelParanoia, the individual may engage in Type 4 catatonic stupor and excitement in which the individual tends to accept the appearance of the good others. He or she also has to neutralize the sense of delusive superiority in grandiose delusion and hallucination by the sense of inferiority in RepDelParanoid. Thus, in comparison with Type 3 catatonic state, the Type 4 one should be more endurable and more reality-oriented. Compared with type 1, Type 2 and type 3 catatonic state, Type 4 is more positively-oriented. Instead of warning and observing the threat or the delusive, bad others in the immediate social and physical environment, the individual is keen in looking and observing good others in supporting him or her. In doing so, his or her sense of insecurity decreases accordingly. By means of that, it allows the individual to transform grandiose delusion and hallucination to paranoid delusion and hallucination. To facilitate the change and transformation, the individual may first return to Type 2 paranoid delusion and hallucination (GS2 + BS2 + BO2) in which he or she thinks that he or she is perfect (GS2) and those who criticize him or her should be diminished (BS2). As mentioned above, if the social environment is quite stable, then the individual may further engage in Type 1 catatonic state in shifting among Type 1 and Type 2 paranoid delusion and hallucination.

This process can be illustrated in the above-mentioned case. When the male adult possess a new grandiose and delusive self-identity as James Bond, he needs to maintain it in a repetitive, supernatural ritual by putting James Bond fiction in his head for hours. As he becomes more and more delusive and grandiose, his mental state may become more and more unstable shifting among different newly constructed delusive and grandiose self identities such as "Mr. Handsome Wong," "James Bond," "Lion King Richard." In doing so, he becomes more and more detached from the reality with a delusive presumption that all people, especially beautiful girls and ladies are cunning and non-trustworthy. With the delusive and grandiose self-identity, he thinks all beautiful girls and ladies should fall in love with Handsome Wong, James Bond, or Lion King Richard. But he (all these delusive identities) would abandon them. Underlining these grandiose hallucinations and delusions are severe inferiority and fear of being teased by females as unattractive, ugly, or even impotent. He needs to use the type 3C catatonic state to sustain his shift among different, delusive self identities.

The situation changes when he encounters an empathic and beautiful lady. He certainly feels he is being loved and cared for. This lady may be the social worker in his psychiatric halfway house, the nurse in the mental hospital, or the female volunteer in the service unit. This beautiful and empathic, young lady shows great concern for him, despite his delusive grandiose self-identity. She is mature and empathic, playing a listening ear to the need and inferiority of him. Gradually, he believes there is still a good other (GO) in the actual social environment. He treasures the togetherness of this beautiful and empathic young lady. Bit by bit, he begins to disclose his inferior feeling and sense of inadequacy to the empathic, young lady. The disclosure of his sense of inferiority finally neutralizes his sense of superiority and grandiosity in his grandiose and delusive self-identity. Finally, his repressed paranoid delusion and hallucination (RepDelParanoia) that many girls are actually teasing him about his impotence, ugly appearance and shortness begins to evolve again. The re-bounce of his repressed, paranoid delusions is certainly in conflict with his grandiose delusions and new identity. Facing this inner conflict, he needs to enter into a type 4 catatonic state to ensure that the presence of a good, beautiful, and empathic lady is a reachable reality. He may pick up the photo of this empathic lady from his iPhone and look at it for a period of time. In this state, he tries to recall how warm, understanding, and empathic she was. He also remembered how he himself disclosed the weakness and sense of inferiority to this empathic, young lady. He does all these things in a form of catatonic stupor for one or two hours every day. By means of doing all these for several weeks, the repressed memories of being bullied by others comes back again. He gradually reduces the absorption in his grandiose delusions as well as in his grandiose and delusive self-identity. He becomes less attached to his delusive identities as Mr. Handsome Wong, James Bond, and King Lion Richard. He regains his sense of actual identity as Peter Wong. He gradually shifts back to Type 2 paranoid delusions and hallucinations (GO2 + BS2 + BO2). He properly needs to engage in type 1 catatonic stupor and excitement to facilitate his shifting between type 1 and type 2 paranoid delusions and hallucinations.

CONCLUSION

In conclusion, this chapter is a comprehensive discussion about the interaction and transformation among paranoid, grandiose, and catatonic delusions and hallucinations, which are comprehensively discussed. The chapter starts with a comprehensive case illustration of how a client with paranoid delusion gradually changed to grandiose delusion and identity as a flying fox on a snow mountain. The catatonic excitement helped him to restore his mental energy and concentration to actualize this grandiose identity. In fact, catatonic excitement enables the individual to store up mental and physical energy to change from paranoid to grandiose delusion. In paranoid delusion, the client still harbors a good sense of reality. With a grandiose delusive identity, the sense of reality is greatly restricted. However, in the catatonic state, the sense of reality is minimized. In paranoid delusion, the individual's self consciousness and social function are still good. They gradually decrease in grandiose delusion and least in the catatonic state.

In relating to various theoretical underpinnings in paranoid, grandiose, and catatonic delusions, the following assumptions are verified:

Assumption 1: Catatonic schizophrenia is a further development of paranoid schizophrenia and grandiose schizophrenia.
Assumption 2: Catatonic schizophrenia is a shifting between the change from paranoid schizophrenia and grandiose schizophrenia.
Assumption 3 + 4: Catatonic schizophrenia is a mental state for the restoration of mental and physical energy both in paranoid and grandiose schizophrenia.

According to these assumptions, there should be four main types of catatonic schizophrenia. These are listed as follows:

Type 1: Catatonic stupor and excitement in paranoid delusions and hallucination (CatParDel).
Type 2: Catatonic stupor and excitement facilitating the change from paranoid to grandiose delusions and hallucinations (CatParGranDel).
Type 3: Catatonic stupor and excitement in grandiose delusions and hallucinations (CatGranDel).
Type 4: Catatonic stupor and excitement facilitating the change from grandiose delusions and hallucinations to paranoid delusions and hallucinations.

In addition to that, there should be five subtypes in type 2 and type 3 catatonic schizophrenia.

Type 2A: Catatonic State shifting paranoid delusion to grandiose delusion without a formation of new delusive identity. It usually lasts for a comparable shorter period of time, less durable and less intense in nature.
Type 2B: Catatonic State shifting paranoid delusion to grandiose delusion with a formation of new delusive identity. It usually lasts for a long period of time, durable and intense in nature.
Type 3A: Catatonic State sustaining the appearance of grandiose delusive and delusive identity. It is a recharge of psychic and mental energy. It appears in a form of repeated or daily rituals.
Type 3B: Catatonic State facilitating the individual to transform from one delusive self-identity to a more powerful, but also more delusive, self-identity (for example, from a fairy/angel to almighty God)

Type 3C: Catatonic State, helping the individual to shift among different forms of delusive self-identities (for example, shifting the delusive identities from the chief disciples of the Buddha to Buddha and then to almighty God)

All these have strong implications in clinical practice. It is important for related clinicians to identify specifically which type of catatonic excitement the client has. In addition, an accurate location of shifting of paranoid, grandiose and catatonic schizophrenia also means that the clinician can describe the current change and predict the future movement and changes of related delusion with reference to related changes in the psychosocial environment. With that sort of understanding, a related intervention can be induced by providing a suitable and supportive psychosocial environment to reduce the occurrence of paranoid, grandiose and catatonic delusions and hallucinations in clients with schizophrenia.

In actual intervention, clinicians should work with mental and physical energy, a related sense of reality, self-consciousness, and social functioning behind paranoid, grandiose, and catatonic delusion. Any constructive, healthy means to increase client's substantial mental and physical energy, sense of reality, self-consciousness, and social functioning will certainly reduce the frequency, intensity, and duration of paranoid, grandiose, and catatonic delusion and hallucination in people with schizophrenia.

REFERENCES

Arieti, S. (1974). *Interpretation of Schizophrenia (2nd edition)*: Completely Revised and Expanded, London: Crosby Lockwood Staples.

Kitamina, T., Okazaki. Y., Fujinawa, A., Takayanagi, I., & Kasahara, Y. (1998). "Dimension of schizophrenia positive symptom: An exploratory factor analysis review," *European Archives of Psychiatry and Clinical Neurosciences*, 248: 130-135.

Knowles, R. McCarthyJones, S., Rowe, G. (2011). "Grandiose delusion: A review and theortical integration of cognitive and affective perspective," *Clinical Psychological Review*, 31: 684696.

Laing R. D. (1960). *The Divided Self*, London: Tavistock Publication.

Lake, C. R. (2008). "Hypothesis: Grandiosity and guilt cause paranoia; Paranoid schizophrenia is a psychotic mood disorder, a review", *Schizophrenia Bulletin*, 24(6): 1151–1162.

Sullivan. H. S. (1956). *Clinical Studies in Psychiatry*, New York: W.W. Norton & Company.

Chapter 6

DIAGNOSIS AND ETIOLOGY OF NEGATIVE SYMPTOMS IN SCHIZOPHRENIA: CRITICS OF COGNITIVE DEFICIT AND IMPAIRMENT

INTRODUCTION

The following chapters 9, 10, and 11 are a refined discussion about the second domain in the self-fragmentation. It is the regressive domain. It begins with a full articulation of negative symptoms in forms of blunt affect, anhedonia, avolition as well as alogia. All these are related to deep regression and repression mechanism. Within this defense mechanism, the individual genuine needs are repressed. To avoid facing the traumatic and oppressive reality, individuals' ego functioning as well as ego identity is deeply regressive. Individual fixates to a primitive life stage prior to the onset of schizophrenia. In extreme case, the individual with schizophrenia may even regress to a stage of stagnancy as similar to fetus in the parent's womb. In existential term, the regression and repression mechanism represents an un-embodied false self being divided out from the self system in the process of self-fragmentation. Ontologically, the false self proclaims its deadness without any lively activities including awareness, feelings, and needs. It is a kind of self made caricature. It serves as an external protective mechanism to shield the inner true self from any external oppression and trauma, as well as attack from the external reality. In this regressive domain, the dilemmas of self-fragmentation versus self-integration, self-visibility versus self-concealment, self destruction versus self-preservation also occurs continually. By means of case discussion, all these dilemmas in this domain are fully described and discussed. Their impacts to the self system, mind and body of individuals with schizophrenia are also depicted. In this chapter, the writer first introduces a full critic of cognitive deficit and impairment orientation in describing negative symptoms in people with schizophrenia.

Diagnosis and Etiology of Negative Symptoms

Prevalence of Negative Symptoms

Makinen (et al., 2010) affirmed that negative symptoms are common persons with schizophrenia. He defined negative symptoms as the weakening or lack of normal thoughts, emotions, or behavior in schizophrenia patients. By reviewing related literature on the negative symptoms of schizophrenia. In June 2007 from *Web of Science, PubMed, PsycINFO,* Medline (Ovid) and Scopus. He concluded that about one in three schizophrenia patients suffer from significant negative symptoms. In these patients, negative symptoms constitute a key element of overall symptoms, weakening their ability to cope with everyday activities, affecting their quality of life and their ability to manage without significant outside help. The prevalence in first-episode psychosis is high, 50-90 percent, and 20-40 percent of schizophrenia patients have persisting negative symptoms. Severe negative symptoms during the early stages of treatment predict poor prognosis. Attention should be focused on negative symptoms during the early phase of treatment, because they cause significant impairment to patients' quality of life. So far, no treatment appears to improve substantially negative symptoms narrowly defined. However, according to clinical experience, when treating negative symptoms, the best effect is achieved by optimizing the dose of medication and by complementing it with psychosocial therapies (Makinen et al., 2010)

Definitions, Description and Measurement of Negative Symptoms

As mentioned in the first chapter, apart from positive symptoms, there are also negative symptoms in people with schizophrenia, especially for those chronic ones.

Unlike positive symptoms such as delusion and hallucination that are very disturbing to people with schizophrenia and their significant others, negative symptoms are latent and hidden burdens and impairments in which persons with schizophrenia may not create burdens for people around.

Andreasen (1982) asserted that all these negative symptoms are important indicators of outcome, of response to treatment, and perhaps of a distinct, underlying pathologic process for schizophrenia. She developed a Scale for the Assessment of Negative (SANS) Symptoms. When symptoms are defined by objective, behavioral indices, they have excellent interrater reliability. Furthermore, the five symptom complexes defined by the scale (affective flattening, alogia, avolition, anhedonia, and attentional impairment) have good internal consistency, which indicates that the conceptual organization of the scale is also cohesive.

Kay's Definition and Measurement of Negative Symptoms

Apart from the SANS, Kay, Fizbeing and Opler had also developed a Positive and Negative Symptoms Scale for Schizophrenia (PANSS) for typological and dimensional assessment. Based on two established psychiatric rating systems, the thirty-item PANSS was constructed. It thus constitutes three scales measuring positive and negative syndromes, their differential, and general severity of illness. Related items are listed as follows:

Positive Scale:

P1. Delusion
P2. Conceptual Disorganization
P3. Hallucinatory Behavior
P4. Excitement
P5. Grandiosity
P6. Suspicious/persecution

Negative Scale:

N1. Blunt Affect
N2. Emotional Withdrawal
N3. Poor Rapport
N4. Passive/apathetic withdrawal
N5. Difficulty in Abstract Thinking
N6. Lack of spontaneity and flow of conversation
N7. Stereotyping thinking

General Psychopathological Scale:

G1. Somatic concern
G2. Anxiety
G3. Guilt Feeling
G4. Tension
G5. Mannerism and posturing
G6. Depression
G7. Motor Retarding
G8. Uncooperativeness
G9. Unusual thought content
G10. Disorientation
G11. Poor Attention
G12. Lack of Judgment and Insight
G13. Disturbance of Volition
G14. Poor Impulse Control
G15. Preoccupation

G16. Active Social Avoidance
(Kay, 1991: 230)

That means there are seven items in a negative scale that are regarded as nature of negative symptoms for persons with schizophrenia. In each of these seven items, there are seven degrees of manifestation: absent, minimal, mild, moderate, moderately severe, and severe.

Kay (1991) specifically defined each of these seven items in detail. Blunt affect is defined as poor emotional responsiveness manifested by a reduction of facial expression, modulation of feelings, and communicative gestures. Rating is done by an observation of the client's affective tone and emotional response during an interview. It can range from stilted or artificial facial expressions and gestures to an explicit flatness and deficiency of emotion most of the time (Kay, 1991: 235).

Emotional withdrawal is defined as a lack of interest, involvement, and emotional commitment to life's events. Rating is done by reports from primary care workers or family members of clients and observation of clients' interpersonal behaviors in the interview (Kay, 1991: 235). It can be an insufficient motivation or initiative in doing things to a total withdrawn, being uncommunicative, and neglectful of personal needs (Kay, 1991).

Poor rapport is described as an absence of empathy, openness, intimacy, closeness, interest, or involvement with interpersonal distancing and reduced verbal and non-verbal communication (Kay, 1991: 236). Rating is based on observation of a client's interpersonal behavior and interaction in the interview. It can be an absence of emotional depth to a totally uninvolved interpersonal distance or indifference to others (Kay, 1991).

Passive/apathetic social withdrawal is interpreted as reduction of interest and initiative in social interaction because of individuals' passivity, apathy, poor energy level or avolition. This can be poor interpersonal involvements and a neglect of activities of daily living (Kay, 1991: 236). Rating is based on report by primary caregivers on clients' social behaviors. It ranges from poor initiative with merely occasional interest in social activities to a profound apathy, social withdrawal and personal neglect (Kay, 1991: 236).

Difficulty in abstract thinking is regarded as an inability of the abstract-symbolic mode of thinking in terms of difficulties in comprehension, classification, generalizations, and problem solving. Rating is based on responses to questions on similarities, proverb interpretation, and use of concrete versus abstract modes (Kay, 1991: 237). It ranges from giving personal interpretations or problems in articulating difficult proverbs to an inability to comprehend the abstract meaning of any proverb or related terms.

Lack of spontaneity and flow of conversation is interpreted as a reduction in the normal flow of communication together with apathy, avolition, defensiveness, or cognitive deficit. It can also involve difficulties in maintaining smooth and fluid interaction and communication. Rating is based on an observation of a client's cognitive-verbal process observed (Kay, 1991: 237). It ranges from poor initiative in conversation to very poor verbal response with only a few words (Kay, 1991).

Stereotyped thinking is defined by a decrease of fluidity, spontaneity, and flexibility of thinking. Individuals with stereotyped thinking usually have rigid, repetitive, or barren thought content. Rating is based on an observation of the client's cognitive verbal process (Kay, 1991: 238). It ranges from the rigidity shown in attitudes or beliefs to severe difficulties in thinking, behavior and conversation in which clients have continuous and constant repetition of limited phrases, rigidity, and inappropriateness of individual communication (Kay, 1991: 238)

Kay's descriptions of negative symptoms clearly show that it can both be subjectively and objectively formulated. Subjective formulation means that individuals with schizophrenia subjectively slow down, reduce, and diminish their interest, involvement and commitment in emotional response to external stimuli. Objective formulation implies that individuals with schizophrenia objectively have impairment, difficulties, and retardation in emotional and cognitive response to external objects, issues and persons. A subjective view means that blunt affect, emotional withdrawal, poor rapport, apathetic withdrawal, difficulties in abstract thinking, and lack of spontaneity in conversation and stereotyped thinking, which are all subjectively formulated by the individual with schizophrenia. He or she may be conscious about all these manifestations. He or she may be purposely disguised his or her actual intention or readiness or selectivity in emotional response and contact with others. An objective view showed that all these negative symptoms are manifested that can be objectively measured and observed by others in the external environment. In actual practice, both subjective and objective views of negative symptoms can be sustained. In other words, those difficulties in emotional responses, rapport, abstract thinking, and flow of conversation observed by the practitioners or reported by primary caregivers of individual with schizophrenia can all be consciously, purposely, or selectively expressed by the individual or objectively seen and observed by others.

Study of 101 schizophrenics found the three scales to be normally distributed and supported their reliability and stability. Positive and negative scores were inversely correlated once their common association with general psychopathology was extracted, suggesting that they represent mutually exclusive constructs. Review of five studies involving the PANSS provided evidence of its criterion-related validity with antecedent, genealogical, and concurrent measures, its predictive validity, its drug sensitivity, and its utility for both typological and dimensional assessment. (Kay, Fizbeing and Opler, 1987)

Andreasen's Definition of Negative Symptoms

According to Andreasen (1982), negative symptoms of schizophrenia are defined as the lack of important abilities including alogia, affective flattening, avolition, and anhedonia. Andreason developed the (1984) Scale for the Assessment of Negative Symptoms (SANS).

Alogia

Alogia means poverty of speech. It contains of deficits in speech fluency, blocked thoughts as well as short and empty replies to questions. Andreasen (1984) in her Scale for the Assessment of Negative Symptoms (SANS) describes alogia as follows:

Alogia is a general term coined to refer to the impoverished thinking and cognition that often occur in subjects with schizophrenia (Greek a= none, logos=mind, thought). Subjects with alogia have thinking processes that seem empty, turgid, or slow. Since thinking cannot be observed directly, it is inferred from the subject's speech. The two major manifestations of alogia are nonfluent, empty speech (poverty of speech) and fluent, empty speech (poverty of content of speech). Blocking and increased latency or response may also reflect alogia. (Andreasen, 1984: 5)

For assessment, it consists of the following components:

1. *Poverty of speech (Brief, concrete, unelaborated, monosyllabic, or even unanswered replies to questions).*
2. *Poverty of content of speech (Vague, over-abstracted, over-concrete, repetitive, and stereotyped speech).*
3. *Blocking (Interruption of a trained speech before a thought or idea has been completed).*
4. *Increased Latency of Response (Take a long time to reply to questions than is usually considered normal).* (Andreasen, 1984: 5-7)

Avolition

Avolition is the reduction, difficulty, or inability of persons with schizophrenia to initiate and persist in goal-directed behavior. For example, persons with schizophrenia are no longer interested in going out and meeting with friends and show little enthusiasm. They are no longer interested in much of anything, sitting in the house for many hours a day doing nothing (Schizophrenia.com, 2004).

Andreason (1984) defines avolition as

> Avolition manifest itself as a characteristic lack of energy, drive and interest. Subject are unable to mobilize themselves to initiate or persist in completing many different kind of tasks. Unlike the diminishing energy or interest of depression, the avolition symptom complex in schizophrenia is usually not accompanied by saddened or depressed affect.

> The avolition symptom complex often leads to severe social and economic impairment. (Andreason, 1984: 7)

That means, avolition is a state of physical and mental fatigue, in which the individual has no interest or energy to do anything. It consists of the following components in assessing symptoms of avolition:

1. *Poor Grooming and Personal Hygiene (Infrequent grooming, bath, dirty hand, soiled clothing).*
2. *Impersistence at Work or School (Absence, infrequency in attending school and work).*
3. *Physical Anergia (Physically inert, sitting at home and doing nothing and poor participation in any activities).* (Andreasen, 1984: 7-8)

Anhedonia

In psychology, anhedonia is an inability to experience pleasure from normally pleasurable life events such as eating, exercise, and social or sexual interaction. Anhedonia is also regarded as an important negative symptom commonly seen in persons with schizophrenia, schizoaffective disorder, schizoid personality disorder, and other mental disorders ((Schizophrenia.com, 2004). Andreasen (1984) defines anhedonia as a state of asociality.

> This symptom complex encompasses the schizophrenic subject's difficulties in experiencing interests or pleasure. It may express itself as a loss of interest in pleasurable activities, an inability to experience pleasure when participating in activities normally considered pleasurable, or a lack of involvement in social relationship of various kinds. (Andreasen, 1984: 9)

It consists of the following components in assessing the state of anhedonia

1. *Few or no recreational interest or activities (ranging from few or no hobbies, to loss of interest in passive activities such as watching TV, and finally to complete and intractable inability to become involved or enjoy activities).*
2. *Decrease in sexual interest and activities (loss of activities in sexual intercourse.)*
3. *Inability to feel intimacy and closeness.*
4. *Restricted and poor relationship with friends and peers of either sex.* (Andreasen, 1984: 9–10)

Affective Flattening

Affective flattening is the reduction in the range and intensity of emotional expression, including facial expression, voice tone, and eye contact. Persons with schizophrenia have problems interpreting body language and using appropriate body language in expressing their feelings and cognition.

Affective flattening is the reduction in the range and intensity of emotional expression, including facial expression, voice tone, and eye contact. Persons with schizophrenia have problems interpreting body language and using appropriate body language in the expression of their feelings and cognition. In Andreason's (1984) Scale for the Assessment of Negative Symptoms (SANS), affective flattening is defined as follows:

> Affective flattening or blunting manifests itself is a characteristic impoverishment of emotional expression, reactivity, and feeling. It can be evaluated by observation of the subject's behavior and responsiveness during a routine interview. The rating of some items may be affected by drugs, since the Parkinsonian side effect of phenothiazines may lead to make-like faces and diminished associated movement. Other aspects of affect such as responsivity or appropriateness will not be affected, however. (Andreason, 1984: 2)

In SANS, it consists of the following components:

1. Unchanging Facial Expression (The subject appears wooden, mechanical, frozen).
2. Decreased Spontaneous Movement (The subject sits quietly throughout the interview and shows few or no spontaneous body movements).
3. Paucity of Expressive Gestures (The subject does not use his body as an aid in experience his ideas).
4. Poor Eye Contact (The subject avoids looking at others or using his eyes as an aid in expression. He appears to be staring into space even when he is talking).
5. Affective Non-responsivity (Failure to smile or laugh when prompted may be tested by smiling or joking).
6. Lack of Vocal Inflections (Speech has a monotonic quality, and important words are not emphasized through changes in pitch or volume).
7. Inappropriate Affect (Affect expressed is inappropriate or incongruous, not simply flat or blunted. Most typically, this manifestation of affective disturbance takes the form of smiling or assuming a silly facial expression). (Andreason, 1984: 2–3).

Poor Attention

Apart from avolition, anhedonia, affect blunting, alogia, attention in schizophrenia is also poor and inadequate.

> Attention is often poor in schizophrenics. The subject may have trouble focusing his attention, or he may only be able to focus sporadically and erratically. He may ignore attempts to converse with him, wander away while in the middle of an activity or take, or appear to be inattentive when engaged in formal testing or interviewing. He may or may not be aware of his difficulty in focusing his attention . . . Inattentiveness appears in social situation or activities , , , , He looks uninvolved or unengaged in conservation…poor concentration when playing games, reading and watching TV. (Andreasen, 1984: 11)

Implications of Kay's PANSS and Andreasen's SANS

Both Kay's PANSs and Andreasen's SANS showed that negative symptoms in persons with schizophrenia have the following features.

1. Poor communication and interaction with persons and objects in the immediate social environment (Persons with psychotic negative symptoms have poor rapport, lack of spontaneity in conversation, poverty of speech, poor attention, blocking, and very low response to others).
2. Withdrawal and self-isolation from reality (Individuals with psychotic negative symptoms are emotionally withdrawn, apathetic, and affectively blunt).
3. Fixation and deep involvement in their own inner world (Persons with psychotic, negative symptoms have intense stereotyped thinking and difficulty in abstract thinking).
4. Low mental and physical energy and will power (Poor hygiene, low motivation and action in work and movement, loss of interest in sex, social activities and relationship).

Putting these four features together, it seems that persons with prevailing negative symptoms stay within their own very restricted, inner world. Unlike those with prevailing positive symptoms in which individuals are very active and energetic in creating their delusive objects, persons, issues, and identities in a flexible time and space, in overwhelming negative symptoms, individuals are stagnant and frozen within a certain time and space. The fixation and stagnancy in a certain time and space can have several reasons. They can be listed as follows:

1. The individual can have cognitive impairment because of which they cannot respond or are too low to respond to others.
2. The individual does not want to stay in the oppressive reality. Thus, he or she prefers to be involved with, or engage within, his or her own inner world with a specific time and space.
3. The individual actually regresses and deteriorates within the stagnant, inner world in which he or she feels his or her life is entirely empty, meaningless, and aimless.

In the following section, the writer aims to address the underlying assumptions within related studies and research.

Kraepelin's Praecox—Feelings and Negative Symptoms

Emil Kraepelin, in the fifth edition of his textbook, was the first one to conceptualize schizophrenia as dementia praecox. Kraepelin defined dementia praecox as follows:

> The weakening of judgment of mental activity and of creative ability, the dulling of emotional interest and the loss of energy, lastly the loosening of the inner unity of psychic life would have to reckoned among the fundamental disorder. (Kraepelin, 1913/1919: 248)

Following Kraepelin's orientation, Rumke (1960) further articulates praecox feeling as follows:

> a marked subjective, rather instinctive feeling or intuition induced in the examiner by the schizophrenic patient right after the first second or minutes of their encounter' (Rumke, 1960: 43). That means, Rumke (1960) focus more on others' emotional response toward persons with schizophrenia especially related professional. Ungvari (eta l, 2010) affirmed this as important diagnostic criteria for schizophrenia.

Rumke further articulated this praecox feeling as having four crucial elements:

- impossibility of empathy
- changes in motor behavior or speech
- lack of exchange of affect, and
- an instinctual rapport (Rumke, 1960; Ungvari et al., 2010)

In other words, praecox feeling is a problem in feeling other emotions (empathy), affective response (exchange of affect), as well as a result of being very introversive and egocentric (instinctual rapport).

In the same ways, Bleuler (1911/1950) defined schizophrenia as having three crucial symptoms: autism, Benommenheit, and the pressure of thoughts or thought-overflow. Autism is defined as "detachment from reality together with the relative and absolute predominance of inner life. " (Bleuler, 1911/1950: 63). Benommenheit was defined as,

> slowing up of all psychic process . . . in conjunction with an incapacity for dealing with any relatively complicated or unusual situation... will power seems to be relatively well or completely; preserved with the absence of depression and evidence of a very mild degree of confusion. (Bleuler, 1911/1956: 14)

That means, negative symptoms in schizophrenia described by Kraepelin (1913/1919) and Bleuler (1911/1950) can be interpreted as:

1. praecox feeling (poverty of speech, lack of empathy, and emotional interest)
2. weakening of judgment of mental activity
3. dulling of emotional interest
4. loss of energy
5. autism and absorption in inner life
6. Benommenheit in terms of loss of energy, loosening inner unity of psychic life

These six features in many ways are similar with Kay's PANS and Andreasen's SANS. For example, the praecox feeling can be interpreted as poor communication and interaction with others in immediate social environment in terms of poor rapport, lack of spontaneity in interaction, and blocking and low response with others. Autism and absorption in inner life is similar to deep involvement in one's inner world. Low physical and mental energy are also mentioned. What is interesting is that Ungvari et al. (1993) affirmed that praecox feeling is subjected to others' interpretation. Their studies showed that some psychiatrists are more concerned with detecting patients' praecox feelings than others. They usually spend less time and are less concerned with listening to patients' descriptions of psychotic symptoms, feelings, and needs. *Ungvari's (eta l, 1993) study is vital in understanding negative symptoms. That means, the four dominant features of negative symptoms suggested in PANS and SANS, are subjected to interpretation.* Decrease and slowing down of interest, energy, and will to interact with objects and persons in external reality observed by the clinicians can also be regarded as related to clinicians' loss of interest and patience in understanding, communicating, and interacting with persons with schizophrenia, in particular those in prevailing negative symptoms such as alogia, anhedonia, avolition, and blunt affect. Perhaps, the writer's own personal clinical experiences in encountering a client with schizophrenia may illustrate this point in detail. Relate parties' consensus in using their stories for academic purpose was sought. For the sake of confidentiality, related parties personal identities and information were properly disguised.

Mr. A was a male adult with schizophrenia for more than twenty years. He was currently forty-five years old. Within these twenty years of psychotic illness, he was frequently relapsed and hospitalized. He had stayed in this hospital for more than six years. He had been deeply hospitalized with prevailing negative symptoms. He appeared as inert, withdrawal, and passivity. Because of prolonged hospitalization and mental problems, Mr. A had lost contact with his family members. As a social worker, the writer was responsible for taking care of Mr. A and designed a rehabilitation plan for him. The writer approached Mr. A for dialogue and communication. However, Mr. A refused to interact with the writer. Although the writer tried his best to initiate interaction and dialogue, Mr. A did not answer. He simply sat quietly, staring aimlessly at the writer for several minutes. He murmured some repeated simple sound such as 'hee, hee, yee and yee'. Then he turned his head away from the writer. The writer sat with Mr. A for a short while. As he did not murmur a word, the writer went away. The writer went to meet Mr. A the next day. Mr. A repeated the same response toward the writer. The writer tried to be sure that Mr. A understood his sincerity. He visited Mr. A. daily for around ten times. Nevertheless, Mr. A still turned away from the writer. The writer did not give up. He persisted in his visits. On the fifteenth time, Mr. A suddenly initiated a dialogue. He told the writer that he was so impressed by the writer's effort to relate to him. From that time onwards, it seemed that Mr. A's negative symptoms were much relieved. He was able to share his past experiences and his painful feeling of being hospitalized for so many years.

From the above-described case, it was clear that A's negative symptoms were not cognitive impairment. He appeared to be inert, withdrawing, and passive. If the writer had not been patient enough or persistent enough, A's inertness and refusal to respond could easily have been diagnosed as anhedonia, alogia, blunt affect, and avolition. The encounter between the writer and A could easily be labeled as praecox feeling. In the case of A, it was clear that A was fully aware of the presence of the writer, but he did not want to respond. It was not that he did not have the ability or had lost the ability to respond. In fact, he did not want to respond.

What follows is A's self narration about why he refused to respond to the writer.

A: Certainly, I was fully aware about the presence of the social worker. I did not want to respond simply because I did not trust professionals including social workers. Throughout the years, I had encountered numerous medical professional including social workers. However, none of them were really interested in caring him. They came for making diagnosis. They came to prove that I was chronic, low motivated and did not want to recover. To keep them away, the best way was being non-responsive. To make a good living in mental hospitals, being inert, passive and withdrawal was the best way to survive within an institutionalized hospital. This medical social worker (the writer) was the most patient workers I encountered in my life. No one could tolerate my inertness and non-response for ten times.

This case illustration clearly demonstrates the praecox feeling toward clients with schizophrenia could be very various and subjected to workers' interpretation and interaction. If the writer were not patient enough to continue for ten times, properly he would conclude that Mr. A was very inert, chronic, withdrawn, and non-communicative. Taking this case illustration and Ungvari et al. (1993) finding on praecox feeling together, it is very likely that prevailing negative symptoms in clients with schizophrenia are not due to cognitive impairment. Instead, it should closely related to individuals' urge to escape from contact with an oppressive reality and to remain regressed within his or her delusive, inner world. In the following sections, the writer tries to give a comprehensive review of related concepts and findings within this orientation.

Critics of Cognitive Impairment in Negative Symptoms

NIMH-MATRICS Consensus Statement on Negative Symptoms

Recent research showed that treatment and recovery on schizophrenia focused too much on positive symptoms rather than negative symptoms. Effects on related antipsychotic drugs are not clearly illustrated. Thus, the NIMH had induced a project on the measurement and treatment research to improve cognition in schizophrenia (MATRICS). The data suggested initial answers to the following questions:

1. What are the separate components of negative symptoms?
2. Are they independent, or components of the same latent construct?
3. Which aspect of each domain belongs to the negative symptom construct?
4. Does this area need a separate assessment?
5. What is best assessment method for clinical trial? (Kirkpatrick et al. 2006: 214)

Related parties had formulated 11 consensus statements on answers to these questions. They are briefly listed as follows:

1. Negative symptoms constitute a distinct therapeutic indication area.
2. Negative symptoms and cognitive impairments represent separate domains.

3. Negative symptoms have face validity as disease manifestation and represent loss or diminution of normal functions.
4. Persistent and clinically significant negative symptoms are an unmet therapeutic need in a large proportion of cases.
5. The distinction between primary and secondary negative symptoms is not essential for the purpose of testing therapeutics for negative symptoms… . (Primary negative symptoms are those that are part of the disease process itself, that is, are not secondary to such factors such depression, drug induced akinesia, or a suspicious withdrawal).
6. The paradigmatic design for clinical trials of persistent negative symptoms would include clinically stable patients whose negative symptoms persist with adequate antipsychotic drug treatment.
7. The paradigmatic design for a co-administered drug is less satisfactory when testing with a broad spectrum antipsychotic agent, that is, one that may have superior efficacy for both positive and negative symptoms… . In such a study, superiority for negative symptoms would be established if the experimental treatment's advantage were limited to negative symptoms, which psychosis and other key symptoms remaining stable and similar to comparator drug.
8. Within negative symptoms, the definition of a clinically meaningful effect size needs further review.
9. The length of a clinical trial will vary with the purpose of a trial. Proof of concept studies may be brief. Preliminary efficacy studies may be 4–12 weeks. Registration trials are likely to be substantially longer (in the range of 6 months), in order to document persistent efficacy.
10. As currently understood, the domains of negative symptoms include blunted affect, alogia, asociality, anhedonia, and avolition… . The structure of relationships among these domains and their predictive validity require further study.
11. The structure of the Scale for the Assessment of Negative Symptoms (SANS)22 is preferred to that of the Positive and Negative Symptom Scale (PANSS) in that several negative symptom constructs are ascertained, with multiple items related to each. (Kirkpatrick et al., 2006:214-217)

All these showed that negative symptoms embrace the following characteristics:

1. They are distinguished from positive symptoms.
2. They are different from cognitive impairment.
3. They intermingle with institutionalized natures such as passivity, inertness, withdrawal and drug induced akinesia.
4. Negative symptoms are unmet therapeutic agents.

5. Related current research design fails to study the symptomatic effects and treatment of negative symptoms.

The consensus statement also affirmed the current SANS plays an important role in assessing negative symptoms.

> 'The SANS has played an important role in the study of negative symptoms. Its inclusion of more than 1 item improves the psychometric properties of the scale. Although an instrument with multiple domains and multiple items in each domain should be considered preferable when negative symptoms are the primary focus of a clinical trial, important and valid information can result from the use of other instruments.' (Kirkpatrick et al., 2006:217-218)

That means, negative symptoms should be assessed separated from positive symptoms. Thus in the development of treatment of negative symptoms, there are three unresolved issues and future directions.

At the Consensus Development Conference, there was also agreement on three recommendations that were intended to facilitate future work on the development of treatments for negative symptoms.

1. Development of a new instrument that included the 5 agreed-upon domains would advance work in this area. Such an instrument needs to be applicable in both in-patient and outpatient clinical trials and needs to be sensitive to change. The negative symptom domains need to be clearly defined for the purposes of instrument development. This task is also essential to encourage development of preclinical models and laboratory-based, human assessments of negative symptoms, and to stimulate translation from neuroscience to the clinical study of negative symptoms.
2. There is a need to establish a framework, leadership, and financing to accomplish the following:
   a. form a work group for the development of a negative symptom instrument for clinical trials;
   b. test the instrument and assess its reliability and psychometric properties; and
   c. test the instrument in a clinical trial to assess its sensitivity to change.
3. There is also a need to establish a framework to promote the identification and testing of drugs for a negative symptom indication. It is likely that this process would be similar to the MATRICS process for drug discovery for the treatment of cognitive impairment in schizophrenia. (Kirkpatrick et al., 2006:219)

All these suggestions clearly showed that further research, treatments and concepts should be developed for negative symptoms in the future.

In response to the NIMH-MATRICS Consensus Development Conference on Negative Symptom recommendation, the Brief Negative Symptom Scale was developed. It was a scale with thirteen items organized on six subscales. They are listed as follows:

Ahedonia
Item 1: Intensity of pleasure during activities
Item 2: Frequency of pleasure during activities
Item 3: Intensity of expected pleasure from future activities
Distress
Item 4: Distress
Asociality
Item 5: Asociality behavior
Item 6: Asociality inner experience
Avolition
Item 7: Avolition behavior
Item 8: Avolition inner experience
Blunted Affect
Item 9: Facial expression
Item 10: Vocal expression
Item 11: Experience gestures
Alogia
Item 12: Quantity of speech
Item13: Spontaneous elaboration

The scale has good interior, test/retest, and internal consistency. It also has good concurrent validity, construct validity, discriminant validity, and predictive validity.

Negative Symptoms and Cognitive Deficits: A Weak Correlation

In the MATRICS study, it showed that cognitive impairment and negative symptoms should be on separate domains and their correlation is weak. Harey, Koren, Reichenberg, and Bowie (2006) tried to outline the actual relationship between these.

Model 1: Cognitive Impairment and Negative Symptoms Are the Same

The first model proposes that these two dimensions are in fact identical features of the illness, or alternate manifestations of the same basic underlying process, and would therefore be improved by the same treatments. (Harey et al., 2006: 254). That means, cognitive impairment and negative symptoms embrace similar natures and characteristics. They occur in the same time are all closely related to the etiology and the process of schizophrenia. Harvey et al. (2006) affirmed that related studies show that the *correlation between negative symptoms and cognitive impairment is limited.* Longitudinal studies clearly illustrated that they can change independently to one another in different treatments and in the natural course of schizophrenia. A complex model may be required to explain the association between these two dimensions. In doing so, more information is needed about:

1. The reliability and stability characteristics of the measure in assessing negative symptoms.
2. Long term data regarding the general stability of negative symptoms and cognitive impairments.

Model 2: Negative Symptoms and Cognitive Impairment are Separate Domains but with Similar Etiological Factors

The second model holds that these features of the illness are, in fact, separable but that they share similar underlying etiological factors, which leads to observed correlations between variables and suggests that treatments for one may also impact the other' (Harey et al., 2006: 254). That means, cognitive impairment and negative symptoms in schizophrenia have different features but share similarities in etiology. It seems that a dysfunction of the thalamus result in people with cognitive impairment and in people with schizophrenia. Harvey et al. (2006) affirmed that results of related cross sectional studies showed moderation correlation between cognitive impairment and negative symptoms in people with schizophrenia. Nevertheless, *there is no longitudinal correlation in changes between these two domains.* In other words, model 2 cannot be supported unless more studies of the joint course and linkage between these domains can be provided.

Model 3: Cognitive Impairment and Negative Symptoms Have Separate Etiology

The third model proposes that each of these symptom dimensions has a separate etiology but that these etiologies might be related, which would suggest that treatments for one domain might impact the other, but not to the same extent as in Model 1 or 2'. (Harey et al., 2006: 254). In model 3, negative symptoms and cognitive symptoms in schizophrenia should be in different domains. They have different etiology. They may be commonly related to etiology in other dimensions due to outside influences. Harvey et al. (2006) affirmed that existing studies seem to support this model. In fact, most longitudinal studies showed similar overlapping course of negative symptoms and cognitive impairment. Also, recent studies suggested that **cognitive performance is strongly related to disorganized symptoms as to negative symptoms showing that cognitive impairments are related in severity to multiple features of schizophrenia**. Furthermore, both negative and cognitive symptoms appear to change at different rates in related studies of the progression or treatment of schizophrenia. However, the overall level of impairment of each of them is correlated at successive longitudinal assessments (Harvey et al., 2006: 255). To develop model 3 further, more similar studies are needed. Identification and longitudinal assessment of putative etiological factors in related to these two domains should be done in these studies (Harvey et al., 2006: 255).

Model 4: Cognitive Impairment and Negative Symptoms are Different from One Another, but They Correlated with the Other Features (The Third Variable) in Schizophrenia

The final model views these symptom dimensions as distinct from each other, with separate etiologies. Thus, correlations between these domains, if detected, are influenced by measurement and definitional issues or ''third variable'' **relationships with other features of the illness**, which could induce and observed correlation that is actually indirect' (Harey et al., 2006: 254). In this model, cognitive impairment and negative symptoms are correlated to other distal outcome and measurement in the features of schizophrenia. It tends to explain the fact that deficit syndrome patients show a different signature of cognitive impairments than nondeficit patients. Related studies show that objective measures of emotional experience are uncorrelated with cognitive symptoms is also consistent with this model. This model is supported by more recent path analysis studies that demonstrate that the zero-order correlation between negative symptoms and cognitive impairments is explained by correlations with distal outcome measures. This model can be further consolidated by pharmacological and psychosocial treatments that enhance cognitive functioning (Harvey et al. 2006: 256).

Conclusion

In conclusion, this chapter is a comprehensive discussion on diagnosis and etiology of negative symptoms in schizophrenia. Andreasen's (1982) SANS affirmed negative symptoms consist of affective flattening, alogia, avolition, anhedonia, attentional impairment. Kay's (1991) PANS described that there are seven components in negative symptoms including blunt affect, emotional withdrawal, poor rapport, passive/apathetic withdrawal, difficulty in abstract thinking, lack of spontaneity and flow of conversation, and stereotyping thinking. Both of them showed that negative symptoms has the following features.

1. Poor communication and interaction with persons and objects in immediate social environment
2. Withdrawal and self-isolation from reality
3. Fixation and deep involvement in their own inner world

4. Low mental and physical energy and will power (poor hygiene, low motivation and action in work and movement. Loss of interest in sex, social activities and relationship).

Putting these four features together, it seems that persons with prevailing negative symptoms stay within their own very restricted inner world. He or she may have cognitive impairment to respond, does not want to stay in the oppressive reality, or regresses and deteriorates in his or her stagnant inner world. Negative symptoms in terms of praecox feelings in schizophrenia described by Kraepelin (1913/1919) and Bleuler (1911/1950) can be interpreted as:

1. praecox feeling (poverty of speech, lack of empathy and emotional interest)
2. weakening of judgment of mental activity
3. dulling of emotional interest
4. loss of energy
5. autism and absorption in inner life
6. loss of energy, loosening inner unity of psychic life

These six features, in many ways are similar with Kay's PANS and Andreasen's SANS. What interesting is that Ungvari et al. (1993) affirmed that praecox feeling is subjected to others' interpretations. That means, the four dominant features of negative symptoms suggested in PANS and SANS, are subjected to interpretation. In 2005,

NIMH had induced a project on the measurement and treatment research to improve cognition in schizophrenia (MATRICS). The data suggested initial answers to the following questions:

1. What are the separate components of negative symptoms?
2. Are they independent, or components of the same latent construct?
3. Which aspect of each domain belongs to the negative symptom construct?
4. Does this area need a separate assessment?
5. What is best assessment method for clinical trial? (Kirkpatrick et al., 2006: 214)

Eleven consensus statements were formulated. All these showed that negative symptoms embrace the following characteristics:

1. They are distinguished from positive symptoms.
2. They are different from cognitive impairment.
3. They intermingle with institutionalized natures such as passivity, inertness, withdrawal and drug induced akinesia.
4. Negative symptoms are unmet therapeutic agents.

5. Related current research design fails to study the symptomatic effects and treatment of negative symptoms.

All these have important implications in interventions and the recovery of people with severe negative symptoms. First, many family caregivers or related professional workers in mental hospitals and psychiatric rehabilitation services regard severe positive symptoms such as acute or confused, paranoid delusions or hallucinations as very annoying and troublesome. However, they regard severe, negative symptoms such as anhedonia, avolition, and blunt affect as less annoying and controllable. Some may even wrongly treat negative symptoms as mentally stable and tranquilizing. Thus, there is a common malpractice that forcing a client with acute or severe positive symptoms into inappropriate or involuntary large dosage of antipsychotic medication or injection until the client become passive, withdrawn and inert. That means, clients' negative symptoms are a result of malpractice of prolonged inappropriate large dosage of antipsychotic drugs induced on the client.

Secondly, as negative symptoms are wrongly regarded as cognitive impairment by most professionals and family caregivers, they may conclude that clients with severe negative symptoms are unrecoverable. It may further moralize and justify very institutionalized practice. It finally become a vicious circle, the more intense negative symptoms are, the more moralized for institutionalized practice and the more severe negative symptoms become.

Thirdly, negative symptoms are unmet by therapeutic agents. Anti-psychotic medication only has curable effect on positive symptoms. In other words, psychosocial orientation and perspective are very important in understanding, interpretation, and treatment of negative symptoms. In the coming chapters, the writer is going to mention it in details.

References

Andreasen, N. C. (1982). "Negative symptoms in schizophrenia: Definition and reliability," *Archives of General Psychiatry*, 39: 784–788.

Andreasen N. C. (1984). *Scale for the Assessment of Negative Symptoms (SANS)*. Iowa City, University of Iowa.

Bleuler, E. (1911/1950) (Trans. J. Zinkin), *Dementia Praecox or the Group of Schizophrenias,* New York, NY, International Universities Press.

Harvey, P. D., Koren, D., Reichenberg, A., Bowie, C. R., (2006). "Negative symptoms and cognitive deficits: What is the nature of their relationship?," *Schizophrenia Bulletin*, 32(2) pp. 250--258, 2006.

Kay S. R., Fiszbein A., Opler L. A. (1987). "The positive and negative syndrome scale (PANSS) for schizophrenia." *Schizophrenia Bulletin*. 13 (2): 261–276.

Kay, S. R. (1991). *Positive and Negative Syndromes in Schizophrenia,* Routledge Mental Health, pp. 33–36.

Kirkpatrick, B., Fenton, W.S, Carpenter, Marder, S. R. (2006). "The NIMH-MATRICS consensus statement on negative symptoms," *Schizophrenic Bulletin*, 32(2): 214-219.

Kirkpatrick B., Strauss, G. P., Ngyen, L., Fischer, B. A. Daniel, D. G., Clenfuegus, A., & Marder, S. R. (2011). "The brief negative symptom scale," *Schizophrenia Bulletin*, 37(2): 300-305.

Kraepelin, E. (1911/1919). *Dementia Praecox and Paraphrenia*,; translated by R. M. Barclay, Edinburgh: E. & S. Livingstone.

Makinen, J., Miettunen, J., Jaaskelainen, E. et al. (2010). "Negative symptoms and their predictors in schizophrenia within the Northern Finland 1966 Birth Cohort," *Psychiatry Research*, 178:121–125.

Rume, H. C. (1960). "Contradictions in the concepts of schizophrenia," *Comprehensive Psychiatry*, 1:331–337.

Ungvari, G. S., Xiang Y-T, Hong, Y., Leung, H. C. M., Chiu, H. F. K. (2010). "Diagnosis of schizophrenia: Reliability of an operationalized approach to praecox-feeling," *Psychopathology*. 2010; 43(5):292-299.

Chapter 7

A Multi-Dimensional Articulation of Negative Symptoms in People with Schizophrenia and Its Implication to Mental Health Recovery

Introduction

In the previous chapter, the assessment, diagnosis, and etiology as well as the findings of MATRICS are thoroughly discussed. Related findings show that negative symptoms are not cognitive impairment. Instead, it is a deep involvement in one's inner world with a serious detachment from reality. Prolonged and severe negative symptoms also imply low mental and physical energy, inertness, passivity, and withdrawal. In this chapter, the writer describes related theoretical underpinnings of negative symptoms in schizophrenia. It begins with a cognitive interpretation, then follows by developmental perspective in terms of desocialization and devaluation. Then, psychodynamic interpretation by regression and repression is fully articulated. Existential and phenomenological interpretation such as existential boredom and false self system is mentioned. Negative symptoms in terms of traumatic numbing, repression and fixation is comprehensively depicted. Finally, based on related theoretical underpinnings, the writer will construct a comprehensive and multidimensional model in understanding, interpreting negative symptoms in schizophrenia. Its implications on recovery and related intervention are also discussed.

NEGATIVE SYMPTOMS AND SOCIAL COGNITION

Lincoln et al. (2011) carried a study to investigate association between negative symptom and social cognition including theory of Mind (ToM), attribution, empathy, self-esteem, and interpersonal self concepts in seventy-five patients with schizophrenia spectrum disorders and seventy-five healthy controls. Related findings showed that negative symptoms are significantly correlated with difficulties in theory of mind including empathy and self esteem. People with schizophrenic negative symptoms are less empathic, with less self-esteem, less self serving bias, poor interpersonal abilities, and dysfunctional acceptance beliefs. Difficulties in ToM were associated with negative symptoms in persons with *low but not in persons with medium or high levels of self-esteem*. Taken together, the social cognition variables and their hypothesized interaction explained 39 percent of the variance in negative symptoms after controlling for neurocognition and depression. The results highlight the relevance of self-concepts related to social abilities, dysfunctional beliefs, and global self-worth alone and in interaction with ToM deficits for negative symptoms and thereby provide a helpful basis for advancing psychosocial interventions (Linclon, 2011:S23). The result clearly showed that Linclon et al.'s (2011) study clearly showed negative symptoms do not relate with cognitive impairment but rather relate a fragmented self system (low self-esteem) in which the interpersonal show poor interpersonal ability and dysfunctional beliefs. People with psychotic negative symptoms, within a fragmented self system, isolate themselves from the outer reality.

DEVELOPMENTAL PERSPECTIVE: ARIETI'S DESOCIALIZATION AND DEVALUATION

In cognitive behavioral terms, negative symptoms are interpreted as cognitive deficits and impairment. Although recent studies showed that cognitive impairment and negative symptoms are of separated domains and their correlations are mild, negative symptoms are still regarded as impairment in one psychosocial functioning. In psychodynamic terms, negative symptoms are interpreted as regression, desocialization, and repression in which the individuals because of former traumatic experiences, tends to isolate and dissociate themselves from the oppressive reality that triggers their former traumatic experiences.

Regression from Interpersonal Relation

> 'I feel that schizophrenic cognition is not illogical or senseless, but that is can be interpreted. The schizophrenia patient adopts cognitive mechanisms that are different from those used by human being generally... .' (Arieti, 1974: 221)

Arieti (1974) affirmed that people with schizophrenia adopt another type of cognitive mechanism to adapt the external reality. Arieti (1974) affirmed it as desocialization and regression. In Arieti's terms, they regress from interpersonal relationship and interaction.

> Almost every schizophrenic retreat from society to a mild, moderate, or pronounced degree. The patient seems to *live in a shell, or in a world of his own, or behind what has been called autistic barrier*.... The patient communicates with visible effort. He *prefers to be by himself, to replace with his inner experiences the actions that require a social exchange.* If he is addressed, he resents even simply questions as if they were intrusions or attacks. He indulges in an extreme degree of privacy, so extreme that nobody, even his roommate, his closest relative, or his best friend can touch it. In every schizophrenic, there is an impairment of the ability to communicate with others and to share experiences with others. The most pronounced and obvious form of this desocialization are seen in regressive patients in back ward of state hospital ... . A group of schizophrenics in reality is not a group; it is a number of separate individuals ... . Their ability to share experiences is so disturbed that they cannot spontaneously initiate any plan with any other human being. (Arieti, 1974: 332)

Conceptual Review of Desocialization

Arieti (1974) has reviewed various theories in described desocialization in schizophrenic before 1974, which can be briefly summarized in Table 7.

Table 7. Related Theories in Describing Desocialization in Schizophrenia

	Views of Schizophrenic Desocialization
Freud's libido theory	Schizophrenic withdrawal as a withdrawal of libidinal cathexes form mental representation of objects when instinctual drives become unmanageable (Arieti,1974: 334)
Fairbairn (1952)	Schizoid patient has an infantile, undeveloped, weak ego. He escape from all the bad objects, whether they are external or internal (Arieti, 1974: 334) Regression as an advanced type of withdrawal, which is reached when schizoid state becomes very pronounced. The realities of the day are experienced as intolerable because of the bad objects are projected into them. Psychotic condition, like myths and dreams, represent flight back in the womb (Arieti, 1974: 334).
Szasz (1975)	Schizophrenia is largely the result of deficiency in internal objects, or deficiency of introjected objects. The client has no model to use in his life. He is awkward and inadequate (Arieti, 1974: 335)

Table 7. (Continued)

	Views of Schizophrenic Desocialization
Becker (1962)	Schizophrenia is due to a deficiency of external objects. External objects are organized behavioral responses to specific situations. Clients are unable to reduce problematic situations into habits, in converting the multiplicity of experience into meaningful objects (Arieti, 1974: 336)
Sullivan (1954)	The self is created by the ensemble of the social relations. if these interpersonal relations are unhealthy and create an excessive anxiety, the psychological development is disturbed and the process of socialization is altered (Arieti, 1974: 336).
Cameron (1947, 1951)	Individuals with socially inadequate development progressively fail to maintain a level of intelligible communication. They have the tendency to separate themselves from their community and to indulge in their private thinking, which does not requires conformity to the thinking of others. Through a process of progressive desocialization, they replace the social language habits with personal, very individual habits. In these people, the social community, which is a realistic interpretation of the interaction of the individuals with others is replaced by the pseudocommunity (Arieti, 1974: 336)

Symbolization and Desocialization

Desocialization and negative symptom are actualized through symbols. Arieti (1974) affirmed for human being several types of symbols are used in communicating meaning between two actors in language. They are:

1. *Images*
2. *Private symbols (paleosymbols)*
3. *Social (or verbal or common or communicable) symbols (Arieti, 1974: 345)*

Arieti (1974) described that desocialization occurs when the individual abandons the use of social symbols and indulges more and more in private symbols. Gradually, he or she becomes more and more alienated from the reality. Arieti (1974) labeled this as a psychotic mechanism.

> The psychosis most of the time occurs when the patient adopts a paleological way of thinking, use paleosymbols more and more, and drops at times gradually, at other times acutely - common symbols. By giving common or socially shared symbols he desocialize himself. Although he may use common symbols predominantly, the symbols that are involved in his delusions and more intensely experienced by him are his own paleosymbols . . . many of the symbols used by the patient are often distortions of social symbols. As long as the patient uses private symbols, at least for the life situations that are most important to him, he cannot integrate socially. However, even the most regressed schizophrenic will retain expression, words, and ways that belong to the interpersonal world. A total abandonment of what is obtained from others is not possible.' (Arieti, 1974: 345)

Arieti (1974) suggested that in persons with schizophrenia, a total abandonment of common symbols is not possible. Instead, it should be a minimal use of common symbol and an increasing usage of private symbols so to keep a distance from the social environment in which they cannot integrate into it. Interestingly, the private symbol used by them is always a purposeful or meaningful distortion of the social symbols.

The Use of Nonverbal, Private Symbols

> when we take into consideration common symbols, for the sake of simplification, we have considered only verbal symbols, but even gestures and motions are being desocialized by the schizophrenic, and they become mannerisms, grimaces, and stereotyped movements, whose meaning society does not understand. The patient is no longer an integral part of the society. . . . (Arieti, 1974: 346)

Arieti (1974) firmly assumed that symbols used in socialization and communication should not be limited by verbal symbol. Instead, non verbal symbols are used also. For persons with schizophrenia, the use of nonverbal gestures, motions are even more applicable in the use paleosymbols (private symbols). In forms of mannerism, grimaces, stereotyped behaviors, persons with schizophrenia are free to express their own meaning without being discovered by others. This is particular true in negative symptoms and in catatonic behaviors in which verbal communication and the use of language is slim and rare. The nonverbal symbolization allows them to stay in their own inner reality without being connected or integrated with the dominating society. The more private nonverbal symbols they use, the more they become desocialized and isolated from the external reality, the more they are confused and involved in their own private, inner life. It is an inner life that differs from philosophers or thinkers. Their inner life is full of unresolved. primary process. In fact, they still retain the ability to communicate with others in forms of common symbols. However, in doing so, their emotions are very detached and apathetic. That means persons with schizophrenia have dual consciousness in daily social interaction. On the one hand, they are involved in limited communication with external reality with very restricted use of common symbols. On the other hand, they are very alienated from the external reality by expressing and responding most in their own private symbols

> Desocialization, as part of the loss contact of reality, is not just a physical separation from others or even an emotional detachment. It is also a relinquishing of common ways of experiencing the world and relying on his own individualistic one. It is giving supremacy to inner life, but not the inner life of the philosopher… . It is an inner life that follows the rules of the primary process…In majority of cases of schizophrenic retains the intellectual understanding of these symbols, but to him they are emotionally remote:

> they are like foreign bodies and do not arouse in him the strong reactions that his won paleosymbols do. Therefore, the schizophrenic, especially at the beginning of the illness, may still retain a capacity to socialize, or to check somehow the process of desocialization, but this will only be at the expense of a strenuous intellectual effort. . . .

Symbol and Projection

Desocialization also occurs in positive symptoms in which the individual employ private symbol to project his own unacceptable part of self outward in forms of paranoid delusion and hallucination. This unacceptable part of self system reflects others' negative and rejecting comment toward the individual with schizophrenia.

> The process of desocialization of the schizophrenic does not operate only in the sense of a loss of common symbols. There is also a tendency to reject or to diverse the self of those attitudes, role and tendencies that become part of the self and that were reflected from others. ...the self is not rejected, but also projected, or given back to the persons who originally gave it to the self. (Arieti, 1974: 346)

That means, in terms of desocialization, positive symptoms (paranoid as well as grandiose delusion and hallucination) work together with negative symptoms, in which common symbols are disregarded by the individual with schizophrenia. Within negative and positive symptoms, only private symbols are used to express the unfulfilled needs of the individual. Strictly speaking, positive symptoms are manifested private symbols in which verbal symbols and non-verbal symptoms are expressed and can be observed and interpreted by others. However, negative symptoms are latent private symbols in which nonverbal symbols may not be expressed. That means, they may not be observable and interpretative. Comparing with manifested verbal symbols, latent nonverbal symbol are more private and hidden. In other words, the individual with prevailing negative psychotic symptoms are more desocialized and they are more alienated from common social symbol.

Symbolization, Desocialization, and Psychotic Symptom

Based on this, a process in psychotic desocialization can be constructed with the stages detailed in Table 8.

Table 8. Process and Stages of Desocialization in Positive and Negative Symptoms

	Use Common Social Symbol	Use of Private Verbal Symbol	Use of Private Non-Verbal Symbol
Stage 1: Development of Positive Symptoms	Begin to withdraw from frequent use of common social symbol. As the social environment is very oppressive and abusive	Begin to indulge in the use of limited private verbal symbol to express and communicate ones' unfulfilled needs, frustration and negative emotion in life. The private verbal symbols formulate in forms of initial paranoid delusion and hallucination	The use of private non-verbal symbol is not facilitated as the individual still want to maintain main realistic contact with others in the social environment
Stage 2: Active Positive Symptoms and First Rank Symptoms	Active withdrawal from the use of common social symbol in communicating with others. Together with this is an active, self-isolated, and very confused mental state	Frequent use of private verbal symbol in expressing one's unfulfilled needs, frustration, and emotions. The private verbal symbols formulate active paranoid and grandiose Delusions and hallucinations. In certain situation, the paranoid and grandiose delusion and hallucination are represented by very distorted common symbol that can only be understood by the individual him- or herself.	Begin to engage in frequent use of non-verbal, private symbols in building up odd and bizarre. catatonic delusion and hallucination. as well as behaviors.
Stage 3: Constant Positive Symptoms and Development of Negative Symptoms	Restricted use of common symbol in the social and physical environment. For example, clients only respond to simple daily activities and routine interpersonal transaction.	The use of verbal private symbols is also restricted and limited. Individuals do not bother to communicate with others. They begin to lose their interest, motives, energy and will power in communicating with others	The use of nonverbal private symbols can also manifest in forms of mild negative symptoms. In being isolated from the actual reality, individuals begin to be emotionally, cognitively and behaviorally alienated from others.
Stage 4: Mild Constant Positive Symptoms and Active Negative Symptoms	Very restricted use of common symbols for minimal survival. Individuals appear inert and withdrawn from the external social and physical environment. Apart from basic living such as sleeping, eating, standing, and sitting, they are alienated from the reality.	The use of private verbal symbol becomes very restricted and very limited. Individuals lose their interest, motives, energy, and will power to communicate with others. They also do not bother others do not understand their views, ideas, and thinking. They prefer to absorb in their delusive but very passive inner world.	Nonverbal private symbols are very introvert and hard to be interpreted by others. Prevailing negative symptoms such as blunt affect, anhedonia, alogia and avolition are concealed by clients' use of strange private nonverbal symptoms. such as staring at certain things, maintaining certain posture, reciting certain sentences.
Stage 5: Prevailing Negative Symptoms	The use of common symbols is really rare. Individuals appear as very inert, withdrawn and out touched of reality. In extreme case, the individuals may even refuse to eat, sleep, and any response to external reality. They may appear as paralyze and lying in bed doing nothing.	The use of private verbal symbol is nearly diminished. Individuals may make some meaningless voice or sound. They keep still and quiet in most period of time	The use of private non-verbal symbol is also restricted. They appear as totally absent from feeling, motion, or even thinking.

Desocialization, Loneliness, and Loss of Self in Schizophrenia

Artieti (1974) further articulated that desocialization is a process of isolation from social isolation to self-isolation. That means, the individual with schizophrenia not only tries to use private symbols to express his or her meaning and views, he or she tries to isolate him- or herself from others.

> By desocialization he loses a great part of himself. This loss is compensated to a minimal degree by the individualistic restitution symptoms, but this compensation is inadequate and in many case transitory. To be alone, as schizophrenic is, does not mean only to be without others, but to be less of himself. The meaning of loneliness, as experienced even by normal people and by neurotics, may be fully understood, in my opinion, if we think of the tragic effect of desocialization in schizophrenia. (Arieti, 1974: 349)

Artieti (1974) affirmed that people with schizophrenia try to be alone in the process of desocialization. It is the only way to avoid being isolated, abused and oppressed by others. However, in doing so, he also isolated him from normal communication, normal self-identity, normal social interaction, and recognition. In other words, in being desocialized, he or she is actually suffering from deviation to normal self-identity, social interaction, and recognition. That means, he or she is going to lose part of his or her self system. Such self-isolation and deviation is a kind of self-induced loneliness. On one hand, the client with schizophrenia wishes to be alone. On the hand, being alone he or she has to lose part of him- or herself. That means, the client with schizophrenia not only isolates him- or herself from others, he or she is also losing part of him- or herself in being avoided to contact others within a very oppressive environment. Or we can say, this is the only way they can maintain a minimal survival.

> Loneliness means fear of losing oneself partially or totally. This meaning reveal itself fully in the panoramic dimensions and in intensity of the schizophrenic devastation; but the ghost of loneliness that also haunts normal people may include, to minimal degree, some of the qualities of these extreme and ultimate consequences. (Arieti, 1974: 349)

Within this line of thinking, for people with schizophrenia, negative symptoms in the form of full indulging in one's inner world and blocking communication from the external world by abandoning the use of common symbols and private, verbal symbols, as well as very restricted use of private, nonverbal symbols, make their whole life a vacuum. They feel extremely lonely and empty inside. The urges to refuse to communicate and the fear of being stimulated by external reality are fully exercised. For them, this is the only way to retain their own autonomy within a very oppressive, abusive, and manipulative reality.

> This brings up another problem. The schizophrenic is alone in the world even in the 'world' of his own making; but is he lonely. Recovered schizophrenics have stated that they felt terribly lonely when they were sick, and there is no ground for thinking that this is a retrospective falsification. However, the fear of interpersonal relations was even greater that loneliness. (Arieti, 1974: 349)

That means, for persons with schizophrenia, there are only two choices. One is being totally swallowed or oppressed by others so that their entire self system of sense of existence is being threatened and denied within the very oppressive and depowering social environment. Another one is being alone and self-isolated from actual reality. As they cannot physically separate from the oppressive reality, they can only desocialize themselves so that they are physically present but mentally absent and isolated from the oppressive and debilitating social environment. In doing so, they also paralyze part of their own self system so that even they are physically connected with the oppressive reality, they do not feel frustrated, painful, and oppressed by others. Along this line of thinking, negative symptom in persons with schizophrenia should not be regarded as a cognitive impairment or without any skills or ability to be social and connective with others. Instead, persons with schizophrenia are lack of will power, motivation, aspiration, or motives to be connected and socialized. They do not have sufficient trust and interest on others. Even though others do not separate from them, they tend to separate themselves from others. It is a stage of social inertness and self-isolation from others. In doing so, it appears that they do not have cognitive skills or mechanisms to relate to others. In fact, they repress all these cognitive skills or mechanisms properly because of their unpleasant, past experiences in connecting with others. The desocialization process mentioned by Arieti (1974) demonstrated a firm determination for persons with schizophrenia to isolate themselves from the unpleasant external world by engaging in using nonverbal symbol in communication. Related negative symptoms such as alogia, anhedonia, avolition, and blunt affect are only external consequences of disengagement in the oppressive reality.

Negative Symptoms, Regression, Devaluation, and Repression

Psychotic negative symptoms can also be understood in terms of regression and devaluation and repression.

Regression and Devaluation Before Self-Fragmentation

Regression and devaluation are ego-defense mechanism for the ego system in facing threat in the oppressive reality. Yip (2013) affirmed regression and self-devaluation is a painful process molding the individual to become very primitive, withdrawn, and retarded in responding to the very oppressive and threatening, external environment. The more regressive and devaluating one is, the more one become inert and withdrawn to an extent that crucial ego-functioning, and activities of the self system are frozen, delayed, and retarded. It certainly speeds up the process of self- fragmentation in schizophrenia. After the self-fragmentation, important ego- functioning, memories, and activities are even repressed. The individual, being engaged in negative, psychotic symptoms, he or she turns him- or herself into an non-being so that others cannot oppress and humiliate them (Yip, 2013).

Regression is an ego-defense mechanism in which the individual temporarily transfers the ego to an earlier stage of development rather than behave in an adult and mature way (Freud, 1965; Freud, 1954).

Meisssner (1981) defined regression as:

> return to a previous state of development or functioning to avoid the anxious or hostilities involved in later stages; return to earlier points of fixation, embodying modes of behavior previously given up. This defense mechanism is often the result of a disruption of equilibrium at later phase of development. (Meissner, 1981: 137)

Regression, as a defense mechanism, embraces the following ingredients.

1. An unconscious response to inhibit internal desire or numb oneself in facing external adverse stimuli.
2. A disruption of equilibrium in later stage of development.
3. A fixation on certain primitive or childlike behaviors that have been given up.
4. An emotional tension and frustration that blocks normal and mature responses.
5. A retardation or slowing down of normal mature response or habitual defense toward frustration and tension.
6. Substitution with simplified behaviors or thought in facing fear, tension, loneliness, and emptiness.
7. A non-attention or neglect of sense of time and space. (Corradi, 1981; Greenacre, 1960; Lewin et al., 1941; Loewald, 1981)

Within these seven characteristics, individuals with schizophrenia, in the process of regression, numb themselves in facing adverse stimuli. Their mature and normal responses and behaviors were slowed down. They absorb themselves within childlike or primitive behaviors as substitutes or involvement shield in displacing their fear, tension, loneliness, and emptiness within the oppressive, psychosocial environment. In doing so, their sense of time and space is distorted, and they can easily adapt frustration within the oppressive environment.

Together with regression, devaluation is also another mechanism used by the individual in facing oppression by others before the process of self-fragmentation. It is “a mechanism in which the person attributes exaggeratedly negative qualities to self or others.” (American Psychiatric Association, 1987). Perry (1990) defined it as

> the individual deals with emotional conflicts or internal or external stressors by attributing exaggeratedly negative qualities to oneself or others. Unlike reaction formulation, devaluation may conceal admiration or possible feelings toward others. (Perry, 1990: 256)

Salter-Pedneault (2008) refers devaluation as:

> a psychological process of coping with the anxiety caused by ambivalent feelings by having period of time in which object of ambivalence is instead viewed as completely flawed, worthless, or as having exaggerated negative qualities. It alternates with another defense mechanism, idealization, in which the object of ambivalence is viewed as perfect or having exaggerated positive qualities. (Salter-Pedneault, 2008:1)

According to related literature, devaluation consists of several characteristics:

1. Emotional tension in facing stress and conflict.
2. An unbearable state of ambivalence and anxiety.
3. Exaggerating negative attribution toward self (sense of worthlessness, powerlessness, or impotence).
4. Exaggerating negative attribution toward others (idealizing others). (American Psychiatric Association, 1987; Perry, 1980)

In other words, in facing the oppression by others, the individual admits and internalizes that he or she is worthless, inferior, and even impotent in a stage that he or she should be neglected and depersonalized. At the same time, he or she may also idealize others. Devaluation is a form of negative attribution toward self. However, this form of exaggeration is not an externalization or outburst of anger or hatred toward oneself and another. Instead, it is a self-absorption of exaggerating negative attribution quietly and gradually. By doing so, the individual does not need to fight back others’ oppression and depersonalization. Instead, he or she simply accepts it quietly in a form of blunt affect, concluding that he or she deserves that kind of oppression and depersonalization.

For persons with schizophrenia, in facing external threat and oppression, both ego-defense mechanisms, regression, and devaluation may be used together. While regression makes the individual return to a primitive stage with fixation of childish behavior and thinking, devaluation tends to deflate the self-identity, image, and boundary of the individual. In fact, regression can be regarded as a distancing of self by involvement in previous pleasant experiences, memories, and behavior patterns in childhood and adolescence so as to neutralize the sense of inferiority in the oppressive environment. All these experiences, memories, and behavior patterns are involvement that shields the individual so as to isolate him or her from unpleasant experiences in the immediate, oppressive environment. Severe self-involvement may intensify regressive behavior, mood, and cognition, or vice versa. As a consequence, the ego functioning, ego-identity, ego-awareness as well as ego-response to the external environment is decreased to an extent the integrity of ego is threatened. In other words, while devaluation is a way to absorb external oppression, regression is a way to ease out the pain of devaluation (Yip, 2013).

Regression, Devaluation, and Repression after the Self- Fragmentation

As the oppression in the immediate environment increases and persists but the ego-functioning decreases and impairs, former ego-mechanisms such as regression and devaluation may not be strong enough to defend the individual. Instead, a more intense, defense mechanism repression is needed to help the individual to detach him- or herself from oppression.

Freud (1917/1954) was the first scholar articulating that repression is a mechanism to conceal unpleasant affect from the ego-system.

> The affect from which the ego has suffered remains as it was before, unaltered and undiminished, the only difference being that the incompatible idea is kept down and shout out from recollection. The repressed ideas from the nucleus of a second psychical group, which I believe, is accessible even without the help of hypnosis. (Freud, 1917/1954:54-55)

> Hysteria originates through the repression of an incomplete ideas from a motive of defense. On this view, the repressed idea would persist as a memory trace that is weak (has little intensity), while the affect that is torn from it would be used for a somatic innervation. (Freud, 1917/1945: 285)

McCullough (1992) defined repression as:

> Repression is seemingly inexplicable naïve, memory laps, or failure to acknowledge input form a selected sense of organ. This defense protects the subject from being aware of what he or she is feeling. The emotional elements are clearly experienced, but his or her cognitive elements remain outside of consciousness. (McCullough, 1992: 176)

In DSM IIIR, repression is briefly defined as follows:

> Repression is a mechanism in which the person is unable to remember or be cognitively aware of disturbing wishes, feelings, thoughts, or experiences. (American Psychiatric Association, 1987:394)

Meissner (1981) further described two types of repression, primary repression, and secondary repression.

> Expelling and withholding from conscious awareness of an idea or feeling. It may operate by excluding from awareness what was once experienced on a conscious level (secondary repression), or it may curb ideas and feelings before they have reached consciousness (primary repression). The forgetting of repression is unique in that it is often accompanied by very symbolic behavior, which suggests that the repressed is not really forgotten. (Meissner, 1981:137)

From all these definitions, repression seems to consist of the following natures:

1. The existence of disturbing ideas, wishes, cognitions, memories, and experiences.
2. The awareness of certain ideas, cognitions, memories, and experiences are expelled and withheld.
3. The affect related to these ideas, cognitions, memories, and experiences are torn and dissociated.
4. Possible repression of previous conscious ideas or cognition (secondary repression).
5. Possible repression of ideas that have never come up to consciousness or awareness.
6. Symbolic behavior possibly accompanying repressed cognitions, ideas, memories, and experiences.
7. Recollection of repressed cognitions, ideas, memories, and experiences by relating to correlated affect and emotion.

In the process of self-fragmentation, regression, and devaluation can no longer face the tremendous negative effects caused by the oppressive environment with a result of splitting of ego-boundary, ego-identity, and ego-functioning. Repression seems to be an effective mechanism in which the individual separates him- or herself from previous disturbing and very oppressive and negative cognitions, ideas, experiences, and desires. It can start with secondary repression in which those negative experiences, causing emotions that were previously and painfully conscious and fearsome, are gradually repressed so to make the person with schizophrenia feel much better in the unavoidable, oppressive environment. Gradually, primary repression occurs in which the individual tries to repress those who never come up to his or her consciousness such diminishing oneself or related issues, persons, and events in the oppressive environment. In the severe process of repression, the individual represses not only those unpleasant memories, experiences, ideas, and cognition, other pleasant ones are also repressed to any extent the individual feels that he or she has a lot of thoughts and ideas that he or she cannot reach them (primary repression). They are far from them. For persons with schizophrenia, after the process of self- fragmentation, the effects of repression, together with intense regression and devaluation may make their sense of self very detached, with an intense sense of ambivalence whether he or she or his or her thought, ideas, cognition is there (Yip, 2013).

Along this line of thinking, positive symptoms can be understood as primary repression where the repressed ideas, images, and traumatic experiences are re-bounced in forms of delusions, hallucinations, and odd and bizarre behaviors. The manifestation of all these may not be directive representation. Instead, it should be done in forms of symbolic ways. A client with repressed experience of traumatic experiences of artificial abortion in an operation threat may harbor a visual hallucination of a dim, white light and a strong sense of being suffocated by white matter into her nose. Together with that sort of primary repression is also an intense sense of fear and loss. It is understandable that the dim, white light should be the unforgettable image of light from the operation theater, and the white matter sucking into his nose should be anesthetics put her into an unconscious condition for the abortion operation. The sense of loss and fear should be the sense after the abortion. Together with this primary repression is secondary repression in which the individual's experience of abortion operation is severely repressed and submerged. Apart from feeling of loss and fear, the individuals' social and ego-functioning is greatly hindered.

Meissner (1981) further described two types of repression, primary repression and secondary repression.

> Expelling and withholding from conscious awareness of an idea or feeling. It may operate by excluding from awareness what was once experienced on a conscious level (secondary repression), or it may curb ideas and feelings before they have reached consciousness (primary repression). The forgetting of repression is unique in that it is often accompanied by very symbolic behavior, which suggests that the repressed is not really forgotten. (Meissner, 1981:137)

From all these definitions, repression seems to consist of the following elements:

1. The existence of disturbing ideas, wishes, cognitions, memories, and experiences.
2. The awareness of certain ideas, cognitions, memories, and experiences that are expelled and withheld.
3. Affect related to these ideas, cognitions, memories, and experiences that are torn and dissociated.
4. Possible repression of previous conscious ideas or cognition (secondary repression).
5. Possible repression of ideas that have never come up to consciousness or awareness.
6. The repressed cognitions, ideas, memories, and experiences accompanied by symbolic behavior.
7. Recollection of repressed cognitions, ideas, memories and experiences by relating to correlated affect and emotion.

Persons with schizophrenia usually have their onset when the external environment is extremely oppressive, humiliating, and unbearably painful. Under those conditions, individuals not only regress from the external environment with a devaluation of their own ability, self-image, and ego- functioning. They tend to conclude that they do not have enough ability to deal with the oppressive external environment. To ease the unbearable pain of being spontaneously oppressed, abused, and ignored, individuals need to repress all related affect, memories, cognitions, and actions within current and past traumatic experiences. Together with this comes an intense dissociation and detachment from the oppressive reality. This is the dissociation/detachment from related ideas, cognitions, affect, and responses from related issues, objects, and persons from actual reality. In other words, within negative symptoms, several defensive mechanisms work closely together. They are regression, devaluation, repression, and dissociation/ detachment. All these can be shown in the following figures 10 and 11.

From Figure 10 it is clear that negative symptoms in schizophrenia consist of four layers of ego defense mechanism. The *first layer is dissociation and detachment* in which the individuals try to dissociate and detach from the oppressive reality. Underlying this layer is the *second layer of devaluation* in which the individual tries to devaluate him- or herself thinking that he or she is unable or powerless in dealing the oppressive reality. As it is covered up by the layer of severe dissociation and detachment, the individual's feelings of inferiority and shame together within devaluation cannot be surfaced out or felt by others. In chronic schizophrenia, the sense of inferiority cannot be released as the dissociation from reality totally hinders the ventilation of mood and effect of the individual.

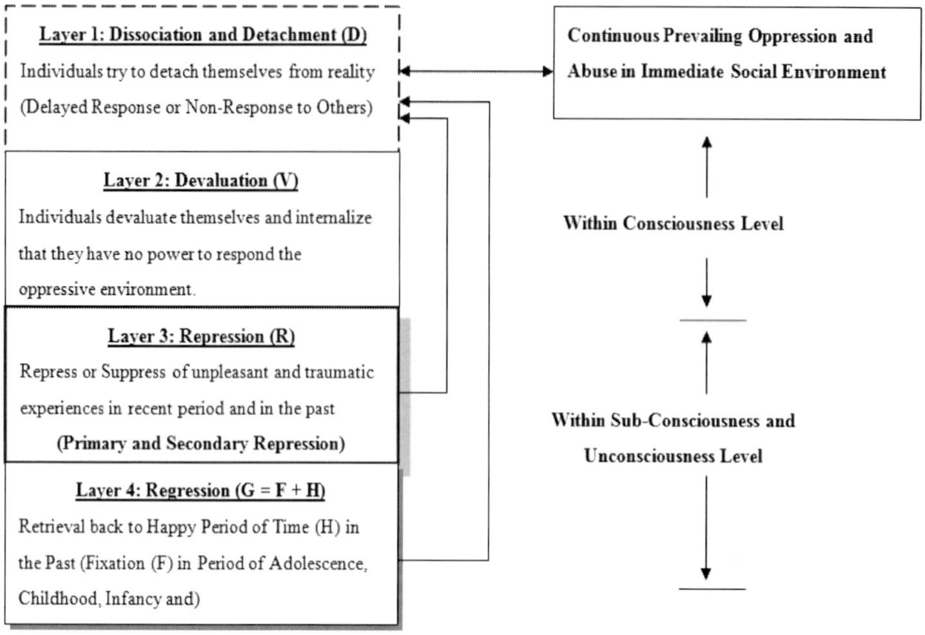

Figure 10. Negative Symptoms in Terms of Detachment, Devaluation, Repression, and Regression.

The *third layer is repression* in which unpleasant memories and traumatic experiences are repression. Within the mechanism of repression, the individual tries not to be conscious about all these unpleasant memories and traumatic experiences. However, as there are two types of repression, primary and secondary repression, in a state of negative symptoms, primary repression is used to repress all related, unhappy experiences from the past. In doing so, related life experiences and memories are also repressed.

Prolonged repression and devaluation are very uncomfortable and unbearable for individuals. Thus, underlying the layer of repression should be the fourth layer of regression in which the individual tries to fixate within certain periods of past time in which he or she had happy and enjoyable experiences. That can be happy experiences in infancy, childhood, adolescence, youth, or adulthood. In severe and extreme regression, the individual can fixate into a state of infancy and babyhood in which he or she is totally dependent and immobile. Only with the retrieval of happy experiences in early childhood experiences, the individual can face the very oppressive social environment.

A close look at negative symptoms may further articulate Layer 1 (D = detachment and dissociation of external oppressive reality), Layer 2 (devaluation of oneself), Layer 3 (repression of unpleasant or even traumatic recent and past experiences) and Layer 4 (regression in terms of fixation and retrieval of happy past experiences) are closely related to one another. Their relationship can be shown in the following figure.

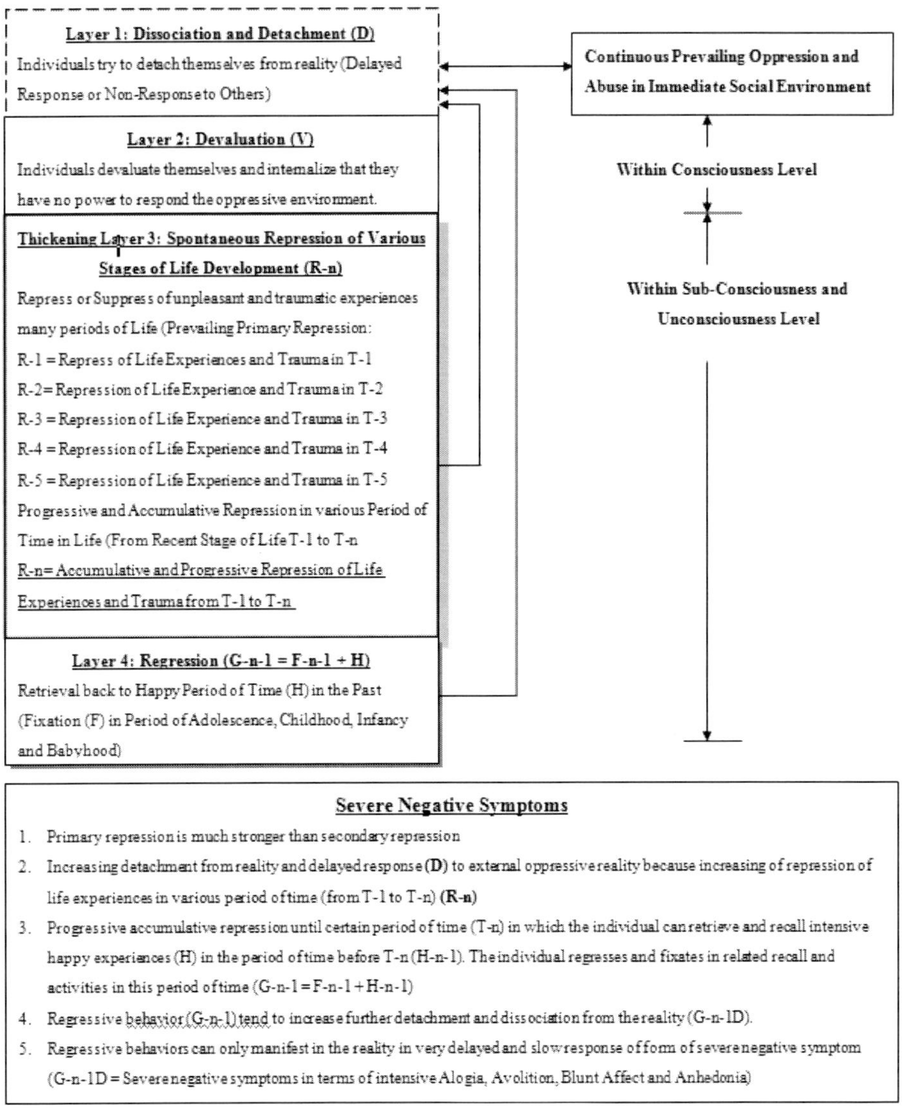

Figure 11. Development of Severe Negative Symptoms in Terms of Detachment, Devaluation, Repression, and Regression

From Figure 11 it is clear that the individual with psychotic negative symptoms suffers pain from the prevailing, oppressive social environment. He or she has nowhere to escape. Instead he or she has to undergo a process of self-fragmentation. Mentally, he or she has to detach him- or herself from the oppressive environment. Prolonged and severe detachment should be accompanied by spontaneous dissociation and devaluation as well as repression. Dissociation implies a body/mind splitting, in which, while the body is still in the oppressive social environment, the mind is detached. Following this a devaluation of self- image, self- identity and ego-functioning in which the individual fully admits the oppressive environment is far from his or her ability to tackle it. The devaluation is intensified by repression in which unpleasant past and recent oppressive and even traumatic experiences are totally repressed within one's own consciousness. Severe repression of recent and past experience also implies a repression of one's life development within all these repressed period of time (R-n). Thus, the individual should regress back to certain period of time (T-n) in which he or she can find sufficient, good experiences to sustain his or her will to minimal survival in daily life.

In extremely severe negative symptoms, individuals may even regress in a form of prenatal state. Sullivan (1962) has a comprehensive description on this prenatal regression.

> 'The mental structure is dissociation in such a fashion that the disintegrated portions *regress in function to earlier level of mental ontology,* without parallelism in individual depth of regression. This disparity of depths seems the essence of that which is schizophrenia, as distinguished from other mental disorders . . . . (Sullivan, 1962: 13)
>
> *The depths of regression in this disorder* greatly exceed that in other forms of mental upset, this too, may be found to be an essential feature. That there is any necessity for accepting the notion of phyletic regression of mind structure is not proven. . . . (Sullivan, 1962: 14)
>
> In a large number there had been markedly psychopathic traits in *the childhood of the patient. Ungovernable temper tantrums, destructiveness, malicious behavior, emotional instabilities of high degrees, excessive sensitiveness, extreme Self-Consciousness and severe neuroses* . . . . (Sullivan, 1962: 14)
>
> An improvement from self- contained, or pent-up attitude with lack of the ability to use available outlets for the expression of distressing content, to one in which the patient was relatively open and able frankly to discuss some his life problems, was generally observed . . . . (Sullivan, 1962: 14)
>
> There was in fact at least two types of content in the general clinical group of hebephrenics. *There was one in which fecal, anal, and urinary interest* dominate the personality. In these, the mannerism was of great interests. So far, it has seemed that the hostile, egoistic desires stirred in opposition to the perverse infantile craving were the motivation of the mannerism. . . . The appearance of a mannerism, as well as the time of its repetition, the exaggeration of its manifestations and the available content before is appearance and subsequent to an occasional disappearance, has led to the rather startling surmise that mannerism is *a regression* to almost purely physiological existence of a mental content, the distinguishing nature of which was to conflicts with the perverse adaption... Silliness is not a criterion, probably being the effect of perverse infantile behavior is contempt of external approval.' (Sullivan, 1962: 16)

> *The regressive process goes deeper* in the mental structures; the functions appearing in content and behavior become lower and lower in the scale psychologic ontogenesis... . (Sullivan, 1962: 18)

> 'The theoretical consideration which has prompted such objective interpretation in the *regressive prenatal state* is also a reflection from the ontogenic viewpoint - viz that the patient, having reverted to the beginning of the mind, nothing further regression could occur and that, therefore, the vital impulse might safely be directed from without to the end of retracing the genetic pathway to adulthood, with the assistance of such experience as could be directed objectively after study of the patient and his pre-psychotic environment... (Sullivan, 1962: 18)

According to Sullivan's (1962) description, regression in persons with schizophrenia can be summed up in the following points:

1. Regression in schizophrenia is far more serious than other forms of mental problems.
2. The depth of regression in schizophrenics has a very substantially impact on the mental structures of the individual.
3. Regression occurs in many aspects of the individual including behaviors (mannerism), physical condition, energy level, mental structures (personality), as well as emotions.
4. As regression goes further, individuals' ego functioning as well desires control is lessened accordingly.
5. Individuals can regress into different stages, such childhood, infancy and even prenatal state.
6. In childhood regression, individuals become a child with temper tantrums, destructiveness, malicious behaviors, emotional instabilities of high degrees, excessive sensitiveness, extreme Self- Consciousness and severe neuroses.
7. In infancy regression, individuals become infants with *fecal, anal and urinary interest* dominating the personality.
8. The final regression can be pre-natal stage in which an individual remains stagnant just like being a fetus in the mother's womb.

According to Sullivan's (1962) descriptions that means, negative symptoms in persons with schizophrenia can be interpreted as severe regression in primary stages of life, childhood, infancy or prenatal fetus. For each stage of regression, components in level 1, level 2 and level 3 as well as features of alogia, avolition, blunt affect and anhedonia can be described as follows:

Positive and Negative Symptoms in Regression to childhood

In Level 1: Dissociation and Detachment in Regression to Childhood (C1)

For persons with schizophrenia, dissociation and detachment make them isolate from any activities and relationship in adulthood. That means, he or she may not conclude or admit that he or she needs to work, to fulfill adult responsibility as a caregiver and bread winner for his or her children and parents. He or she may not think that he or she should behave like an adult in a way that he or she takes up obligations as an adult. Even if he or she is married, he or she is withdrawn and detached from marital relationship and activities. He or she is unable to take of his or her spouse. He or she is unable to engage in meaningful activities with his or her spouse. He or she fails to build up his or her own family. Even if he or she is a parent, he or she is withdrawn ad detached from parent child relationship. He or she is unable to take care of his or her children. He or she fails to support the whole family. He or she does not engage in family activities. Even if he or she is an employee, he or she is withdrawn and detached from work and related duties.

In Level 2: Devaluation in Regression to Childhood (C2)

In devaluation, individuals with schizophrenia because of various unpleasant experiences in adolescence or in adulthood, they conclude that they cannot or is unable to perform various roles of an adult/youth/adolescence. This can include finding a stable job in youth and adult; building their own families, but having good courtship, marriage and rearing children; contributing to their communities and society. Because of past failure in adolescence, youth and adulthood, they affirmed that they are unable to be mature adolescents and/or young adult. They think that their lives deem to be fail in family, work, peer and society. They are over shadowed by past failure and traumas in life. All they can affirm that they may be functional children. They feel safe to be children rather than being mature and good functioning adults.

In Level 3: Spontaneous Repression in Regression to Childhood

In regression to childhood, individuals tend to repress those unpleasant and even traumatic experiences in adolescence, youth and adulthood. It can be traumas such as abuse, bullying and being oppressed in adolescence, youth and adulthood. It can also be painful divorce or separation in courtship. It can be unemployment, workplace bullying and/or oppression in work and employment. Furthermore, it can be unpleasant experiences, suffering and even hardship in prolonged institutionalization or maltreatment in treatment and rehabilitation services. In time of serious repression, even normal and positive experiences and memories are also partially or heavily condensed.

In Level 4: Regression and Fixation in Childhood

For a person with psychosis, regression and fixation in childhood implies that he or she behaves like a naughty child with 'ungovernable temper tantrums, destructiveness, malicious behavior, emotional instabilities of high degrees, excessive sensitiveness, extreme Self- Consciousness and severe neuroses (Sullivan, 1962: 14). In other words, he or she may embrace very disturbing positive symptoms such as confused paranoid or grandiose delusions, hallucinations and odd and bizarre behaviors. Together with this is also the occurrence of mild negative symptoms in which the individual does not have inappropriate emotional, cognitive and psychic response to external demands in family, work and in social circle. He or she may not have any will power and energy to take up obligations and responsibilities in adulthood (mild avolition), to speak clearly and express soundly about their views and opinions (mild alogia), to respond correctly to others' emotion (mild blunt affect) and emotionally and relationally quite distancing from others (mild anhedonia).

Negative Symptoms in Regression to Infancy

In Level 1: Dissociation and Detachment in Regression to Infancy

For persons with schizophrenia, in regression to infancy, the individual fails to recognize, to admit and to perform social and ego functioning in adulthood, adolescence, and childhood. Being regression in infancy implies that the individual is even more naive than a naughty child. He or she is very egocentric caring only about his or her desires and needs such as food, drink, sleeping and egestion. He or she is very dissociated from others' needs. He or she is very detached to external reality. He or she may not able to distinguish safety and risk. He or she is very absorbed in his or her own thinking and desires. His or her mobility is quite limited. He or she behaves like an infant being dissociated from the adult world.

In Level 2: Devaluation in Regression to Infancy

In regression to infancy for persons with schizophrenia, they devaluate their ego and social functioning in adulthood, youth, adolescence and childhood. In devaluating ego functioning in adulthood and youth, they are unable to go out for work or fulfilling any duties and responsibility of being adults and youth. They do not have confidence to speak for their right, to reject others' unreasonable demand and request. They are unable to fulfill developmental tasks of courtship and marriage. Their developmental tasks in being an adolescence is being devaluated in which they fail to have proper self- care, going outside and taking public transport, learning and education, as well as striving for an unique self- and gender identity for themselves. Furthermore, their developmental attainment in childhood is also denied.

In Level 3: Spontaneous Repression in Regression to Infancy

For persons with schizophrenia, in regression to infancy, they tend to repress related memories and experiences in adulthood, youth, adolescence and children, in particular those unhappy and traumatic experiences. Many of them may have unpleasant experiences in adulthood such as being institutionalized and neglected in mental hospitals, being controlled and ignored by related workers and professionals in mental health services. Some also experience unemployment, oppression and bullying in adulthood and youth. Some may be abused by their family members in their childhood and adolescence. In negative symptoms, individuals, in severe repression of unpleasant experiences, they also repress those normal experiences in adulthood, youth, adolescence and childhood. In other words, their life experiences are mostly frozen and condensed, leaving only those experiences in infancy.

In Level 4: Regression and Fixation in Infancy

In persons with schizophrenia with prevailing negative symptoms, it implies that the individual fails to address and express his psychosocial needs in even in a childhood state. Instead, physiological needs totally absorb the individual in which he or she simply becomes a baby. In Freud's term, the individual's superego and ego are greatly hindered or repressed. Thus, only his or her id prevails. In doing so, the individual may be dominated by anal and oral needs. Apart from eating, his or her daily life and personality may be dominated by fecal, anal and urinary interest. He or she may crave for food, being touched and cared or simply stay or sitting aimlessly for the whole day (Sullivan, 1962). All these may appear in a form of mannerism in which the individual constantly engages in repetitive infant like behaviors struggling for basic survival such as eating, crying, poor self- care and personal hygiene. Some may even play around urine and faeces. All these were very unacceptable to people around the individual thinking that the individual is 'crazy' and 'silly'. In terms of alogia, the individual regresses to a state that he or she can only murmur some babyish sound or simple wordings. In terms of avolition, the individual only regresses to will power and behaviors such as eating, sucking and egestion. In terms of anhedoina, the individual regresses to only very primitive intervention like a baby attach to his or her mother, cry to his or her mother's holding and yell for food and get rid of uncomfortable means. In terms of blunt affect, the individual simply shows no emotional response to others even if others try all means to interact with him or her.

Negative Symptoms in Regression to Prenatal Fetus

In Level 1: Dissociation and Detachment

For persons with schizophrenia, regression to prenatal fetus is the final stage of regression in which the individual can regress no more. He or she is fixated in a state of fetus in mother's womb. This is a state of both physical and mental inertia. In terms of dissociation and detachment, the individual totally dissociate from external environment. Regression in childhood implies dissociation and detachment from adult world. Regression in childhood strives for egocentric expression can childish satisfaction. Regression in infancy means even losing one own self- identity and ability to outreach to outside world. Regression in prenatal fetus means the individual can no longer function as an independent being. He or she total dissociates from all sort of external stimuli. He or she may be lying on bed for whole day long. He or she cannot be attracted or motivated even by primitive desires such as food and sex.

Level 2: Devaluation in Regression to Prenatal Fetus

In the regression to prenatal fetus, and individual with schizophrenia tens to devaluate his or her ego, social and physical functioning. He or she does not have any confidence or even motivation to perform any ability in adulthood, youth, adolescence, childhood and infancy. In other words, he or she is entirely malfunctioning in being an adult, a youth, an adolescent, a child and an infant. In other words, the individual does not have confidence to behave like a human being. He or she is only confident in lying on bed, being inert and motionless for nothing.

In Level 3: Spontaneous Repression in Regression to Prenatal Fetus

In prenatal fetus regression, an individual with schizophrenia tends to repress all his or her ego, social, psychological and physical functioning in adulthood, youth, adolescence, childhood, and infancy. At first, the individual only represses those unhappy experiences in adulthood, youth, adolescence, childhood, and infancy. As the repression moves on, the individual also represses all related experiences in his or her life. Finally, the individual may only appear as an unborn child with repressed memories, ego functioning and social functioning. He or she represses his or her own identity, his or her ability to be a human being. Occasionally, related residual memories, ego and social functioning in life, especially those unpleasant and traumatic experiences may re-bounce making the individual suddenly become emotional and sentimental. In some cases, he or she may even manifest some sorts of aggressive and disturbing behaviors.

In Level 4: Regression and Fixation in Prenatal Fetus

Fixation in Prenatal Fetus for persons with schizophrenia implies that they fixate in being in a comfort state as a fetus in the mothers' womb. In other words, they enjoy doing nothing or being totally inert as a fetus in their mothers' womb. In terms of alogia, the individual with schizophrenia will never murmur any words. In terms of avolition, he or she has no motivation or will power to do anything. In terms of anhedonia, he or she has no interest in establishing any social and interpersonal relationship. In terms of blunt affect, he or she shows no response to anyone. In fact, the prenatal fetus is the final state of regression in which no further regression can be attained.

All these showed that the severity of psychotic negative symptoms depends really on how deep the individual regresses into different stages of life. All these can be demonstrated in the following figure.

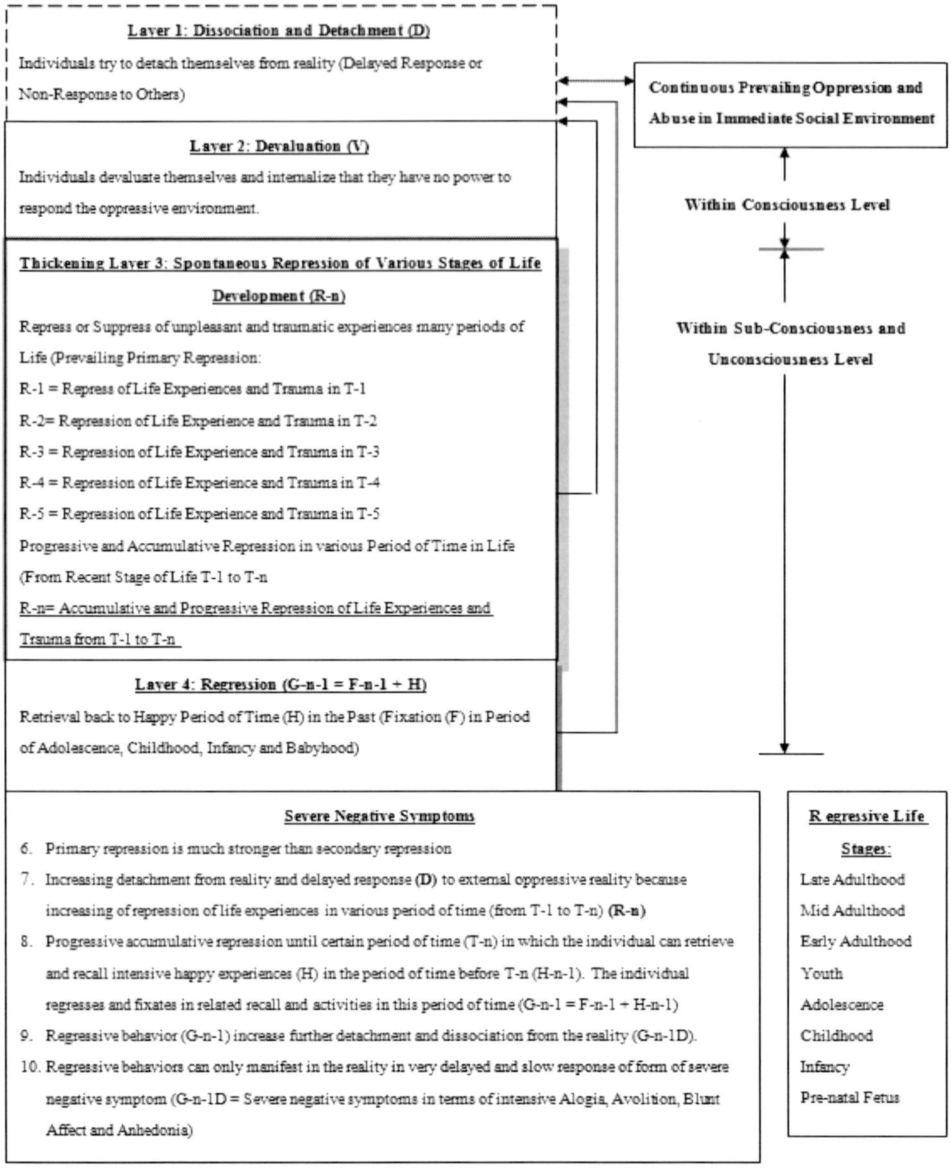

Figure 12. Development of Severe Negative Symptoms in terms of Detachment, Devaluation, Repression and Regression.

LAING'S DESCRIPTION OF FALSE SELF SYSTEM

The Normal False Self (Mask)

Laing (1960) has a full description about the false self system. He described that false self (mask) is also commonly used by individuals in daily social functioning. In normal daily life, individuals use the false self to serve the following purpose:

1. To comply with the will of others but without expressing one's own different view in facing difficulties and challenges in the social environment.
2. To protect one from being trapped, pinpointed, and grasped by others.
3. To cope with others' unreasonable demands so that he or she can be basically survive psychologically and socially in hardship and challenges.
4. To manage and control others by hiding his or her actual intent with a socially acceptable mask.

However, for normal people, the use of the false self (mask) is limited in the following ways so that the self system will not be destructed:

1. The time of using the false self should be limited and under control.
2. The use of the false self is to serve the living of the true self. That means the true, inner self can still stay in contact with the reality and get fulfillment from the use of false self.
3. In complying the will of others, the individual can still exercise his or her own will in most aspects of life.

Psychotic False Self System

For persons with schizophrenia, Laing (1960) affirmed that the false system is extensively developed with the following natures:

1. The use of false self becomes an autonomous and compulsive way in which the individual is unable to control it. It becomes an involuntary, negative conformity of others.
2. The false self of the schizoid persons is compulsively compliant to the will of others, just for the doing what others want in forms of being others' puppets, robots and machines.
3. Individuals tend to lose their will and autonomy as the false self develops further.

4. The use of the false self is felt as alien, the unrealness, meaninglessness, purposeless. These sorts of feelings permeate his or her perceptions, thoughts, feelings, and actions.
5. They represent a deadness not only for defensive purpose but for the dynamic structure of the individual's being.

Impersonation and Identification in the False Self System

In losing one's will and autonomy, the false self can also means losing one's identity with others' identity as the individual's "false identity" with the following stages.

1. In compliance with others' will and wants, it goes together with a fear of being killed or destroyed by others.
2. The false self assumes more and more of the characteristics of the person or person upon whom its compliance is based.
3. Gradually the hatred of impersonation by others may turn into a caricature.
4. The impersonation is a form of identification whereby a part of the individual assumes a personality he or she is not.

In impersonation, the whole of the impersonation is not necessarily implicated. It is usually a sub-total identification limited to assuming the characteristics of another person's behaviors. (Laing, 1960: 100-105)

Destruction of Self and Others in the Impersonation of False Self System

The increase of the extent of impersonation represents the growth of false system in psychotic development with the following harmful consequences:

1. Both the false system and others becomes unreal and dissociated.
2. The false self system is felt to encroach more and more, to make deeper and deeper inroads into the individual's being until practically everything is conceived to belong to this system.
3. It becomes more and more extensive, autonomous, harassed by compulsive behaviors fragments.
4. All that belongs to it becomes more and more dead, unreal and mechanical.
5. As the false self system links with others in immediate reality, the false self system not only complies with others but is also possessed by others. That means, the individual is beginning to be in a position to feel not only that his or

her perceptions are false because he or she is continuously looking through other people's eyes but they are playing him tricks.

6. In response to this, the false self system in destroying one's own will, it also destroys the parts that comply with others. That means, he or she destroys the reality (others) that being constructed by it. The self tries to destroy the world by reducing it to dust and ashes, without assimilating. Its hatred reduces the object to nothing, without digesting it. (Laing, 1960:144-145)

The false self system needs to reside on others, but instead of taking them in, it destroy them together with destroying itself. *It is a way of killing oneself so as to kill others. In doing so, the individual avoids being killed by others.*

Gradually, the power to destroy the realness of others grows in a way the individual thinks that he or she embraces magical power to destroy others and things in the environment by touching, copying, imitating, and stealing them.

In the process there is loss of others and hence a loss of the sense of me and you together, of we-ness (Laing, 1960:150).

From Deadness of Self and Others to Regression and Repression

In existential terms, the co-destruction of false self and others implies a destruction of reality. It also implies a total collapse of immediate reality. The total collapse of the current reality means that the individual is staying in a complete vacuum. To fill out the current vacuum, individuals within psychotic fragmentation may prefer to stay within good memories from the past. In psychodynamic terms, it is regression within which the individual stay within one's good past experiences. The more regressive one becomes, the more primitive developmental age one would stay in. In existential and phenomenological terms, existence in the current state is destructive and empty. Instead, existence in a previous and former period of time is far more meaningful and substantial. In the case of Julie, in facing an externally oppressive and unpleasant childhood and adolescence, she was spontaneously engaged in her dolls which she dressed, clothed, and played with in her room. Julie Doll was her regressive self who had happy moments that could be recalled and enjoyed. However, all this meaningful past existence in which Julie could stay away from her current torture and oppression was stolen by her bad mother.

> Until the age of seventeen, Julie had a doll. She had had this doll from infancy; she dressed and clothed it, played with it in her room, no one knew quite in what way. It was a secret enclave in her life. She called it (Julie Doll). Her mother became more and more insistent that she should give up this doll, because she was a big girl now. One day the doll was gone. It was never known whether Julie had thrown it out, or whether her

> mother had put it away. Julie accused her mother. Her mother denied that she had done anything to the doll and said that Julie must have lost it herself. It was shortly after this that Julie was told by a voice that a child wearing her clothes had been beaten to pulp by her mother, and she proposed to go to the police to report this crime. (Laing, 1960: 194)

It was clear that Julie's false and regressive self of Julie Doll (negative symptoms of withdrawal) was denied by the active fear of being engulfed by her "bad mother." In pathological terms, there was a rebound from negative symptoms to positive symptoms in which Julie felt very irritated that her only regressive shelter as well as her own happy but childish self was spoiled and killed by her bad mother.

Regressive self and sense of existence can also happen when the individual loses his or her only significant other. This happened in Mrs. R's case mentioned by Laing (1960).

> Mrs. R... Briefly, her story was as follows: She was only and a lonely child. There was no open neglect or hostility in her family. She felt, however, that her parents were always too engrossed in each other for either of them ever to take notice of her. She grew up waiting to fill this hole in her life but never succeeded in becoming self sufficient, or ascribed in her own world. . . . She grew up to a very attractive girl was married at seventeen to the first man who really noticed her. ...She was triumphant and self confident under the warmth of her husband's attention. ... But he was an army officer and was shortly posted aboard. At this separation she experienced severe panic. . . . Again, one notes the absence of grief at her mother's death. At this time she began to reckon up the chances of her being alone in the world be her father; possibly her husband; beyond that-nothing. This did not depress her, it frightened her. She then joined her husband abroad and led a gay life for a few years. She craved for all the attention he could give her but this became less and less. She was restless and unsatisfied. Their marriage broke up and she returned to live a flat in London with her father. . . . (Laing, 1960: 55)

Mrs. R's case clearly showed that her self-confidence and self-integrity based on craving attachment with her significant others. Within constant concern and care of these figures, R could function normally. However, once these figures faded out, R's sense of existence became threatened. Instead, she regressed herself to be a small insecure child who craved for love and concern. It is an ontological fear of being depersonalized.

> Mrs. R who was threatened with depersonalization when she could not be recognized or imagine herself recognized and responded to by someone who knew her sufficiently well for their recognition of the response to her to be significant. Her need to be seen was based on the equation that 'I am the persons that other people know and recognize me to be. (Laing, 1960: 119)

Intense depersonalized experiences create a sort of self-fragmentation that the false self gradually turns dead and the whole self system regresses from current oppressive reality and to a childish, simple, and naive but more secure past experience. The more traumatic and oppressive the current reality, the more regressive the individual becomes.

NEGATIVE SYMPTOMS AND BOREDOM

A Conceptual Review of Boredom

Yip (2013) asserted that negative symptoms in schizophrenia should be closely related to boredom. According to related literature, there are two types of boredom: situation-dependent boredom (SDB) and situation- independent boredom (SIB) (Todman, 2003 & 2007a) SDB is a kind of reactive boredom with response to under-stimulating or repetitive environment. If the under-stimulating conditions are removed, the sense of boredom may also be diminished (Neu, 1998; Todman, 2003). The sense of boredom can be arousal due to risky environment or risky individuals that more vulnerable to the onset of boredom (Todman, 2003; Watt and Vodanovich, 1992 & 1999) Farmer and Sundberg (1986) constructed the boredom proneness scale consists of the following items:

1. *insufficient concentration on activities*
2. *frequent worry about things*
3. *time passes slowly*
4. *do not know what to do*
5. *trapped in meaningless things*
6. *feel bored looking at home movies and slides*
7. *do not have projects or things to do*
8. *hard to entertain oneself*
9. *do things repetitively and monotonously*
10. *need stronger stimulation to get going*
11. *get a kick out of most things*
12. *difficulty feeling excited about work*
13. *difficulty finding something to do or keep interested*
14. *sitting around and do nothing*
15. *unable to wait patiently with nothing to do on hand*
16. *becoming restless waiting*
17. *waking up with no ideas*
18. *difficulty finding job that is exciting*
19. *unable to find a job that is challenging*
20. *work following one's abilities*

21. *others regard as not imaginative or creative*
22. *unable to have many interests and have too much spare time*
23. *keep doing thing over long period of time*
24. *like to do things that are exciting and dangerous or else would become dull*
25. *need change and variety so to feel happy*
26. *movie and television programs are getting old*
27. *always find things boring and monotonous as a young person (Summarized and slightly modified from Farmer and Sundberg, 1986: 7)*

Todman (2003) has successfully sum up various natures of SDB and its correlation with. They are briefly mentioned as follows:

1. Correlates to Cognitive/Attentional Dysfunctions including:
   a. high level of distractibility
   b. low level of enjoyment
   c. poor ability to seek enjoyment
2. Correlates to Emotional/Motivational Dysfunctions in terms of:
   a. high levels of negative affect such as hostility
   b. decreased levels of persistence
   c. high levels of restlessness and a need for change or excitement in some people
   d. reduced motivation and feelings of apathy
3. Correlates to Social/Interpersonal Dysfunction in terms of:
   a. reduced sociability
   b. poor peer relationship
   c. increase interpersonal sensitivity
4. Correlates to Impulse Control Dysfunction in terms of:
   a. reduced impulse control
   d. alcohol dependence
   e. pathological gambling or heroine usage
5. Correlates to Neurotransmitter Dysfunction in terms of:
   a. dopamine receptor sensitivity
6. Correlates with Problem in Autonomous Arousal
   a. less than optimal levels of autonomic arousal (Todman, 2003: 148)

SIB is regarded as a kind of endogenous boredom (Neu, 1988). It is a kind of ontological boredom originated from the Greek word "alyosis" (alys) (Bergler, 1945). This is a kind of chronic boredom resulting from an inability to utilize the coping mechanisms needed to provide escape from monotony and to give meaning to routine activities in daily life (Todman, 2003:149). Frankl (1969) articulated that it is a kind of existential vacuum. It involves two types of loss, the loss of basic animal instincts as well as the loss of one's traditions. That means, one can do what other people do (conformism) or does what other people wish him or her to do (totalitarianism) (Frankl, 1969: 139). That means, people do not know how to manifest their ontological existence, identity, and meaning. As this sort of boredom is very unbearable and intolerable, people may like to mask that sort of boredom with an endless pursuit of power, money, and pleasure like activities in forms of sex, addiction, and risky behaviors (Frankl, 1969).

In that kind of boredom, as Svendsen (2005/1999) described it, it is to be bored without being aware of the act, without being able to offer any reason or cause. It is a kind of profound boredom in which people not only cannot do what they want to do or do what they do not want to do but have no idea of what they want to do. There is a loss of one's bearing and anchoring in life. It is also a loss of one's will power and determination to do anything (Svendsen, 2005/1999: 19). Without stimulus or focus, the individual is confronted with nothingness, the meaninglessness of existence and experiences existential anxiety. Heidegger states this idea nicely: "Profound boredom, drifting here and there in the abysses of our existence like a muffling fog, removes all things and men and oneself along with it into a remarkable indifference. This boredom reveals being as a whole." Svendsen (2005) further articulated that boredom is closely related to personal meaning, interest, and information. Ontological boredom or existential crisis occurs where one is not able to articulate his or her own meaning in life. Thus, he or she inclines to define or search his or her own meaning from others. The more he or she depends on this, the more serious his or her boredom will become. Svendsen (2005) refers this type of meaning that is inextricably linked to being meaningful for someone. Together with the interpretation of meaning is related action, the sense of what is interesting and the way of processing related information. Interest provides the direction for one's action. However, as Heideggar pointed out, today's interest is only directed by what is currently interesting. The sense of being currently interesting does not imply that sort of interesting feelings can be long lasting. Once the feeling of interest diminishes, the sense of boredom prevails. That means, life has to be interesting to avoid the unbearable sense of boredom (Yip, 2013).

In other word, ontological boredom is an existence vacuum in which the individual fails to make meaning out of their life and out of their environment in which there is overwhelming information. They are only passive observers or actors following others' will. The sense of boredom out of meaningless life is unbearable. Without any stimulus or focus, the individual is confronted within a state of nothingness. It is a state of meaninglessness of existence in the form of existential anxiety. Heidegger affirmed that "profound boredom, drifting here and there in the abysses of our existence like a muffling fog, removes all things and men and oneself along with it into a remarkable indifference. This boredom reveals being as a whole. (Heideggar, 1929). The only outlet is to make things currently interesting. Nevertheless, the sense of what is interesting comes and goes, leaving the individual can only be endlessly pursing a sense of what is interesting or has secular stimulation.

Boredom and Schizophrenia

When Todman (2003) had analyzed five cases with schizophrenia, he came to the following conclusions distinguishing boredom and schizophrenia:

1. Hallucination is a coping response for boredom. When hallucination increases, boredom levels decrease. (Todman, 2003).
2. For persons with paranoid schizophrenia, boredom is the result of competition of attention between novel tasks and the objects of hyper-vigilance for limited attentional resources. It is a misattribution of sources of distractibility. (Todman, 2003: 154)
3. For persons with post-psychotic mood disturbance, boredom is the consequence of the attempt to maintain or to reduce processing capacity and to prevent an overextension during recovery. This can be explicitly demonstrated by those clients who have rapid recovery of processing capacity in an under-stimulating treatment environment. (Todman, 2003:154)
4. Boredom can also use an adaptation mechanism for facing related symptoms such hypohedonia. It diminishes the individual's processing capacity and competency with the consequence of reducing sensitivity to change and misattribution of sameness to internal, stable, and global factors (Todman, 2003: 153). In other words, boredom is regarded as a *negative symptom,* in which persons with schizophrenia develop a kind of tolerance for the monotony associated with the generalized lack of interest and involvement in activities, interaction, and people around. Individuals become absorbed in the sense of boredom to ignore the passage of time and reduce the input of stimuli from their immediate environment. This can end up a state of stable boredom in which individuals believe that positive reinforcement or interesting things, issues, and events in reality is forever unavailable. (Todman, 2003)

Boredom and Negative Symptoms

Boredom as a Mechanism to Ignore the Passage of Time

Todman (2008) summed up related research and concluded that individuals who were most bothered by boredom (functionally and affectively) were also the individuals who were more likely to be hallucination-prone (Todman, 2008: 166). However, the findings that negative symptoms (anhedonia) or post-psychotic mood is related to boredom in the form of a mechanism to ignore the passage of time and demonstrate a generalized absence of interest in any person, event, affairs, or objects happening in immediate reality. That is actually a sort of active withdrawal from reality with ontological implications that the individual with schizophrenia tends to lose meaning and interest as well as information in contacting reality. The absorption in a state of ontological boredom is in fact a way to demonstrate this sort of loss of hope and interest in encountering anyone, events, and affairs.

Boredom and Anhedonia

In later writings, Todman (2007b) further elaborated the relationship of boredom with anhedonia, the negative symptom, of schizophrenia. He defined anhedonia as a state of boredom with three dimensions:

1. Extensiveness and ubiquity of anhedonia
2. Intensity of unpleasantness of anhedonia
3. Frequency and duration of anhedonia

That means that in the state of boredom individuals with schizophrenia have a high level of anhedonia. Their inability to seek interests, pleasure, and enjoyment extends everywhere (ubiquity and extensiveness). Their sense of unpleasantness is high and intense. The duration and frequency of their inability to seek pleasure and the sense of unpleasantness is prevailing and high. In other words, individuals with schizophrenia may be very absorbed in their inner world with very low or even no interest, no ability, or no urge to seek any pleasure or even stimuli in external environment in their sense of boredom. Todman (2008) further articulated that in the state of boredom, individuals with schizophrenia effectively shut down their own mechanism for seeking for pleasure and a positive environment in their psychosocial environment and in their everyday life. As anhedonia and a state of boredom is also closely related to blunt affect for persons with schizophrenia, it is very possible that they are so frustrated with external issues, events, persons and affairs happening in the external reality that they tend to find no meanings, no hope, and no interest within themselves. For them, boredom tends to be the only mechanism or way to withdraw from this meaningless and hopeless world. In other word, the state of ontological boredom involves using nothingness to replace meaninglessness and hopelessness.

Boredom and Alogia

Within Todman's concept, alogia in clients with schizophrenia can also be described in three dimensions:

1. Extensiveness and ubiquity of alogia
2. Intensity of unpleasantness of alogia
3. Frequency and duration of alogia

Alogia means poverty of speech in negative symptoms. In terms of boredom, it means that the individual, in the withdrawal from the reality and the ignorance of space and time, not only interest in persons, issues and objects of the reality. He or she also loses interest in making verbal connection with them. Being heavily absorbed in his or her delusive inner world, he or she has no interest to express any inner idea, to listen to or speak to the outside world. In some ways, his or her inner delusive world is far too complicated, delusive or even fragmented to express to others. In terms of extensiveness, the individual inertness to express his or her view extends to every aspect of life. He or she has poverty of speech (inertness to express him- or herself) in work, in family and in social circle. Underlying this is an extensive spread and diffusion of ontological boredom. The individual concludes that every aspect of life is meaningless and boredom. It is entirely meaningless and useless to communicate with family members as they are still oppressive, manipulative, uncaring, apathetic, hypocritical, and/or lack understanding toward them. Similar situations occur among related professionals in mental hospitals and psychiatric rehabilitation services. In work setting, he or she feels that his or her values and meaning in work is in vain and people around do not care or even oppress him or her. Thus, any form of interaction and communication is futile.

In terms of intensity, he or she becomes more and more reluctant to voice out his or her thought, to connect with others verbally and to speak less and less clearly. That means, the individual simply concludes that life is entirely boring, empty, and meaningless. People are oppressive, apathetic, and abusive. He or she becomes more and more inert toward the expression of his or her ideas, views, and perspectives in front of others. For him or her, being quiet and silent tends to be the most secure and comfortable way to survive in a very oppressive world.

In terms of frequency, his or her alogia occurs in every sentence of his or her speech. In more severe cases, even within one sentence, there are three or four times of hesitation or interruption. Even within the short period of time in speaking one sentence, the sense of ontological boredom disturbs the individual so much and in a way he or she is unable to think, to speak, and to communicate clearly. He or she is totally kept in a state of stagnancy.

Boredom and Avolition

Avolition is a state of mental and physical fatigue in which the individual has no interest, energy, or will power to do anything. It consists of severe social and economic impairment (Andreasen, 1984: 7). Along Toman's thinking, avolition in clients with schizophrenia also has three dimensions:

1. Extensiveness and ubiquity of avolition
2. Intensity of unpleasantness of avolition
3. Frequency and duration of avolition

In terms of extensiveness of avolition, that means the individual's sense of mental and physical fatigue extends to many aspects of life. At first, he or she may only feel mental and/or physical fatigue in work, family, or school, in particular in the social circle that mostly oppresses and excludes him or her. Gradually, it extends to other social circles as well. Finally, it extends to all aspects of social life. He or she becomes inert and unmotivated in almost every aspect of daily life. In extreme cases, his or her personal hygiene and self-care are deeply affected. He or she did not have any motivation to clean him- or herself, to change his or her clothes, and to move out of his or her room. His or her physical and mental fatigue come a sense of ontological boring in which he or she concludes that no matter how hard and how diligent he or she has been in his or her life, his or her effort is still in vain because of the very exclusivity, oppression, and criticism of others. In doing so, it is better for him or her to do nothing. Also, previous struggles in his or her life seems to sap all his or her energy in life making him or her feel that he or she has no ontological energy to do anything.

In terms of the intensity of avolition, the individual's mental and physical energy was exhausted gradually, from having limited interest and involvement in daily activities to experiencing extreme fatigue and stagnant involvement in any daily activities. In extreme cases, persons with severe avolition may sit quietly in the house doing nothing. Within an intense sense of ontological boredom, individuals may conclude that there is no meaning to engage in any activities in social environment. In mild intensity of avolition, individuals with schizophrenia may still find interest to engage in activities and interaction to objects, issues and persons in relation to their prevailing delusion and hallucination. In moderate intensity, they know that all these interactions with these objects, issues and persons are also meaningless and empty. Life is entirely boring ontologically for them. Thus, it is better to remain inert in most of their life.

In severe intensity of avolition, the individual does not possess any will power, physical and mental energy to engage in any activities in life.

In terms of frequency and duration of avolition, an individual frequently feels exhausted and tired in most of the day. Every day, he or she gets up with a boring mind. He or she fully aware that everything he or she does is meaningless, empty and ends up with nowhere. Thus, it is better to remain inert. He or she may refuse to get up. Even he or she gets up, he or she does not have energy and will power to comb his or her hair, to take a bath, to engage in daily life. In severe avolition, the sense of severe ontological boredom appears frequently in every moment in life. Its duration makes the individual fully absorbed in his or her sense of ontological boredom rather than responsive to any activity and stimulus in the immediate physical and social environment. In severe cases, persons with schizophrenia may sit at home doing nothing for hours or for the whole day.

Boredom and Affective Flattening

Affective flattening or blunt affect implies the reduction of emotional expression and response including tone, gestures, eye contact, and voices. (Andreasen, 1984: 7). Along Toman's thinking, blunt affect in clients with schizophrenia also has three dimensions:

1. Extensiveness and ubiquity of blunt affect
2. Intensity of unpleasantness of blunt affect
3. Frequency and duration of blunt affect

In terms of extensiveness of blunt affect, it means that the sense of affective flattening first may start in one aspect of life, in particular in an immediate, oppressive environment. Gradually, even in the absence of oppressive immediate social environment, individuals with schizophrenia spread their blunt affect in every aspect of life including colleagues at work, family members, and peers in their social circle. Because of a growing sense of boredom and fixation of the chronic, ontological boredom, the individual with schizophrenia simply concludes it is better to show no emotional response to others because all of them are oppressive, exclusive, and even abusive. Social interaction with them is entirely meaningless and empty. Life is simply a vacuum.

The intensity of blunt affect implies that the emotional response to others' encounter can gradually slow down from with some slow, selective, and passive emotional response to gradually no emotional response to others. In extreme cases, even facing others' strong emotions such as intense anger and sadness or happiness, the individual with schizophrenia still have no affective response. For instance, while everyone is crying in funeral for the death of the client's father, the client still has no affective response. In the same way, even in a social gathering when everyone is very happy and laughing, the individual with schizophrenia still feel inert and has no emotional response. In terms of boredom, the sense of chronic boredom is so intense that the individual feels everything, include emotional response and emotional expression is entirely meaningless and worthlessness. The sense of ontological boredom simply fixates in his or her mind and body freezing any emotional response to the external environment.

Regarding the frequency of blunt affect, it implies that the sense of blunt affect happen can range from a low frequency to a high frequency. For those persons with mild negative symptoms in schizophrenia, their affective flattening may only occur rarely, perhaps, only once or twice in a week and in particular when he or she is alone and in times of physical and mental fatigue. In some cases, low, frequent blunt affect happens when the client's prevailing positive symptoms such as paranoid and grandiose delusions and hallucinations decline or fail to deal with stressful situation. The individual has high situational boredom (in which the individual cannot communicate well with others) and mild, ontological boredom (in which the individual begins to feel that he or she is excluded by oppressive others. No matter how hard he or she attempts to defend him- or herself within delusive world, he or she still feels that the oppressive others are very powerful and diminishing).

For moderate frequency of blunt affect, the individual certainly feels bored and inert every day, and he or she concludes there is quite meaningless to respond to others' emotion and affect. In that situation, he or she only rarely shows his or her emotions and only to those he or she feels very accepting cases, he or she only says a few words to these significant others. His or her sentences and answers are usually short with very inert and flat affect, no facial expression.

For high frequency of blunt affect, the individual not feel boring and inert in everyday life, but also in his or her whole life. What he or she has done in the past, the present and the future are meaningless and empty. In addition to that, he or she also feels that time is stagnant and life is a vacuum. Whether he or she does or does not do anything, responds or does not respond to other is all the same. His or her sense of ontological existence is frozen as well as his or her emotions. He or she does not show any emotion to anybody anytime. He or she simply does nothing, lives his or her daily life just like a corpse without any emotions and feelings.

Ontological Boredom, Positive Symptoms, and Negative Symptoms

Yip (2013) concluded that in the process of schizophrenia, ontological boredom, positive symptoms, negative symptoms, and effects of institutionalization are closely linked with one another. Before the occurrence of psychotic symptoms, the individual actually has situational boredom induced by an oppressive environment in which the individual fails to have meaningful involvement. As the oppressive environment turns worse, the situational boredom is very intensified. As the individual cannot escape from the oppressive environment, he or she tends to develop positive symptoms to cope with or conceal the intense, situational boredom.

In the process of self-fragmentation, intense situational boredom becomes ontological boredom in which related senses of emptiness, confusion, and ontological insecurity prevailed. Well-developed, active paranoid, grandiose, and catatonic delusions and hallucinations enable the individual to absorb him- or herself in escaping from ontological boredom on one hand. A diffused self-boundary and intense negative feelings from delusions and hallucinations further intensify a sense of ontological boredom on the other hand. Within this dilemma, the individual's psychic and physical energy decline quickly. As a consequence, the individual's response toward external reality is deeply affected. He or she does not possess enough will power and energy (avolition) to interact or form meaningful interpersonal relationship with others (anhedonia). Within a prevailing sense of ontological boredom, ventilation, and expression of one's feeling and ideas are entirely meaningless (alogia). Even though the external environment may be happy or sad; tense, or relaxed; and/or excited or boring; emotional connection or sharing with other becomes unnecessary and meaningless (blunt affect). That means, the individual develops active negative symptoms because of the destructive effects of intense ontological boredom.

Thus, it is common for individuals to develop negative symptoms after an overwhelming manifestation of positive symptoms such as paranoid, grandiose, and catatonic delusions and hallucinations because of the following reasons:

1. The process of self-fragmentation destroys the individual's self boundary and ego function in which he or she fails to respond to the external environment in an appropriate way.
2. The prevailing manifestation of first-rank symptoms in an acute mental state exhausts the individual's mental and physical energy in which his or her ability to respond to the external environment is reduced and even suppressed.
3. Situational boredom is intensified into ontological boredom in the self-fragmentation process. In prolonged self-fragmentation, ontological boredom in which the individual conclude life is entirely empty and meaningless prevails. It is useless to do anything, to say a word, to relate anyone, or to show any emotional response to the external environment.
4. In terms of a very institutionalized service context, the individual's ontological boredom prevails. Individuals may feel that time and related issues and persons are stagnant. Interpersonal interaction among patients and between professionals and patients are reduced or very minimized. As a consequence, they may conclude it is better to remain inert, passive, and withdrawn rather than become active and involved in institutionalized life. In other words, the institutionalized effect is intermingled with negative symptoms making the individual feels very inert, passive, and withdrawn.

TRAUMA AND NEGATIVE SYMPTOMS

Mental Structure and Mechanisms in Trauma and Schizophrenia

As mentioned in previous chapters, there are three major groups of concepts and studies that describe how individual's self system being fractured by the traumatic experiences:

1. Breaking down of the ego system in traumatic experiences and recall (Individual's weak and fragile ego system is gradually or abruptly broken down by traumatic experiences and related recall. (Garland, 1991)
2. Failure of dissociation mechanism (Dissociation of traumatic experiences protect the individual from traumatic recall and allow the individual absorb the negative impact of traumatic experiences gradually. However, the failure of the dissociation mechanism implies an overwhelmingly negative impact on the individual. The loss of a protective mechanism leads to a final fracture of the individual's self system). (Sullivan, 1956)
3. Spontaneous evidence and co-morbidity between traumatic experiences (child abuse, bullying, victimization) and psychosis (Morrison et al., 2006). (There are numerous studies in this decade showing that trauma is one the major psychosocial causes leading to psychosis in which positive symptoms, negative symptoms, and first-rank symptoms are closely related to process, details, contents of traumatic experiences, individual experiences in abuse, victimization, bullying, and disasters. In particular those happen in childhood and adolescence.

Also, the breaking down of the individual's ego system in traumatic events is based on four groups of related factors:

Group A: Destructive effects of the traumatic experiences (intensity, duration, and frequency of harm created).

Group B: Durability of the ego system in facing external threat (stability and integrity of the ego system, unsettled and unresolved emotional complex).

Group C: Related support from the external environment (support, care, comfort, and acceptance from others. Or rejection, isolation, stigmatization, exclusion, and punishment from others).

Group D: Inner processing of traumatic experiences (filtering, containing, interpreting, repressing, and recalling of traumatic experiences. (Yip, 2013)

Yip (2013) concluded that the breakdown of the ego system includes the following;

1. The breakdown of an established way of going about one's life,
2. a breakdown of established beliefs
3. a breakdown about the predictability of established mental structures
4. a breakdown of established defensive organization.
5. a breakdown of the trust in the fundamental goodness of one's objects,
6. a breakdown of the protective function of the good objects
7. a breakdown of the world itself are shattered (modified from Garland, 1991: 10)

According to Sullivan (1956), the total failure of dissociation dynamism, as summarized by Yip (2013) consists of the following stages of development:

1. Unpleasant or traumatic past experiences or covered desire or drives that need to be covered up and prevented from coming to consciousness.
2. The individual's need to keep all these out of his or her consciousness to maintain the integration and normal functioning of his or her self system.
3. Any encounter of related objects, events, and persons that possibly trigger his or her well-concealed desires and traumatic past experiences may can arouse anxiety.
4. The feeling of anxiety and uneasiness that is an unconscious warning signal that the dissociation mechanism may come to a point of fracture that requires taking immediate action.
5. The individual's conscious or unconscious efforts try to avoid or separate him- or herself from related objects, events, and persons that possibly trigger his or her well-concealed desires and traumatic past experience so as to maintain his or her deteriorating dissociation dynamism and eliminate his or her sense of anxiety.
6. Well-justified, rationalized excuses and personalized reasons and preferences that mask avoidance acts which appear as normal and natural in interpersonal interaction (As a result, the individual's unpleasant, traumatic, past experiences or covered desires or drives can be further covered up and come up into his or her consciousness).
7. Continual fear and avoidance of related triggering objects, events, and persons that gradually limit or restrain the whole life of the individual so as to achieve equilibrium and ego-functioning maintained by the deteriorating dissociation dynamism.
8. The emergence of an endless cycle of being triggered, getting away, and using rationalization to justify these actions of avoidance (Gradually, the individual's daily activity and concentration in achieving normal and important duties may be more and more disturbed by the deteriorating dissociation dynamism).
9. As the deteriorating dissociation dynamism becomes more and more fragile and the individual's ego disturbance is more and more serious, a state in which the individual is not only disturbed substantially by the existence of related objects, events, and persons in the actual environment but is also disturbed by unrelated objects, events, persons imaginatively or even delusively constructed (In this process, the deteriorating dissociation dynamism is complicated by the individual's use of symbolization and fantasy).

Fowler (et al., 2006) tried to speculate the pathway from trauma to psychosis within four cognitive routes:

1. Direct associations between intrusive memories of traumatic or stressful experiences and delusion and hallucination.
2. Indirect association between trauma and persecutory delusions and hallucinations mediated by negative evaluation of self and others (the schema route).
3. Indirect association between trauma and hallucination mediated by negative and self-critical rumination concerning the relationship between the voice heard and the voice's identity.
4. Speculations about potential catastrophic interactions between trauma processes and information-processing abnormalities which characterize psychosis which may magnify vulnerability to psychosis. (Fowler et al., 2006: 100)

Hemsely (1994) asserted that information process models of PTSD and psychosis are similar in a way that both have intrusive thoughts that hinder the incoming information from related reality. That means, the distortion and problems of information-processing can be manifested in several ways:

1. Regarding past traumatic experiences as a current one. Senses of anxiety, fear, and being threaten in PTSD from traumatic experiences are still felt as real and spontaneous by the individual. (Ehlers and Clark, 2000)
2. Problems in placing moment to moment experiences within appropriate context (Fowler et al., 2006) (Individuals are either totally occupied by the recall of traumatic experiences or the present situations are still too still traumatic and stressful that the individual tries to avoid or isolate).
3. Failure of the individual to construct a coherent whole in shifting from past memories and new information input from related contexts. (Squire, 1992)

Along similar lines of thinking, Romme and Escher's (2006) concluded that there are seven paths in turning traumatic experiences into the onset of psychosis. They are as follows:

1. The dissociative pathway
2. Turning the suffered powerlessness and aggression toward oneself
3. The abolition of all emotions or becoming like a robot
4. A flight reaction from the existing problems into a fantasy solution
5. Trying to fulfil impossible expectations
6. Denial of or transforming what has happened
7. To surrender to a higher power (Romme & Escher, 2006: 171-173)

Breaking, Dissociation, and Loss in Trauma and Schizophrenia

Putting all these together leads to the conclusion that, within traumatic experiences there are three mechanisms involved in transforming the individual having schizophrenic symptoms in the process of self-fragmentation. They are as follows:

- Breaking mechanism (B)
- Dissociation mechanism (D)
- Loss and identification with the lost object (L)

All these three mechanisms have definite destructive effects on one's mental structure:

- Meaning of life and will power (m)
- Self/ego system (ego identity, boundary, and functioning) (s)
- Emotion (feeling, sense, affect, and mood) (e)
- Values, cognition, morality, and reflectivity (v)
- Social functioning (role, social interaction, and responsibility) (f)
- Internalized object (0)
- Memory and past experiences (p)

The breaking effect implies the breaking of the ego system, emotionality, belief, social functioning, internalized object, and memory. Within the breaking effect, there are still three components:

1. The splitting of the mental structure (B1)
2. The confusion of the mental functioning (B2)
3. The malfunctioning of normal mental functioning (B3)

The dissociation effect implies the dissociation of the ego system, emotionality, belief, social functioning, internalized object, and memories. Within the dissociation effect, there are still repression and splitting in three:

1. Repression and numbing of one's sense of reality (external numbing) (D1a), as well as splitting of oneself and the outside environment (D1b)
2. Repression and numbing of one's own being (internal numbing of sense of self, body, mind and growth) (D2a), as well as splitting and separation among the senses of self, body, mind, and growth (D2b)

3. Repression and numbing of unpleasant and traumatic experiences and memories (D3a), as well as splitting one's integrated sense of present, past, and future (D3b)

Within the loss and identification of lost objects, there should be several components:

1. Loss of part of the ego system that merges with the lost object (L1)
2. Splitting part of the ego system to compensate the lost part (L2)
3. Letting the split part of the ego identify with the lost object (L3)
4. In severe traumatic loss, loss of the boundary and mental structure of the ego system (L4)

For positive psychotic symptoms, including grandiose, paranoid, and catatonic delusion and hallucination, it should be a combination of the following components with the breaking, dissociation, and loss and identification mechanisms. They can be described as follows:

1. the splitting of the mental structure (B1)
2. splitting and separation among senses of self, body, mind, and growth (D2b)
3. To compensate the lost part, splitting part of the ego system (L2)
4. Letting the split part of ego identify with the lost object (L3)

Negative Symptoms and Mental Mechanism in Trauma and Schizophrenia

For negative, psychotic symptoms, including alogia, blunt affect, anhedonia, and avolition, there should be the following components within the breaking, dissociation, loss, and identification mechanisms:

1. The malfunctioning of normal mental functioning (B3).
2. Repression and numbing of one's sense of reality (external numbing) (D1a).
3. Repression and numbing of one's own being (internal numbing of sense of self, body, mind, and growth) (D2a).
4. Repression and numbing of unpleasant and traumatic experiences and memories (D3a).
5. Loss of part of the ego system that merges with the lost object (L1).

From the above five components, the repression mechanism plays a more crucial role in the formation of negative psychotic symptoms than those in breaking, dissociation and loss and identification mechanism. All these components certainly have a vital impact on individual's mental structure and functioning including:

- The meaning of life and will power (m)
- The self/ego system (ego identity, boundaries, and functioning) (s)
- Emotions (feeling, sense, affect, and mood) (e)
- Values, cognition, morality, and reflectivity (v)
- Social functioning (role, social interaction, and responsibility) (f)
- Internalized objects (o)
- Memory and past experiences (p)

In line with this thinking, negative psychotic symptoms can be understood as combinations of related components in these three mechanisms as well as in the related mental structure and functioning. For example, the malfunctioning of normal mental functioning (B3) can combine various components in the mental structure including the meaning of life, self system, emotion, values, social functioning, internalized object, internalized object, memory and past experience malfunction (B3m, B3s, B3e, B3v, B3f, B3o & B3p). In other words, the following may exist:

- Malfunctioned will power (B3m)
- Malfunctioned ego system (identity, boundary, and functioning (B3s)
- Malfunctioned emotion (feeling, sense, affect, and mood) (B3e)
- Malfunctioned values, cognition, morality, and reflectivity (B3v)
- Malfunctioned social functioning (roles, social interaction, and responsibility (B3f)
- Malfunctioned internalized object (B3o)
- Malfunctioned memory (B3p)

Alogia in Mental Mechanisms in Trauma and Schizophrenia

Alogia can be interpreted as poverty of speech. It implies deficits and latency in speech fluency, content, and responses as well as empty speech (Andreason, 1984). In terms of three mechanisms in trauma and schizophrenia, difficulties in speech imply the blocking of normal cognitive functioning. The blocking can occur in the reception, process, and response to incoming messages and stimuli.

In the reception process, D1a (repression and numbing of one's sense of reality) means that a person with alogia tends to numb incoming messages, information, and stimuli from objects, issues, events, and persons from the immediate external environment. Because of that sort of numbing, the individual does not care or simply ignores any incoming messages and stimuli. Even though it is very sensitive, risky, or even threatening, the individual does not take that or even ignore it. That means, numbing of one's sense of reality also implies numbing one's cognitive reception toward external stimuli. The numbing can be in various degrees ranging from a full numbing of all environmental responses to partial and selective responses to certain issues, persons, and events.

The blocking also occurs in the processing of incoming messages and stimuli. It can be malfunctioning of one's normal mental functioning (B3) in terms of one's cognitions, will power, and ego functioning, as well as related memories and past experiences. The blocking of the process implies that the individual is unable to have a full process of incoming messages and stimuli. The individual is unable to reflect, to interpret, and to get the meaning out of the incoming message and stimuli. Even if the incoming message is able to trigger his or her pleasant or unpleasant experiences, the repression and numbing of one's own being (internal numbing of sense of self, body, mind and growth) (D2a) and the repression and numbing of unpleasant and traumatic experiences and memories (D3a) completely or partially block the processing of incoming messages, and stimuli greatly hinder or even suffocate the triggering effects. As a consequence, the individual is quite passive and inert in expressing his or her thoughts toward the incoming stimuli and message.

Finally, the blocking of speech and cognitive functioning can also occur in the response and reaction toward incoming messages and stimuli. Anyway, malfunctioning of normal mental functioning (B3), repression and numbing of one's own being (D2a) can diffuse to one's meaning of life and will power (m) as well as emotion (e) and values, cognition, and morality (v) causing the individual to lose all will power, emotion, cognition, and the moral virtue to respond to the outer world. In the process, his or her speech becomes very hindered with poor content, fluency, and continuity.

Avolition in Mental Mechanism in Trauma and Schizophrenia

Avolition is defined as deprivation of the ability to persist in goal-directed behavior. Individuals with avolition have no interest in doing anything in the outside world (Schizophrenia.com, 2004). It is a state of physical and mental fatigue, in which the individual has no interest or energy for doing anything. In avolition, the state of physical and mental inertia can roughly be divided into three main components:

1. Physical and mental inertia to external reality
2. Physical and mental inertia to the inner world
3. Physical and mental inertia to connect external reality and the inner world

These three components correlate and intermingle with one another, making the individual become seriously stagnant both inside and outside. In the process of schizophrenia, individuals tend to spend all their mental and physical energy in the sereve manifestation of positive symptoms of delusions and hallucinations as well as first-rank symptoms. Thus, within negative symptoms of avolition, the individual's mental and physical energy are deeply exhausted.

In terms of traumatic experiences, avolition resembles a state of acute stress disorder in which the individual's sense of his or her own being is partially or seriously numbed. It is common that persons during, or immediately after, a traumatic event such as a disaster, earthquake, or rape usually appear inert and numbed (D1a). The numbing of emotion, cognition, and social functioning make the individual become very tolerant and enduring to external trauma, torture, and harm. In avolition, the individual enters into a state of inertia so that he or she becomes very tolerant, enduring, and non-responsive to the external environment that, in the eyes of the individual, is very oppressive and abusive.

Within the physical and mental inertia toward the inner world, the individual with avolition usually is numb to his or her own being, including the senses of self, body, and growth (D2a). The numbing serves two important functions: First, it helps the individual suppress or repress all unpleasant memories and former traumatic experiences. In doing so, his or her own mental functioning at that period of time is also repressed and suppressed. If related, unpleasant mental functioning should be deeply hindered, he or she appears inert and stagnant. Secondly, it helps the individual to tolerate continual oppression, abuse, and unpleasant treatment from external reality. Once the individual's senses of body, mind, and self are numbed, the sense of being humiliated, oppressed, abused, and isolated can be enlightened. In severe psychotic negative symptoms, individuals always stay in a stage of serious inertia showing no response to others' oppression, blaming, cursing, and insulting.

In normal daily life and interpersonal interaction, individuals need to consume a significant amount of mental and physical energy in establishing connection between external reality and the internal world. On one hand, he or she needs to perceive, interpret, and relate incoming messages. On the other hand, according to such perceptions and interpretation, he or she has emotion, and action. There may be inconsistency and consistency among the reception of incoming messages, perceptions, and interpretation, as well as related response. It is clear that extra mental energy and physical energy are needed in dealing with inconsistency far more than with consistency. Inconsistency can also occur with the reception of incoming messages. For example, while one clearly hears some words that are negative and very critical from significant others, his or her own self-image, good memories, and positive emotion may not accept this negative incoming message. Instead, the individual may tend to ignore or undermine this incoming message. Similarly, inconsistency also occurs in the perception and interpretation process as well as in the process of response. That means a need to spend physical and mental energy on each of the following:

1. Reception of incoming messages (Er1)
2. Resolving inconsistency on reception of incoming message (Er2)

3. Perception and interpretation (Ep1)
4. Resolving inconsistency on perception and interpretation (Ep2)
5. Showing related response (Es1)
6. Resolving inconsistency on showing related response (Es2)
7. Connecting reception, perception, interpretation, and showing response to incoming message (Erps1)
8. Dealing with inconsistency among reception, perception, interpretation, and response (Ersp2)

That means, an individual with avolition not only loses a lot of his or her mental and physical energy in reception, interpretation, and response to external reality. He or she also spends his or her residual psychic and physical energy in facing the inconsistency in various levels (Er2, Ep2, Es2 and Ersp2). As a consequence, the individual's mental and physical energy was mostly exhausted. The individual does not have any will power to commit or engage in any goal-directed activities. He or she becomes inert, passive, and withdrawn. In terms of traumatic experiences, apart from mental and physical energy spent on the above-mentioned items, the individual also needs to spend extra mental and physical energy on repressing past traumatic memories to avoid being triggered by external events, objects, and issues. In other words, the individual has to spend extra energy (T) in trauma-related triggers (incoming stimuli), perception, interpretation, and response (Er1T, Ep1T, Es1T and Ersp1T). That means, the individual does not have any residual mental energy to commit to anything. He or she is entirely motionless and immobile both psychologically and physically.

Anhedonia in Mental Mechanisms in Trauma and Schizophrenia

As mentioned above, anhedonia is an inability to experience pleasure from normally pleasurable life events such as eating, exercise, and social or sexual interaction. Andreasen (1984) defines anhedonia as a state of asociality.

> This symptom complex encompasses the schizophrenic subject's difficulties in experiencing interests or pleasure. It may express itself as a loss of interest in pleasurable activities, an inability to experience pleasure when participating in activities normally considered pleasurable, or a lack of involvement in social relationship of various kinds. (Andreasen, 1984: 9)

Normal persons, in facing something, someone, or some issues they like or favor normally have the following responses:

1. Actively approach them
2. Try to focus or attend to them
3. Engage and connect with them
4. Become concentrated and involved in the connection and engagement
5. Recall similar positive experiences and memories
6. Feel happy and enjoyable in the engagement, concentration, and involvement
7. Express and share related happy and enjoyable experiences as well as feelings
8. Expect and try to continue all these enjoyable engagements

In terms of traumatic experiences, anhedonia can be described as an acute stress disorder or a numbing of a client's feeling and urge to connect with the external reality as well as numbing one's ability to experience and express positive feeling in relating to issues, persons, objects and events in the external reality. It can be anyone of the problems in the above mentioned items. They can be as follows:

1. Numbing of motives, intention, and energy to approach anyone
2. Difficulty focusing or paying attention to others even if others approach the individual
3. Failure to focus, attend and connect with others
4. Deep engagement in the individual's own inner world regardless of any situation
5. The appearance of stagnation and apathy within self-absorption
6. Inability or difficulty for the individual to express his or her absorption in his or her own inner world
7. Lack of intention, motivation, or energy to connect with any person, thing and/or events
8. Continuation of a state of stagnancy and self-absorption regardless of time, environment, and the presence of others

All these eight components are certainly a product of repression and numbing of the individual's sense of reality as well as their sense of self, body, mind, and growth. The repression and numbing tends to occur in most dimensions of life, in particular social functioning and meaning of life in which the individual has very low intention, will power, energy, and motivation to connect with others and become involved in any meaningful interaction and activities.

While avolition implies mental and physical fatigue in facing inconsistency in reception, perception, interpretation, and response to incoming messages and stimuli, anhedonia implies that the individual does not possess any interest, motivation, emotion, intention, and will power to connect with external persons, issues, objects and events in external reality. In both traumatic experiences and in psychotic, negative symptoms, avolition and anhedonia come together. Facing intolerable traumatic experiences, the breaking effects can destroy the individual's mental structure. The dissociative effect enables the individual to conceal traumatic experiences and related memories. These two powerful mechanisms certainly exhaust the individual's physical and mental energy (avolition) as well as hinder the individual's power to connect external reality and their inner world (anhedonia). The state of stagnancy serves as a protective mechanism enabling the individual to prevent triggering concealed traumatic experiences and memories.

Blunt Affect in Mental Mechanism in Trauma and Schizophrenia

Affective flattening is the reduction in the range and intensity of emotional expression, including facial expression, voice tone, and eye contact. In Andreason's (1984) Scale for the Assessment of Negative Symptoms (SANS), affective flattening is defined as follows:

> Affective flattening or blunting manifests itself is a characteristic impoverishment of emotional expression, reactivity, and feeling. (Andreason, 1984: 2)

In other words, the individual's emotional response toward his or her external reality is partially or totally blocked. In terms of traumatic experiences, it is similar to anyone who is overstressed by painful experience to an extent that he or she has lost both painful feeling and response. It is common to observe some survivors who are saved from a traumatic earthquake after several days searching appear numbed and feelingless. Even though their bodies may be seriously wounded, it seems that they do not cry or ease out any painful feelings. The numbing of the emotional mechanism serves several important protective functions. First of all, it lessens the pain of the individual so that painful feelings would not disturb his or her cognition and rationality in finding ways to escape from disastrous situations and conditions. Secondly, it freezes the individual's sense of time in torturing experiences. He or she does not feel bored, empty, sad, or meaningless. By doing so, the individual is able to wait for rescue.

In terms of trauma, blunt affect can be occurred within three different period of time. They are the following:

1. Blunt affect within the original traumatic experience
2. Blunt affect after the traumatic experiences
3. Bunt affect within the rebounce of traumatic experience
4. Prolonged blunt affect long after the traumatic experience

Each of them has its own unique natures. For the first type, as mentioned above, blunt affect within the first/original traumatic experiences, it is certainly the numbing of one's sense and feelings so that one can survive pain and torture within very traumatic experiences. In terms of negative psychotic symptoms, it implies that the individual tries to numb his or her feelings so that he or she is not being hurt or humiliated within a very oppressive environment.

For the second type of blunt affect, it is also the repression and numbing of one's own sense of reality (D1a) as well as one's own being (D2a) so that one can have capacity to regain the ability to face normal daily life by repressing and numbing emotions and loss in recent traumatic experiences. In terms of negative psychotic symptoms, it can be the numbing and repression of one's recent traumatic experiences. It can be the outburst of first-rank symptom in times of severe and horrible paranoid hallucination and delusion in which the individual feels deeply threatened and fearful.

In both type 1 and type 2 blunt affect within an immediate conclusion of traumatic experiences, repression effects can be intensified by antipsychotic medication, in particular those that require high-dosage injection. They not only alleviate the active positive and first-rank symptoms but also repress their own mental system especially emotions and affect.

In type 3 the blunt affect occurs within the rebounce of a traumatic experience. The rebounce of traumatic experiences, in fact, are very painful. In times of post-traumatic stress disorder, traumatic memories rebounce in forms of spontaneous flashbacks, reoccurrence of nightmares, and unconscious bodily responses are, in many ways quite intolerable to individuals. With the togetherness of supportive others, then the traumatic rebounce is intermingled with positive feelings of genuineness and warmth and comfort. If not, to lessen the traumatic effects, individuals may need to numb their emotional response further. That means, they have to repress both the original traumatic experiences and second traumatic rebounce (D1aO + D1aR + D2aO + D2aR). D1aO is the repression and numbing of one's sense of reality in the original experiences of trauma. D1aR is those in the rebounce of traumatic experiences and memory. D2aO is the repression and numbing of one's own sense of being in original traumatic experiences. D2aR is the repression and numbing of one's sense of being in the rebounce of traumatic experiences. In other words, the numbing and repression goes further than the first traumatic experiences. In terms of blunt affect in psychotic symptoms, the individual has severe numbing of emotionality so to repress the following traumatic experiences and recall:

1. Memories and traumatic experiences happening in life long before the onset of schizophrenia including those in childhood, adolescence, and adulthood.
2. Memories and traumatic experiences in the rebounce from traumatic experiences in childhood, adolescence, and adulthood.
3. Memories and traumatic experiences happening in life at the onset or immediately after the onset of schizophrenia including threatening paranoid delusion and hallucination or first-rank thought insertion or thought-broadcasting.

4. Memories and traumatic experiences in the process of involuntary admission, detention, and treatment within very institutionalized hospital and service settings.

In the repression and numbing of all these memories and traumatic experiences, individuals' ego functioning, including emotionality, is severely hindered. Individuals appear as inert, blunt, and withdrawn without any emotional response to most incoming stimuli. Even others tried to insult and humiliate them, they showed no response. Even if others showed gratitude and appreciation to them, they showed no response.

In type 4 blunt affect, symptoms occur long after the traumatic experiences. That means related memories and traumatic experiences happening in lifelong experience, in rebounce, in related paranoid symptoms and in the process of involuntary admission, detention, and treatment have been repressed and numbed for a long period of time. Furthermore, related ego functioning and social functioning have been hindered for a long time. The longer all these are repressed and hindered, the harder it is for the individual to recover normal social and ego functioning. In other words, their repression and numbing of a sense of reality and being including emotionality gradually become a habitual and daily practice for the individual. The individual, especially those who have stayed in the mental hospital, have negative symptoms including blunt affect that prevail seriously. They may sit in a chair or stand in the sitting room aimlessly and motionless for a hours without giving any response to anyone around him or her.

Psychotic Negative Symptoms: A Multi-Dimensional View

The Inner Negative Trip

As mentioned above, negative symptoms can be defined in terms of alogia, avolition, anhedonia, and blunt affect. Related studies by the National Institute of Mental Health (NIMH) in the Measurement and Treatment Research to Improve Cognition in Schizophrenia (MATRICS) showed that psychotic, negative symptoms are not related to cognitive impairment. Instead, they relate to other variables. Clinical practice with clients with severe psychotic, negative symptoms shows they are closely related to:

1. Low psychic and physical energy
2. Intense withdrawal from reality
3. Strong involvement in an inner world
4. Poor communication with the external environment

Arieti (1974) asserted that a person with schizophrenia undergoes a process of desocialization in which he or she gradually desocializes him- or herself from the main society by applying private meaning to social symbols within his or her delusions and hallucination. In negative symptoms, individuals with schizophrenia are accustomed to use nonverbal, private symbols to indicate their own meaning and interpretation. In doing so, they may be purposefully isolated from the outer world.

The Self-Induced Deadness in Most Dimensions of Life

The Deadness of the Psychotic, False Self

Within an existential phenomenological perspective, in Laing's (1960) terms, negative symptoms are the manifestation of the psychotic, false self. It represents the part of the self serving as a cocoon to shelter the inner self from outer, oppressive reality. The individual loses his or her autonomy and is obliged to comply with the will and ideas of others. In doing so, the false self represents the deadness of self in which the individual destroys oppressive reality by diminishing his or her own authenticity.

In terms of the psychodynamic defense mechanism, negative symptoms represent the product of several processes. They are dissociation and detachment from reality and self-devaluation, repression of traumatic experiences and of reality, as well as regression to happy experiences in previous life stages.

The Deadness of the Sense of Being and Ontological Boredom

In terms of boredom, negative symptoms imply the manifestation of ontological boredom in which the individual concludes that it is entirely meaningless, useless, and empty to interact, relate, or connect with any person, issue, object, or thing in the external environment. That means it is entirely meaningless and useless to speak (alogia), to feel and give affective response (blunt affect), to do anything (avolition), and to interact with others (anhedonia). The sense of ontological boredom can be very extensive, frequent, and intense in everyday life, making the individual's negative symptoms severe and uncontrollable.

The Deadness and Freezing of Mind and Body

Under the influence of the deadness of the senses of being and existence as well as the self system, the individuals' minds and bodies are also deeply frozen with four withdrawal mechanisms. They are the following:

1. *Dissociation and detachment from reality* (D=Individuals try to detach themselves from reality and have delayed responses or non-responses to others).
2. *Self-devaluation* (V=Individuals devaluate themselves and internalize that they have no power to respond to the oppressive environment).
3. *Repression of traumatic experiences and reality* (R-n= spontaneous repression of various stages of life development)
4. *Regression and fixation to happy experiences in previous life stages* (G-n-1= F-n-1 + H = Retrieval back to a happy period of time (H) in the past (fixation (F) in the period of adolescence, childhood, or infancy).

Within these four mechanisms, severe negative symptoms can be understood as products of the following dimensions:

1. Primary repression is much stronger than secondary repression.
2. Increasing detachment from reality and delayed response *(D)* to external, oppressive reality because of the increasing repression of life experiences in various period of time (from T-1 to T-n) *(R-n)*
3. Progressive, accumulative repression until a certain period of time (T-n) in which the individual can retrieve and recall intense, happy experiences (H) in the period of time before T-n (H-n-1). The individual regresses and fixates in related recall and activities in this period of time (G-n = F-n-1 + H-n-1).
4. Regressive behavior (G-n-1) tends to increase further detachment and dissociation from reality (G-n-1D).
5. Regressive behaviors can only manifest in reality in very delayed and slow responses in the form of severe, negative symptoms (G-n-1D=severe negative symptoms in terms of intense Alogia, Avolition, Blunt Affect, and Anhedonia)

Prolonged Repression of Past Trauma and Oppressive Reality

In terms of traumatic experiences, negative symptoms including alogia, blunt affect, anhedonia, and avolition is a manifestation of the following components within the breaking, dissociation, and loss and identification mechanisms. They are described as follows:

1. the malfunctioning of normal mental functioning (B3)
2. repression and numbing of one's sense of reality (external numbing) (D1a)
3. repression and numbing of one's own being (internal numbing of sense of self, body, mind, and growth) (D2a)
4. repression and numbing of unpleasant and traumatic experiences and memories (D3a)

5. Loss of the part of the ego system that merges with the lost object (L1)

In terms of three mechanisms in trauma and schizophrenia, *alogia* (difficulties in speech) implies a blocking of normal, cognitive functioning. The blocking can occur in the reception, process, and response to incoming messages and stimuli.

Individuals with *avolition* are in a state of physical and mental fatigue, in which the individual has no energy and interest in doing anything. In avolition, the state of physical and mental inertia can roughly be divided into three main components. They include:

1. Physical and mental inertia to external reality
2. Physical and mental inertia to the inner world
3. Physical and mental inertia to connect external reality and the inner world

It is clear that extra mental energy and physical energy are needed in dealing with inconsistency far more than with consistency. That means, an individual with avolition not only reduces a lot of his or her mental and physical energy in reception, interpretation, and response to external reality. He or she also spends his or her residual psychic and physical energy in facing the inconsistency in various levels (Er2, Ep2, Es2 and Ersp2).

1. Physical and mental energy spent on resolving inconsistency on reception of incoming message (Er2).
2. Physical and mental energy spent on resolving inconsistency on perception and interpretation (Ep2).
3. Physical and mental energy spent on resolving inconsistency on showing related response (Es2).
4. Physical and mental energy spent in dealing with inconsistency among reception, perception, interpretation and response (Ersp2).

As a consequence, the individual's mental and physical energy is mostly exhausted. The individual does not have any will power to commit or engage in any goal-directed activities. He or she becomes inert, passive, and withdrawn. In terms of traumatic experiences, apart from mental and physical energy spent on the above-mentioned items, the individual also needs to spend extra mental and physical energy in repressing past traumatic memories to avoid being triggered by external events, objects, and issues. In other words, the individual has to spend extra energy (T) on trauma-related triggers (incoming stimuli), perceptions, interpretations, and responses (Er1T, Ep1T, Es1T and Ersp1T). That means the individual does not have any residual, mental energy to commit to anything. He or she is entirely motionless and immobile both psychologically and physically.

In terms of traumatic experiences, anhedonia can be described as an acute stress disorder or a numbing of a client's feelings and an urge to connect with external reality as well as a numbing of one's ability to experience and express positive feelings in relating to issues, persons, objects, and events in external reality. It can be any one of the problems in the above-mentioned items. They can be as follows:

1. Numbing of motives, intention, and energy to approach anyone.
2. Difficulty in focusing or paying attention to others, even if others approach the individual.
3. Fail to focus, attend, and connect with others.
4. Deep engagement in his or her own inner world regardless of any situation
5. The appearance of stagnation and apathy within self-absorption.
6. Inability or difficulty in expressing his or her absorption in his or her own inner world.
7. No intention, motive, or energy to connect with any person, thing and/or events.
8. A continued state of stagnancy and self-absorption regardless of time, environment, or the presence of others.

In terms of trauma, blunt affect can occur within three different periods of time. They include:

1. Within the original traumatic experience (The individual tries to numb his or her feeling so that he or she does not being hurt or humiliated within a very oppressive environment).
2. After the traumatic experiences (The numbing and repression of one's recently happened traumatic experiences. It can be the outburst of first rank symptom in times of severe and horrible paranoid hallucination and delusion in which the individual feels deeply threatened and fearful).
3. When the rebounce from the traumatic experience (Severe numbing of emotionality so to repress memories and traumatic experiences happening in: life long before the onset of schizophrenia; in rebounce of traumatic experiences in childhood, adolescence and adulthood; in the onset or immediate after the onset of schizophrenia; and in the process of involuntary admission, detention and treatment).
4. Long after the traumatic experience (Related memories and traumatic experiences happening in life long experience, in rebounce, in related paranoid symptoms and in the process of involuntary admission, detention and treatment have been repressed and numbed for a long period of time, and together with long hindered ego and social functioning).

A Multi-Dimensional View of Psychotic, Negative Symptoms: Self-Induced Deadness of Being, Self, Mind, and Body

Putting all these together, the writer tries to construct a multi-dimensional model in describing negative symptoms in persons with schizophrenia. In fact, psychotic, negative system represent a dissociation, splitting, and stagenancy in various dimensions of life.

1. *Ontological emptiness and boredom about the meaning of life* in which the individual feels entirely meaningless, useless, and empty in interacting, relating, and connecting with any person, issue, object and thing in the external environment. That means, it is entirely meaningless and useless to speak (alogia), to feel and give affective response (blunt affect), to do anything (avolition), or to interact with others (anhedonia).
2. In Laing's (1960) terms, negative symptoms are *the manifestation of the psychotic, false self.* It represents the part of the self being serves as a cocoon to shelter the inner self from outer oppressive reality. The individual loses his or her autonomy and is obliged to comply to others' will and ideas. In doing so, *the false self represents the deadness of self* in which the individual destroys the oppressive reality by diminishing his or her own authenticity.
3. Within the ontological boredom, emptiness, and deadness of the psychotic, false self, the *individual's mind and body undergoes a process of internal withdrawal.* Within the process of withdrawal. There are *four defensive psychological mechanisms.* They are *dissociation and detachment from the reality* (D=Individuals try to detach themselves from reality and have delayed response or non-response to others); *self-devaluation* (V=Individuals devaluate themselves and internalize that they have no power to respond the oppressive environment); *repression of traumatic experiences and reality* (R-=spontaneous repression of various stages of life development); as well as *regression and fixation to happy experiences in previous life stages* (G-n-1 = F-n-1 + H=retrieval back to happy period of time (H) in the past (fixation (F) in period of adolescence, childhood, and infancy). In other words, severe psychotic, negative symptoms occur in dissociation and detachment of reality, repression of an unhappy life in adulthood, youth, adolescence, and childhood, and regression and fixation to a happy life stage in early childhood, infancy, and even prenatal stages in which the individual fails to speak fluently (alogia), to have enough will power to perform normal daily activities (avolition), to interact with others (anhedonia), or to express his or her emotions and to respond to others' emotions (blunt affect). In other words, the ontological emptiness and boredom, as well as deadness of the psychotic, false self system *creates a frozen body and mind over most of the period of time in one lifespan.* There is a freezing of the unhappy, present reality

and unhappy past events to a very stagnation of the regressive but happy, earliest past such as early childhood, infancy, and the even prenatal human state.

Frozen body and mind in most period of time in one life span.

(Freezing of unhappy present reality and unhappy past events. Fixation on a highly stagnancy regressive and happy life stage of early childhood, infancy and even prenatal stage. It has four mechanisms

1. **dissociation and detachment from the reality** (D = Individuals try to detach themselves from reality and have delayed response or non-response to others)
2. **self devaluation** (V = Individuals devaluate themselves and internalize that they have no power to respond the oppressive environment)
3. **repression of traumatic experiences and reality** (R-n = spontaneous repression of various stages of life development)
4. **regression and fixation to happy experiences in previous life stages** (G-n-1 = F-n-1 + H = retrieval back to happy period of time (H) in the past (fixation (F) in period of adolescence, childhood, infancy and babyhood).

Severe psychotic negative symptoms occur in dissociation and detachment of reality, repression of unhappy life in adulthood, youth , adolescence and childhood, and regression and fixation of happy life stage in early childhood, infancy and even pre-natal stages in which fails to speak fluently **(alogia),** to have enough will power to perform normal daily activities **(avolition),** to interact with other **(anhedonia)** and to express his/her emotions and to response with others emotiions **(blunt affect).**

↕

Ontological emptiness and boredom in meaning of life

Entirely meaningless in life, useless and empty in interacting, relating and connecting with other person, issue, object and thing in the external environment. Individuals are entirely meaningless and useless to speak **(alogia)**, to feel and give affective response **(blunt affect)**, to do anything **(avolition)** and to interact with others **(anhedonia)**

The manifestation of the psychotic false self.

Psychotic false self serves as a cocoon to shelter the inner self from outer oppressive reality. The individual losses his/her autonomy and is obliged to comply to others' will and idea. **Alogia, blunt affect, avolition and anhedonia represents the deadness of false self** in which the individual destroys the oppressive reality by diminish his/her own realness.

↕

Deep repression of past experiences in oppressive reality and trauma.

1. Numbing one's sense of reality, sense of own being (body, mind and growth) and unpleasant traumatic experiences
2. Loss of parts of ego system that mergest with the loss object.
3. Mental and physical energy is easily exhausted **(avoliton)**.
4. Repression blocks off cognition and expression in reception, interpretation and response of incoming stimuli **(alogia).**
5. Prolong stagnancy in numbing one's feeling and urge in connecting with others in external reality **(anhedonia).**
6. The numbing of emotionality **(blunt affect)** in original, after (outburst of first rank symptoms and paranoid hallucination), within the rebounce (severe numbing of traumatic experiences in life and in related positive psychotic symptoms) and long after traumatic experiences (all traumatic experiences in life, in psychotic symptoms and in the institutitionalized treatment process).

Figure 13. A Multi-Dimensional View of Psychotic, Negative Symptoms.

4. Within the influence of deadness of the psychotic, false self, as well as the ontological emptiness and meaninglessness in life, individuals with psychotic, negative symptoms tend to create a frozen body and mind in most of the periods of time in their lifespan. In doing so, individuals' experiences in oppressive reality and traumatic past are deeply repressed. Together with this is also the

> numbing of one's sense of reality, sense of own being (body, mind, and growth) and unpleasant traumatic experiences and loss of parts of the ego system that merges with the loss object. As a consequence, individuals' mental and physical energy is easily exhausted *(avolition).* The state of repression prevails in a state that blocks off normal cognition and expression in reception, interpretation, and response of incoming stimuli *(alogia)***.** The deep and prolonged repression can also exist as a form of stagnancy in numbing one's feelings and urges in connecting with others in external reality *(anhedonia).* The numbing of emotionalism *(blunt affect)* can occur in the original, traumatic experiences of life, after the traumatic experience (outburst of first-rank symptoms and paranoid hallucination), within the rebounce of traumatic experience (severe numbing of traumatic experiences in life and in related, positive, psychotic symptoms) and long after traumatic experiences (all traumatic experiences in life, in psychotic symptoms, and in the institutionalized treatment process).

All these four perspectives as well as components of psychotic, negative symptoms are in fact, interrelated to one another and can be represented in Figure 13.

Revitalization of Senses of Body, Mind, Self, and Being of Persons with Severe Psychotic, Negative Symptoms

These four dimensions of life in psychotic, negative symptoms are in fact, interrelated. The emptiness and boredom in the meaninglessness of life implies individuals with negative symptoms lose their sense of existence and being. It gradually extends and connected with the deadness of the self system. The emptiness of the meaning of life and deadness of self diffuses to all levels of life. In everyday life and human interaction, individuals appear as having a totally frozen mind and body in their lifespan and deep repression of past experiences in oppressive reality and trauma. That means severe psychotic symptoms imply a total self-induced deadness of the meaning of life, self system, mind and body in the traumatic past, oppressive reality and hopeless future. It should not be understood as a stage of cognitive impairment. Instead, it should be understood as a self-defense mechanism by repression of past trauma, dissociation from oppressive reality, and regression to a happy past in childhood because of emptiness and the loss of total meaning in life after prolonged traumatic experiences within a very oppressive reality.

In other words, if the external reality is very tolerant, accepting, and supportive, the individual with psychotic, negative symptoms can re-vitalize their senses of self, body, mind, and being and have a good recovery. Loren Moshen's pioneering experiences in running the Soteria residential recovery center for those clients with chronic schizophrenia without using any medication but only total acceptance and caring can demonstrate this sort of acceptance in actual practice.

Recovery of Deirdre's Psychotic Negative Symptom

Deirdre was 17 and was admitted to Soteria for a twelve-week stay. Her early history showed difficulties that stemmed from the feeling of inferiority toward her twin sister. When she was 14, she showed signs of severe disturbance that tended to be originated from her adolescent dating. She had received some medical treatment in a nearby medical center. The medication did not help her much but made her very sleepy. Her parents took her to Soteria so as to free from the negative effects of anti-psychotic medication, and she had a better recovery. Her psychiatrist affirmed that anti-psychotic medication prevented her from regression. Colleagues in Soteria believed that stopping medication made her become regressive for a while and later could recover in a therapeutic environment of tolerance, intense support and genuine caring (Mosher, Hendrix & Frot, 2004). What follows is the extract from a worker's narration about helping Deirdre to work through severe regressive, psychotic blunt affect to recovery into the normal life and functioning of an adolescent.

When she arrived at Soteria in the first week:

> She was very nervous and disorganized at times. She felt that someone was trying to rape her and somehow felt that is would be good for her. She complained of feeling sleepy most of the time... Deirdre was deep into her madness as the drugs were reduced. . . . Another resident told me that she came into his room, and they had sex, without intercourse. In the morning her behavior had regressed: She was speaking "baby talk" and urinated on the kitchen floor and over herself . . . she a had difficult time sleeping, , , , I stayed up with her. I remained with her. A staff member and Deirdre slept together in Deirdre's bed. . . . In the morning, she wanted to breastfeed from me. I gave her a baby bottle instead, which pacified her. For about an hour she was into a deep regression; then she emerged but in continued confusion. . . . On Sunday and Monday, she was very spaced out and scared. Staff stayed with her. Monday night, she slept eleven hours and woke up Tuesday, appearing a lot calmer. She went to the park and played and had a quiet, lucid conversation with me regarding sex. (Mosher, Hendrix & Frot, 2004: 40–41)

From the above description, it was clear that Deirdre was a stage of severe psychotic, negative symptoms. In terms of ontological boredom, her sense of being and existence as an adolescent was totally hindered. Instead, a profound sense of emptiness and boredom prevailed. She felt her life was entirely meaningless, and it was useless to speak (alogia), to feel, and to give an effective response (blunt affect), to do anything (avolition), and to interact with others (anhedonia). In terms of her psychotic, false self, Deirdre's childish behavior and baby talk represent a cocoon to shelter her from the outer, oppressive reality. It is a deadness of self in which the individual loses her autonomy and comply to others' idea. Alogia in a form of baby talk implies a self-induced deadness of cognition and expression of speech. Anhedonia and avolition in terms of restlessness regression without doing anything implies a self-induced deadness of physical and mental energy and will power. Blunt affect implies total babyish emotion without any emotional reponse to external reality and environment. In terms of traumatic experiences, it was clear that she suffered from a paranoid of being raped by others. Also, she was in a state of frozen of body of mind in being an adolescent. Her memory of childhood and infancy was also frozen. Instead, she simply acted like a baby with the gesture for breastfeeding, urination in kitchen and baby talk. That means she was dissociated and detached from reality. She also underwent a process of self-devaluation in which she devaluated herself as a functional, adolescent and child. All unpleasant experiences in childhood and adolescence were totally repressed. She was thus fixated to the comfort zone of being a baby. She did not have will power (avolition), competence to establish interpersonal relationship (anhedonia), speak clearly and emotionality as an adolescent and child (blunt affect).

In terms of deep repression, Deirdre's ego and social functioning were greatly repressed. She exhausted her physical and mental energy (avolition), her emotionality was deeply numbed (blunt affect), her feelings and ability to connect to reality was also blocked (anhedonia), and her reception, interpretation, and response of incoming stimuli are also severely blocked (alogia).

> On Sunday and Monday, she was very spaced out and scared. Staff stayed with her. Monday night, she slept eleven hours and woke up Tuesday, appearing a lot calmer. She went to the park and played and had a quiet, lucid conversation with me regarding sex. She was anxious to talk about her experiences with other resident and staff. (Mosher, Hendrix & Frot, 2004: 41)

After the third week, Deirdre became better:

> Deirdre is continuing to do better, still talking a lot with anyone who is willing. She is able to be alone more, reading, writing, embroidering, and watching TV. Her fears continue but not to point that she loses control. (Mosher, Hendrix & Frot, 2004: 41)

In the fourth week. Deirdre became mentally stable:

> Deirdre is increasingly clear and secure. She participates more and isn't as afraid of noises or intensity. . . . Her sister is coming home from Wednesday to Sunday, and Deirdre would like to visit her at home on Thursday. . . . (Mosher, Hendrix & Frot, 2004: 43)

In the sixth week, Deirdre started to look for work. A staff member in Soteria accompanied her on a job interview, and she got a job as gift wrapper at Penney. In the first day to work, she encountered some problem in transportation. A staff in the Soteria drove her to work. In the tenth week, Deirdre resolved the school issue, and she continued her work smoothly. In the eleventh week, Deirdre was in a good mood. She used the family car and took people to the beach and shopping. She planned to go to school. In the twelve week, Deirdre went to a community college and lived in the dormitory there. Years later, she was able to complete a BA in psychology. She became a forest ranger, living in the state park for several years (Mosher, Hendrix & Fori, 2004: 47–49).

From the above description, it was clear that Deirdre was in a stage of severe, regressive, psychotic, negative symptoms that involved baby talk and urinating in the kitchen. She also had difficulty going to sleep and required a female worker to breastfeed her. Instead of regarding her severe psychotic confusion that needed immediate hospitalized, restraints, heavy medication, or injections, the staff in Soteria created a safe and accepting external, residential holding environment to protect, to care, to accept, and to support her. Certainly, Deirdre's negative, psychotic symptoms were not regarded as irreversible, cognitive impairment. Instead, they were regarded as repressed, traumatic memories and experiences. Once, all these repressed memories were rebounced together with unconditional acceptance as well as warm and genuine togetherness and caring provided by related workers in Soteria, Deiridre was able to regain her own age-appropriate, adolescent self-identity and social functioning. Certainly, it was a gradual process within twelve weeks. In the first week, Deirdre reduced her severe regressive, psychotic, negative symptoms from infancy (urination, breast feeding to sleeping with adult); in the second week, from infancy to childhood (playing in the park and asking questions about sex from the worker); in the third week, back to early adolescence (talking a lot with anyone who is willing, reading, writing, embroidering and watching TV). It was clear that in the third week, Deirdre's severe psychotic negative symptoms gradually turn into positive symptoms in which repressed traumatic experience and memories such unpleasant or even traumatic sex experiences or interpersonal encounter re-bounce. She tried to resolve them by continuous by asking question about sex as well as talking to anyone who was willing. Together with that was the renewal of a sense of reality evidenced by good participation in normal daily activities such as reading, writing, embroidering, and watching TV. In other words, she was no longer detached and dissociated from reality that was oppressive in the past. Instead, it became supportive, caring, and genuine.

At that moment, when she was entirely out of her involvement in severe regressive, psychotic, negative symptoms, the worker facilitated her to visit her happy moments in childhood and adolescence by facilitating a meeting with her sister. That was a firm re-linkage and connection to the actual supportive and caring reality. After the sixth week,

Dierdre was able to regain into her age-appropriate social functioning. She was able to search for a good job, joined with others to the beach, and finally planned to go to college again. As related workers had already helped her to work through her traumatic experiences in her courtship in her college life by sharing her experiences and questions in sex and courtship, she regained enough self-confidence to relate with young males within a college environmental context. She went back to college and graduated with honors in psychology.

Conclusion: Implications for Recovery

In conclusion, this chapter is a comprehensive discussion of the theoretical underpinnings of the negative symptoms of schizophrenia. Related findings showed that the negative symptoms are significantly correlated with difficulties in theory of mind including empathy and self esteem. People with psychotic negative symptoms are less empathic, with less self-esteem, less self-serving bias, poor interpersonal abilities, and dysfunctional acceptance beliefs (Lincoln et al, 2011). Arieti (1974) affirmed people with schizophrenia have retreated from social interaction. It is a form of self-alienation as well as regressive desocialization. Arieti (1974) argued that desocialization occurs when the individual abandons the use of social symbols and indulges more and more in private symbols. Gradually, he or she becomes more and more alienated from reality. Strictly speaking, positive symptoms are manifest private symbols in which verbal symbols and non-verbal symptoms are expressed and can be observed and interpreted by others. However, negative symptoms are latent private symbols in which nonverbal symbols may not be expressed. That means, they may not be observable and interpretative. negative symptoms in forms of fully indulging in one's inner world and blocking communication from the external world by abandoning the use of common symbols and private verbal symbols, as well as very restricted use of private non-verbal symbols, making their whole life a vacuum. They feel extremely lonely and empty inside. The urges to refuse to communicate and the fear to be stimulated by external reality are fully exercised. For them, this is the only way to retain their own autonomy within a very oppressive, abusive, and manipulative reality.

Both Artieti (1974) and Lincoln (et al., 2004) findings showed the recovery of negative symptoms should not depend on medications. Instead, it should be a positive linkage of supportive reality in forms of frequent use of common symbols so that clients with severe and chronic psychosis can retain confidence and interest in expressing their hidden emotions and needs as well as in interacting with others in a meaningful and healthy way.

Negative symptoms can also be interpreted as a severe form of regression, devaluation, and repression. It consists of four layers of an ego defense mechanism. The *first layer is dissociation and detachment* in which the individual tries to dissociate and detach from the oppressive reality. Underlying this layer is the *second layer of devaluation* in which the individual tries to devaluate him- or herself thinking that he or she is unable or powerless in dealing the oppressive reality. As it is covered up by the layer of severe dissociation and detachment, individual's feeling of inferiority and shame together within the devaluation cannot be exposed or experienced by others. In chronic schizophrenia, the sense of inferiority cannot be released as the dissociation from reality totally hinders the ventilation of the mood and effect of the individual. The *third layer is repression* in which unpleasant memories and traumatic experiences are repressed. Within the mechanism of repression, the individual tries not to be conscious about all these unpleasant memories and traumatic experiences. However, as there are two types of repression, primary and secondary repression, in negative symptoms, primary repression is used to repress all related, unhappy experiences in the past. In doing so, related life experiences and memories are also repressed. Prolonged repression and devaluation are very uncomfortable and unbearable for individuals. Thus, underlying the layer of repression should be the fourth layer of regression in which the individual tries to fixate within certain period of past time in which he or she has happy and enjoyable experiences. That can be happy experiences in infancy, childhood, adolescence, youth, or adulthood. In severe and extreme regression, the individual can fixate into a state of infancy in which he or she is totally dependent and immobile.

Along this line of thinking, recovery of psychotic, negative symptoms should be a full articulation of these four defense mechanism. Regarding dissociation and detachment, there should be a very supportive reality with empathetic others who have unconditional regard and high acceptance toward clients with chronic schizophrenia. Only by doing so, they can regain interest, confidence, and initiatives in relating to positive reality. For devaluation, the supportive reality should facilitate clients in developing their potential, strengths, and abilities so that they can re-develop a positive sense of self-identity. When these two layers of defense mechanism are dissolved, repressed, and numbed unpleasant or even traumatic memories and experiences can be recalled and ventilated. In clinical practice, at that moment, there may a rebounce of positive symptoms such as paranoid, grandiose, and catatonic delusion and hallucinations. Undermining all these are hidden, concealed, and unexpressed negative emotions and unfullfilled basic needs. Instead of a further repression of these traumatic symbols through recall and brought about by heavy doses of anti-psychotic medications, related professionals should facilitate clients in ventilating all these needs and unresolved, negative emotions. Finally, by means of a supportive reality (to dissolve dissociation and detachment), development of positive self-identity (to dissolve devaluation) and proper facilitation of unfullfilled needs and negative emotions, the deepest layer of regression can be gradually dissolved. Based on Sullivan's (1962) orientation, psychotic dissociation, devaluation, repression, and regression can go deeper and deeper from childhood, infancy, and finally to the prenatal fetus in which clients' mobility, self-care and personal hygiene can further deteriorate. That means the recovery process from severe, negative symptoms can also be a reversal of prenatal fetus, infancy, childhood, and adolescence. Deirdre's case is a deep regression to infancy. Her recovery was a good illustration of how she could recover gradually from infancy, childhood, adolescence, and back to adult's consciousness and maturity.

In terms of trauma, negative psychotic symptoms, including alogia, blunt affect, anhedonia, and avolition are the consequences within the breaking, dissociation, and loss and identification mechanisms with the following components:

1. The malfunctioning of normal mental functioning
2. Repression and numbing of one's sense of reality (external numbing)
3. Repression and numbing of one's own being (internal numbing of sense of self, body, mind and growth)
4. Repression and numbing of unpleasant and traumatic experiences and memories
5. Loss of part of ego system that merges with the lost object

In other words, the recovery of psychotic, negative symptoms should be a re-development of normal mental functioning, a renewal of one's sense of reality, and a sense of being, a healing of one's traumatic experiences and memories, as well as a healthy development of one's healthy ego system.

In existential terms, psychotic negative symptoms are a manifestation of ontological emptiness and boredom in the meaning of life. Clients feel entirely meaningless in life, useless and empty in interacting, relating and connecting with other people, issues, objects, and things in the external environment. Individuals are entirely meaningless and useless to speak *(alogia)*, to feel and give affective response *(blunt affect)*, to do anything *(avolition),* and to interact with others *(anhedonia)*. Psychotic negative symptoms are also a manifestation of psychotic, false self. The psychotic false self serves as a cocoon to shelter the inner self from outer, oppressive reality. The individual loses his or her autonomy and is obliged to comply with others' will and ideas. Alogia, blunt affect, avolition, and anhedonia represents the deadness of the false self in which the individual destroys the oppressive reality by diminishing his or her own authenticity.

REFERENCES

American Psychiatric Association (1987). *Diagnostic and Statistical Manual of Mental Disorder,* 3rd Edition, rev, Washington D.C.: American Psychiatric Association.

Andreasen N. C. (1983). *Scale for the Assessment of Negative Symptoms (SANS).* Iowa City, University of Iowa.

Arieti, S. (1974). *Interpretation of Schizophrenia (2nd edition)*: Completely Revised and Expanded, New York: Basic Books.

Becker, E. (1962). *The Birth and Death of Meaning*, New York: The Free Press.

Bergler, E. (1945). On the disease-entity boredom ("alyosis") and its psychopathology. *Psychiatric Quarterly*, 79: 38–51.

Cameron, N (1947). *The Psychology of Behavior Disorders, a Biosocial Approach.* Boston: Houghton Mifflin,

Corradi, R. B. (1981). "Psychological regression with illness," *Psychosomatics* 24: 353-362, 1983.

Ehlers, A., and Clark, D. M. (2000). "A cognitive model of post-traumatic stress disorder," *Behavior Research and Therapy*, 38, 319-345.

Farmer, R. & Sundberg, N. D. (1986). "Boredom proneness: the Development and correlates of a new scale," *Journal of Personality Assessment*, 50(1): 4-7.

Fairbairn W. R. D (1952) *Psychoanalytical Studies of the Personality* London: Routledge.

Fowler, D. Freeman, D., and Steel, C. et al. (2006) "The catastrophic interaction hypothesis: How do stress, trauma, emotion and information processing abnormalities lead to psychosis?," in W. Larkin, W. & A. P. Morrison, (Edited) *Trauma and Psychosis: New Directions for Theory and Therapy. pp. 101-124.* London: Routlege.

Frankl, V.E. (2006). *Man's Search for Meaning*, Boston: Beacon Press.

Freud, S. ((2015) "Mourning and Melancholia" in J. Strachey (Edited and Translated), *The Standard Edition of the Complete Psychological Works of Sigmund Freud*, (Volume14), Emeryville, CA: Andesite Press (Origin work published 1917).

Freud, A. (1947). *The Ego and the Mechanisms of Defense*, New York: International Universities Press.

Garland, C. (1998). "Thinking about trauma", in C. Garland (Edited) *Understanding Trauma: A Psychoanalytical Approach,* pp: 9-31, London: Duckworth.

Greenacre, P. (1960). "Regression and Fixation—Considerations Concerning the Development of the Ego," *Journal of the American Psychoanalytic Association*, 8:703-723.

Laing R. D., (1960). *The Divided Self*, London: Tavistock Publications.

Lewin, K. Barker, R., Dembo, T. (1941). "Frustration and regression: an Experiment with young children", R. Barker, T. Dembo, and K Lewin. *Studies in Topological and Vector Psychology II*, pp. 216-219.Iowa: University of Iowa Press, Iowa.

Lincoln, T. M., Mehl, S., Kesting, M. & Rief, W. (2011). "Negative symptoms and social cognition: Identifying targets for psychological intervention," *Schizophrenia Bulletin*, 37(Suppl. 2): S23-S32.

LivingwithSchizophreniauk.org (2004). Negative Symptoms of Schizophrenia, *LivingwithSchizophreniauk.org*. https://www.livingwithschizophreniauk.org/advice.

Loewald, H. W. (1981). "Regression: Some general considerations," *Psychoanalytic Quarterly*, 50:22-43.

Meissner'. W. W. (1981). "Defense mechanism," in Kaplan, H. I., & Sadock, .B J. *Modern Synopsis of Comprehensive Textbook of Psychiatry*, (3rd edition), pp. 137-138, Baltimore, MD, William & Wilkins.

McCullough, L. (1992). "Toward reliability in identifying ego defenses: Clinical techniques," in Valliant, G. E. (Edited) *Ego Mechanism of Defense: A Guide for Clinicians and Research*. pp. 171-179. Washington, D.C. : American Psychiatric Association.

Neu, J. (1998). "Boring from within: Endogenous versus reactive boredom," In W. F. Flack & J. D. Laird eds. *Emotions in Psychopathology: Theory and Research* (pp. 158-170). Oxford University Press.

Perry, J. C. (1990). *Defense Mechanism Rating Scale* (5th Edition), Montreal, Quebec: Institute of Community and Family Psychiatry.

Romme, M. A. J. & Escher, S. D. M. (2006). "Trauma and hearing voices," W. Larkin & A. P. Morrison (Edited) *Trauma and Psychosis: New Directions for Theory and Therapy*. pp.162-191. New York: Routledge.

Squire, L. (1992). "Memory and the hippocampus: A synthesis from finding with rats, monkeys and human," *Psychological Review*, 98, 195-231.

Svendsen, L. (1999/2005). *A Philosophy of Boredom*, (Translated by John Irons) Bath: Reaktion Book.

Sullivan H. S. (1973). *Clinical Studies in Psychiatry,* New York: Norton and Company.

Sullivan, H. J. (1962). *Schizophrenia as a Human Process*, New York: W. W. Norton & Company.

Todman, M. (2003). "Boredom and psychotic disorder: Cognitive and motivational issues," *Psychiatry*, 66(2): 146-167.

Todman, M. (2007a). "Psychopathology and boredom: a Neglected association," *International Conference on Psychology*, July 9-10, Athens.

Todman, M. (2007b). "Self-monitoring, self-assessment and discrepancies with observer ratings in schizophrenia and schizoaffective disorder: a Strategy for negotiating change in symptom unawareness" in W. H. Murray (Edited) *Schizoaffective Disorder: New Research*, pp. 1-34, New York: Nova Science.

Watt, J. D. & Vodanovich, S. J. (1992). "Relationship between boredom proneness and impulsivity," *Psychological Reports*, 70(1): 688-690.

Yip, K.S (2013). "Chapter 4: Sense of Dissociative Fear in Persons with Acute Stress and Post-Traumatic Stress Disorder: Interpretation and Intervention," *Emotionality and Mental Illness: Volume 2,* pp. 145-280, New York: Nova Science.

Chapter 8

SELF-FRAGMENTATION AND SELF- INTEGRATION IN PSYCHOTIC NEGATIVE SYMPTOMS AND ITS IMPLICATION TO MENTAL HEALTH RECOVERY

INTRODUCTION

In the previous chapters, positive and negative symptoms are comprehensively discussed. Within positive symptoms, paranoid, grandiose, and catatonic delusions and hallucination are closely related to one another. Among negative symptoms, avolition, alogia, anhedonia and blunt affect are nurtured by severe ego defense mechanisms in terms of detachment and dissociation, devaluation, repression, fixation, and regression. As positive symptoms are very disturbing to others, related professionals and caregivers may wrongly impose inappropriate high dosage of anti-psychotic medication, making clients become inert, passive and withdrawal. Coupled with institutionalized service settings, clients with chronic schizophrenia usually end up with severe negative symptoms and deep regression into infancy or even pre-natal fixation.

POSITIVE SYMPTOMS AND NEGATIVE SYMPTOMS: A CLOSE RELATIONSHIP

From Positive Symptoms to Negative Symptoms

From Dierdre's case, it is clear that positive and negative symptoms, in fact, are closely related. In mental health practice, persons with schizophrenia, in the stage of onset, are always troubled with active paranoid, grandiose, and/or catatonic delusion and hallucination. Most professionals regard anti-psychotic medication as the best way to deal with active, positive symptoms. Nevertheless, within the very institutionalized and hospitalized, overdose of antipsychotic medication, together with institutionalized or hospitalized setting, prolonged detention and rigidly scheduled and restricted daily activities, easily turn clients' positive symptoms into negative symptoms. As the NIMH-MATRICS consensus statement described, negative symptoms always intermingled with institutionalized natures such as withdrawal and drug trials of akinesia. Antipsychotic medication also has no effect on the manifestation of psychotic, negative symptoms.

> The distinction between primary and secondary negative symptoms is not essential for the purpose of testing therapeutics for negative symptoms.... (Primary negative symptoms are those that are part of the disease process itself, that is, are not secondary to such factors such depression, drug induced akinesia, or a suspicious withdrawal).The paradigmatic design for clinical trials of persistent negative symptoms would include clinically stable patients whose negative symptoms persist with adequate antipsychotic drug treatment. (Kirkpatrick et al., 2006:214-217)

That means, inappropriate and severe anti-psychotic medication and prolonged institutionalization is actually a traumatic treatment experience in which the individual engages in an intense repression and dissociation process from the ontological boring and very oppressive institutionalized reality. In doing so, his or her psychotic positive symptoms transform into severe psychotic, negative symptoms.

Paranoid, Grandiose, and Catatonic-Based Positive and Negative Symptoms

Within the transformation of psychotic positive symptoms to negative symptoms, the traits of paranoia, grandiosity, and catatonia still exist within psychotic negative symptoms. In other words, within severe psychotic, negative symptoms, alogia, anhedonia, blunt affect, and avolition, there are still three different types. They include:

1. Paranoid-oriented alogia, blunt affect, avolition, and anhedonia
2. Grandiose -alogia, blunt affect, avolition, and anhedonia
3. Catatonic-oriented alogia, blunt affect, avolition, and anhedonia

From Paranoid Delusion and Hallucination to Paranoid- Oriented Negative Symptoms

Within paranoid delusions and hallucination, there can also exist forms of both positive and negative symptoms. In terms of clients' subjective experiences, they can prevail in three ways:

P+ = taking delusive action to avoid being persecuted

P0 = no action should be taken so that I cannot be discovered by the persecuted others

P- = even if I have taken every action, there is still no way to avoid being persecuted, so better to remain stagnant and do nothing

It is clear that P+ should be active, psychotic, positive symptoms in each individual take bizarre and odd actions/behaviors to avoid being persecuted by the oppressive but delusive others. P0 and P- should be intense, negative symptoms. In P0, individuals with schizophrenia are trapped with a dilemma. On one hand, individuals with schizophrenia admit the existence of oppressive but delusive others. On the other hand, individuals conclude that no action should be taken. If they do not take any action, related oppressive but delusive others could not discover them (P0). In terms of alogia, individuals do not want to talk too much as all their words and voices are closely watched by oppressive but delusive others (AlP0). In terms of blunt affect, individuals refuse to express their emotions so that oppressive but delusive others cannot discover them (BP0). In terms of avolition, individuals do not have or do not want to show up their physical energy, mental energy as well as will to perform anything so that oppressive others have no trail or way to discover their presence (AvP0). Similarly, he or she has no interest in connecting and interacting with others (AnP0).

In terms of P-, psychotic, negative symptoms turn worse. In P0, individuals assume that no action should be taken to prevent being discovered by their persecuting others. In P-, the situation turns worse, even the individual does everything, he or she cannot avoid being persecuted by others so it is better to remain stagnant and do nothing. In that sense, the individual harbor intense fear even in state of alogia, blunt affect, avolition and anhedoina. He or she is dissociated and numbed within the prevailing fear. In other words, he or she is too fearful to speak clearly. His or her ability to speak and to express his or her idea is numbed (AlP-). Similarly, because of dissociative fear, his or her will power and psychic energy to do anything was numbed (AvP-). His or her interest to connect with others is also numbed within dissociative fear (AnP-). Finally, his or her emotional response toward other is also hindered by dissociative fear (BP-).

From Grandiose Delusion and Hallucination to Grandiose-Oriented, Negative Symptoms

Within grandiose hallucinations and delusion, there can exist both in positive and negative symptoms. In terms of clients' subjective experiences, they can be represented in the following ways:

G+ = I am powerful enough to diminish the related threat
G0 = No action is needed since they do not dare to do any threat. They simply run away
G- = I have to develop my power and existence to diminish threats suddenly

G+ certainly are active grandiose positive symptoms in which the individual embraces a new, grandiose and delusive identity in which he or she becomes a powerful being. He or she can be a famous man/woman or supernatural being. She becomes very powerful in a way the delusive oppressive others can never hurt or harm.

G0 and G- are negative symptoms in which the individual transforms psychotic, positive symptoms into negative symptoms. In G0, the individual believes that no action is needed as their delusive, oppressive others dare not do anything since they know that he or she is very powerful and will demolish them. In that sense, they all go away. In G0, there are also alogia, avoiliton, anhedonia, and blunt affect. In alogia, the individual within his or her delusive and grandiose identity, firmly believes even if he or she does not say any words, his or her delusive, oppressive others have already frightened and will go away (AlG0). In avolition, the individual engages no will power and no interest to fight with the delusive, oppressive others as they are too weak to deal with them. Sooner or later, they will disappear (AvG0). In blunt affect, the individual has no emotional response to any action by such delusive, neglected, oppressive others (BG0). In anhedonia, the individual simply has no interest in relating to such delusive, minimal, oppressive others (AnG0).

Regarding G-, it also exists in alogia, avolition, anhedonia, and blunt affect. In alogia, the individual reminds him- or herself to keep still and not say a word (AlG-) in orderto convince others of his or her power and existence and defeat opponents suddenly. In anhedonia, the individual also hides their interest to connect and to interact with others in order to attack his or her opponents suddenly (AnG-). In avolition, the individual shows no interest and will to do anything so that he or she can be completely invisible in diminishing oppressive others (AvG-). In blunt affect, the indivodual does not show any emotion to disguse his or her appearance in front of the opponents (BG-).

Catatonic Hallucination and Delusion to Catatonic-Based, Negative Symptoms

Within catatonic hallucinations and delusions, there can appear in forms of positive and negative symptoms. In terms of clients' subjective experiences, they can be any of the following:

C+ = I need to store my energy and have a very keen observation before I can fight back or to defend myself from oppressive others.
C0 = The oppressive others are changing and moving. Better watch carefully before taking any action. Inappropriate actions can be wrong and harmful
C- = The oppressive others are moving and changing. Being inert is the only way to disguise oneself from the attack of others

C + certainly is the positive symptoms in which the individual keeps him- or herself in an active, catatonic stupor to have a keen observation on the related, oppressive environment. As mentioned above in the chapter of positive symptoms, the individual is actually assessing how to react so as to shift from different types of grandiose or paranoid delusions and hallucination. However in C- and C+, the individual's catatonic state is actually a sign of psychotic, negative symptoms.

C0 implies that through prolonged and keen observation of a related, oppressive reality, the individual finally conclude that no action is better than any action. Inappropriate actions can be wrong and damaging. In other words, the individual does not change to paranoid or grandiose delusion or hallucination. Instead, he or she affirms that no action is needed. This can be several excuses behind this assumption:

1. The oppressive others are actually changing, we should know how they are changing first before taking any action.
2. The oppressive others disguise their power, influence, and even appearance wisely. Thus, it is better to do nothing so as to recognize their exact forms and ways of attack.
3. The current oppressive others are not the really one. We need to wait until the real one appears.

C0 can also exist in forms of alogia, anhedonia, avolition, and blunt affect. In alogia (AgC0), individuals do not say anything or murmur a full sentence so as to avoid taking any action in facing the oppressive others. It is simply due to the fact that no word can appropriately describe the movement or the change in the oppressive others. In anhedonia (AnC0), individuals prefer to remain stagnant in their interpersonal relationships. As oppressive others may change or appear in forms that will disguise their actual existence.

Thus, any interpersonal relationship may take a risk of falling into the trap of the cunning, oppressive others. In avolition (AvC0), individuals do not show or embrace any will or motivation to do anything. It is simply due to the fact that the oppressive others are so cunning it is better to do nothing or doing anything is also in vain. In blunt affect (BC0), as the oppressive others are changing a lot and moving in many forms, they should be very sensitive to any emotional response performed by the individual with psychotic, negative symptoms. Thus, it is better for them to remain inert, blunt, and unresponsive in their emotional responses.

C- implies that the oppressive others are moving and changing. They are very powerful so it is better to keep oneself in a stage of inertness to avoid being discovered and attacked by the oppressive others. Unlike C+ and C0, individuals with catatonic schizophrenia harbor fear of taking any action. This fear is due to the following:

1. The changes and movement of the oppressive others are too powerful to deal with. If the individual takes inappropriate actions, they would hurt the individual.
2. The changes and movement of the oppressive others may attack the individual all of a sudden. Thus, it is better to remain stagnant so as to avoid being discovered by the oppressive others.
3. The oppressive others can come from any direction or appear in any form. Thus, being stagnant and being invisible is the best way to avoid being attacked.

Within this constant fear, the individual manifests his or her negative symptoms of alogia, avolition, anhedonia, and blunt affect.

In alogia (AgC-), the individual refuses to murmur any words or utter any sound that would arouse the attention of the oppressive others to attack him or her. Furthermore, being quiet is the best way to face the ever changing, oppressive others.

In avolition (AvC-) instead of wasting effort to arouse the attack of the oppressive others, perhaps it is best to remain inert and wait the oppressive others. Once they launch their attacks, their form, position, and power appear. That means they become visible. Only when they become visible, can the individual fight back accurately.

In blunt affect (BC-), the same principle applies, it is better to show no emotional response so that the oppressive first may not be able to find them. Second, emotional response actually provides inner, psychic power to fight back, so it is better to let the oppressive others show their appearance and begin their attack. Then the appropriate affect, together with actions, can be taken promptly.

Similarly, in anhedonia (AnC-), the individual should not show any interest in establishing a normal relationship. Once they do so, they will be discovered by the oppressive others. Also, it is better not to relate to anyone, as the cunning oppressor can change into any form or anyone. Thus it is better to keep away from others so that he or she can observe in what ways the oppressive others plan to attack him or her and in what ways he or she can fight back.

SELF-FRAGMENTATION IN PSYCHOTIC, NEGATIVE SYMPTOMS

Misconception on Self-Fragmentation in Negative Symptoms

Within day-to-day clinical practice with persons with schizophrenia, many professionals still harbor a wrong concept that self-fragmentation occurs within clients' positive symptoms. They regard clients' paranoid and grandiose hallucinations and delusions as signs of a confused mind and fragmented sense of self and reality. However, once these clients are under treatment with an intense dosage of antipsychotic medication or even ECC treatment, they become inert, passive and withdrawn. They are in a state of prevailing, negative symptoms. However, many professionals may wrongly believe that mental stability exists when no harassment or trouble is created for people around them, including human professional. They fail to see that negative symptoms are also signs of self-fragmentation In fact, as mentioned above, psychotic, negative symptoms go together with positive symptoms of self-fragmentation. In the initial process of self-fragmentation, the psychotic positive symptoms go more and more intense. However, as the self-fragmentation goes further, individuals with schizophrenia becomes more and more withdrawn, inert, and stagnant toward reality. Thus, severe, psychotic, negative symptoms actually represent even more severe self-fragmentation than positive symptoms.

Negative Symptoms in the Process of Self-Fragmentation

As mentioned above, self-fragmentation involves seven stages. They are,

Stage 1: Dissociation (dissociation of mind and body, past and present, inner and outer, and self and others).

Stage 2: Splitting occurs when dissociation fails (good and bad self, embodied self and unembodied self, and true and false self).

Stage 3: Molar fragmentation of personality (breaking into more than one partial-self systems within which may or may not be conflicting to one another).

Stage 4: Molecular fragmentation of thoughts within each split/fractured partial-self system (confusion of thoughts, perception and interpretation within every fractured sub-self system).

Stage 5: Further fragmentation of all these divided and fractured partial self systems (Each fractured partial self system may have its own delusive identity, boundary and interpretation of external reality).

Stage 6: There are spontaneous and continuous conflicts and ambiguity within and between these divided and fractured partial self systems (The individual may shift from one delusive identity to another one, has constant manifestation of running tracks of auditory hallucination with one arguing with one another, with thought insertion and thought broadcasting).

Stage 7: The self-fragmentationof all these partial self systems can be continuous until reparation is impossible. (The individual is in a state of severe mental confusion and has a very poor sense of reality that may lead to psychiatric emergency and possible harm to oneself and another).

Within these seven stages, not only positive symptoms are developed, negative symptoms also prevail. The manifestation of psychotic negative symptoms can be roughly described in Table 9.

Table 9. Stages of Development of Self-Fragmentation and Manifestation of Positive and Negative Symptoms

Stages of Development	Manifestation of Positive Symptoms	Manifestation of Negative Symptoms
Stage 1: Dissociation	The individual begins to fixate in own egocentric thought and behaviors that are odd and bizarre to others.	Dissociation prevails in which the individual is quite alienated and inert to external reality because of splitting between mind and body, past and present. Along this line, the individual becomes self isolated from others. The individual's mind was split into real self and unembodied self. The unembodied self appears in a form of dissociation of mind from body, as well as a separation of real self from the reality
Stage 2: Splitting where the dissociation fails	Egocentric thought and behaviors becomes very organized in form of positive symptoms such as paranoid, grandiose, and catatonic delusions and hallucinations	Individuals' mind split into real self, false self and unembodied self. The real self is being separted from the reality by the false self and unembodied self. The hallucination and delusion represent the unfulfilled wish and fantasy of the real self. The false self and unemobided self merge together making the individual become inert, passive and withdrawn from external reality.

Stages of Development	Manifestation of Positive Symptoms	Manifestation of Negative Symptoms
Stage 3: Molar fragmentation of personality	The self system breaks into more than one partial self systems within which may or may not be conflicting to one another. Each partial-self system may have a distinctive self-identity and personality. It manifests in forms of active and full paranoid, grandiose and catatonic delusions and hallucinations	Individual's mind further splitS into inner, real self, inner, false self, outer, false self and unembodied self. The inner, false self, outer, false self and unembodied self merge together in a process in which negative, psychotic symptoms prevail. On one hand, the individual heavily absorbs in active paranoid, grandiose, and catatonic delusions and hallucinations. On the other hand, the individual is alienated from reality. He or she has no emotional response (blunt affect), no interest in doing anything (avoliton), including interpersonal relationshsips (anhedonia), or even speaking any words (alogia) with any person, issue, or object in reality.
Stage 4: Molecular fragmentation of thoughts within each split/fractured partial self system	Positive symptoms possibly turn into a high confusion in which the individual's previously well-organized paranoid, grandiose, and catatonic delusions and hallucinations become loose and confused in time, space and identity.	Within molecular fragmentation, individual negative symptoms prevail. Apart from alienation from reality, individual also represses his or her unpleasant and traumatic experiences in adulthood and in adolescence. He or she is deeply absorbed in his or her blunt affect, avolition, anhedonia, and alogia.
Stage 5 to 6: Further fragmentation of all these divided and fractured partial self systems in which there are spontaneous conflicts and ambiguity within between these divided and fractured self system	As the client becomes more and more confused, and his or her mind is over-whelmed with fragmented delusions and hallucinations, his or her mental and physical energy as well as social functioning decline accordingly. Active grandiose, paranoid and catatonic delusion and hallucination become self absorbed stagnant self talk, Odd and bizarre behaviors are greatly reduced.	The client's negative symptoms intensify. He or she not only represses unpleasant and traumatic experiences in adulthood and adolescen but also those in late childhood. As a consequence, he or she is fixated in those happy experiences in early childhood. Apart from being absorbed in intense blunt affect, avolition, anhedonia and alogia. He or she also appears as a child with dependent, regressive and id oriented behaviors and life pattern.
Stage 7: The self-fragmentation of all these partial self systems can be continual until reparation is impossible.	Within the severe self-fragmentation process, the client exhausts all his or her mental and physical energy. Grandiose, paranoid, or catatonic delusion and hallucination turns inward in forms of very stagnant and unexpressed thinking. Similar to those traumatic experiences, all these grandiose, paranoid, and delusions and hallucinations are well concealed and repressed. Together with this concealment is exhaustion and repression of mental and physical energy. However, all this concealment and repression may rebounce in the state of sub-consciousness and unconsciousness. In some clients, they may appear as very fearful and aggressive (because of paranoid delusion and hallucinations), happy (because of grandiose delusion and hallucination), as well as tense (because of catatonic delusion and hallucination) like nightmare.	Negative symptoms such as alogia, anhedonia, blunt affect and avolition become very severe. They intermingle with very regressive behaviors. Clients appear as infants or even a fetus with intense inert, immobile, passive, and withdrawn behaviors. For alogia, they do not say any words or simply murmur some baby sounds. For avolition, individuals may simply lay on bed without doing any thing. They also have poor personal hygiene. For anhedonia, they may totally depend on others just babies. They need to be fed or cared by others. For blunt affect, they do not any emotional response toward others. Instead, they appear like a baby, crying when they feel uncomfortable and smiling in a silly way.

Psychotic Negative Symptoms and Self-Splitting versus Self- Cohesion

Underlying this self-fragmentation process are three unresolved dilemmas, self splitting versus self cohesion, self concealment versus self visibility and self-destruction versus self preservation. Self-splitting versus self-cohesion exists in a form of pull and push force. The individual needs to split his or her self system so as to maintain a fragile or even delusive cohesion in facing the extremely oppressive social environment. It consists of a process with the following stages of development:

Stage 1: Temporary self-splitting versus self-cohesion to significant others only.
Stage 2: Partial self-splitting versus self-cohesion to persons and events in the reality.
Stage 3: Full self-splitting versus self-cohesion to persons and events in the delusive but organized reality.
Stage 4: Very confused self-splitting versus self-cohesion in very delusive and disorganized reality.

As stated above, the manifestation of psychotic, negative symptoms is very correlated to the self-splitting in terms of unembodied self, outer, false self, inner, false self and inner, real self. Facing the very oppressive psychosocial environment, the occurrence of unembodied self, outer, false and inner, false self serves to protect the inner self so that the initial self system (one's inner morality, dignity, wishes, real need, identity). The more vigorous is the self-splitting, the stronger is the need to have self-cohesion. It is a self-cohesion among one's wishes, needs, identity, and image within the past, the present, and the future. To maintain the invaluable self-cohesion, individuals prefer to split their self systems further and further. As he or she becomes more and more alienated from reality, his or her residual ego strengths decrease further and further. In positive symptoms, the concealed needs, wishwa, identity, and image appear in forms of delusive and self-constructed fantasy. In negative symptoms, the false self and the unemboided self were split out from the original self-system and serve to make the concealed but residual self system cohesive and surviving. According to Laing's thinking, the self-splitting versus self-cohesion can be described in the following processes:

1. The splitting of the self system into inner self and unembodied self so as to maintain the cohesiveness of the inner self (Stage two: partial self-splitting versus self cohesion). In this stage, the splitting can only be situational and contextual. That means in one context, especially the oppressive environment, the individual can appear to be dissociative and alienated in order to preserve his or her own self-cohesiveness. In the other situation and context, he or she can be quite cohesive. For example, an individual is located in an office full of office dynamics and politics in which his or her boss is cunning and hypocritical. To

survive within this oppressive office dynamics and politics, he or she needs to embrace a mask (unembodied self). He or she should appear to be very submissive and obedient. In front of his or her boss, he or she tries to speak as little as possible. Even if his or her boss curses him or her seriously, he or she should appear as calm and accepting. He or she tries to keep a mental and emotional distance from his or her boss's comment. He or she tries to keep a social and physical distance from his or her boss. By doing so, he or she can maintain his or her inner views, emotions, values, and dignity can be concealed without being challenged by his or her boss. It is a sign of "split cohesiveness." However, after office hours, in a bar when his or her supportive peers are there, his real self can air out all his or her feelings of hatred toward his boss. That means the unembodied self in terms being emotionally dissociated (initial and mild blunt affect), mentally dissociated (initial and mild avolition), socially dissociated (initial and mild ahenodia), and verbally dissociated (initial and mild alogia).

2. The splitting of inner self system into real self and false self so as to maintain the cohesiveness of the real self (stage 3: full self- splitting versus self-cohesion). As the oppressive environment prevails, the individual has no way out for escaping from it. Instead, the unembodied self even remains in a permanent form. It cannot have sufficient sheltering power to protect the cohesiveness of the whole system. The individual needs to split further into real self and false self. That means the self system splits in two to protect against shifts in the cohesiveness of the residual self system. The more the self system undergoes the splitting process, the more fragmented the self system becomes, and the more deadly the self system becomes. The deadness and malfunctioning of the permanent unembodied self and false self make the psychotic, negative symptoms occur stably. The individual becomes very inert in speaking (alogia), social interaction (anhedonia), doing anything (avolition), and emotion (blunt affect). The more oppressive the social environment is, the more inert and self isolated the individual becomes; and the more severe the psychotic negative symptoms are. Finally, even without oppressive figures in the immediate social environment, the negative symptoms still prevail. The individual appears as inert, passive, withdrawn in all circumstances. Within this self splitting process, accompanied with the splitting of self system, it is also a paralyzation of various form of ego functioning in the self system. The individual ego functioning, in terms of memories, interaction, will to interact with the reality are also repressed and concealed. As a consequence, individuals may appear as an immature child both in deed and in mind.

3. The splitting of the real self into the inner, real self, and the inner, false self so as to maintain the cohesiveness of the inner, real self (Stage four: very confused self-splitting versus self-cohesion). As the oppressive environment goes on in forms of very institutionalized treatment contexts, very exclusive and isolated work and family environment, the individual's self-splitting has to move forward. The residual real self needs to split further to an inner, real self and an inner, false self. In other words, the self system is divided into four components:

    a. Unembodied self
    b. Outer, false self
    c. Inner, false self
    d. Inner, real self

The whole self system is split into four parts, and the inner, real self is only occupied as one-fourth of the components. The other split components, unembodied self, outer, false self, and inner, false self represent the dissociation, repression, and inertness to the external, oppressive environment and internal, traumatic memories. That means, the whole self system can only sustain a one-fourth lively element to maintain the basic but minimal survival of cohesive elements. Through the splitting of the three faulty self systems, the individual is able to maintain one-fourth cohesiveness of his or her self-dignity, self-respect, self-uniqueness and self-consistency by being heavily dissociated and alienated from the external, social environment and by being intensely repressed from traumatic memories and experiences. As the whole self system is dominated by a malfunctioning false, self system, the individual can only maintain a minimal residue cohesive self system. What conceals and covers the residual, cohesive self system is a very, deadly and split merging of unembodied self (intense dissociation from reality), the outer, false self and the inner, false self in forms of intense alogia (unwilling or unmotivated to speak or express oneself), intense anhedonia (unwilling or unmotivated to relate to other), intense avolition (unwilling or unmotivated to do anything), intense blunt affect (unwilling or unmotivated to express or relate to any emotion). In doing so, the individual's normal ego functioning and social functioning are deeply hindered. He or she may appear as very inert or as a regressive infant or baby. In some extreme cases, the individual may deeply withdraw and lay in bed all day long without any movement at all, just like a fetus in its mother's womb.

Psychotic, Negative Symptoms and Self-Concealment versus Self-Visibility, Dynamic Forces

The second dilemma is self-concealment versus self-visibility in which the individual tries to maintain a dilemma of existence versus non-existence within the oppressive environment. With positive, psychotic symptoms, projective identification is a form of normal social camouflage in which the individual tries to identify with his or her oppressive others. As mentioned above, the whole process of development of this dilemma with psychotic self-fragmentation can be described by the following stages:

Stage 1: Temporary self-concealment versus self-visibility (Reflective concealment Vs actual participatory visibility).

Stage 2: Partial self-concealment versus self-visibility (Detached concealment Vs Dissociative participatory visibility).

Stage 3: Full self-concealment versus self-visibility (Camouflage concealment Vs opponent identified visibility).

Stage 4: Confused self-concealment versus self-visibility (Prevailing paranoid concealment V grandiose visibility).

Stage 5: Very confused self-concealment versus self-visibility (Frequent shifting of delusive identity and paranoid delusion).

In all these five stages, negative symptoms also occur in forms that are very detached and dissociative from the external, oppressive environment as well as from the normal ego and social functioning. As mentioned above, the split, unembodied self, outer, false self, and inner, false self also serve as concealment of the residual, inner, real self system from the external, oppressive environment as well as from inner, traumatic experiences and memories. That means there are actually three types of concealment within psychotic, negative symptoms.

1. External concealment: concealing the residual self system from further harm from external oppressive environment (the unembodied self).
2. Internal concealment: concealing the residual self system from triggering of unpleasant past memories especially those which are oppression, abuse, bullying, and rejection by others in infancy, childhood, adolescence and adulthood (inner false self).
3. Intermediate concealment: separation of the connection of the internal concealment and external concealment. That means the internal concealment system does not affect the external concealment from the external oppressive reality (external false self).

In other words, each of these concealments operates separately from the other. Together with these three sorts of concealment, there are also three types of visibility. As mentioned in a previous chapter, the best concealment is camouflage, so that the individual appears in the same form of their enemies and the related, social environment. In psychotic negative symptoms, visibility exist in forms of following the instruction of the oppressive factors, remaining quiet, calm, and unresponsive to adverse comment, criticism, and oppression; and suppressing and numbing possible triggers of past traumatic experiences and feelings.

1. External concealed visibility: The unembodied self tries be very submissive and obedient in following the instructions of the oppressive others. In doing so, he or she can avoid being blamed, criticized, and oppressed by others. However, as his or her ego and social functioning are strongly hindered by the self-fragmentation, individuals can only follow simple instruction. The more his or her self system is fragmented, the more retarded and simple his or her ability to follow external instruction from oppressive reality.
2. Internal concealed visibility: The inner, false self enable the individual to become dissociated and freeze all sort of traumas and unpleasant events in life. Together with this internal concealment, the individual's unpleasant memories and traumatic experiences are not triggered or rebounded by any abuse, bullying, or oppression. Together with this also occur freezing and concealment of pleasant memories and happy experiences. That means nothing in the external environment, no matter whether it is happy or unhappy, pleasant or traumatic can trigger the inner world of the individual or motivate the individual to do anything (avolition), connect with any persons (anhedonia), display any emotional response (blunt affect), or say anything (alogia). In some situations, if related persons press or provoke the individual intensely for responses, he or she may simply repeat their interaction, gestures, and/or wordings in a very naïve and childish ways. In many ways, the individual appears as a mirror, reflecting others' emotions, relationships, interactions, and speech but concealing his or her own.
3. Intermediate concealed visibility: The external, false self enables the individual to separate the connection of internal concealment and external concealment. That means the individual does not feel that he or she is consciously inert to external environment nor he or she feels that he or she represses his or her unpleasant and traumatic experiences and memories. While externally he or she is following the external oppressive environment in simple and naïve ways, and internally he or she represses all his or her social, emotional, verbal and mental response, he or she is also unaware of such simple naive responses as well as his or her own inertness and

repression. In terms of visibility, the individual's internal mirror (inner, false self) and external simplicity and naïveté are separated by transparent glass (outer, false self). Each of them operates at their own rhythm and pace.

Taking these three symptoms, which are negative-oriented and have concealed visibility, together, individuals within prevailing negative symptoms such as alogia, anhedoina, avolition, and blunt affect, similar to positive symptoms, conceal the residual, real self and exist in social camouflage with their oppressive others. In positive symptoms, projective identification is used in social camouflage in which the individual tries to identify with his or her oppressive others. While the oppressive others always attack the individual as a bad and inferior one to sustain their oppression, in projective identification, the individual merges his or her own bad self with the bad others and projects, it looks outward in forming prevailing paranoid delusion and hallucination. Within the paranoid delusion, as the individual merges with the oppressive others, he or she assumes oppressive others are everywhere. Within grandiose delusions, the individual turns into an even more powerful figure to fight back the oppressive others. However, in negative symptoms, the camouflage turns into a static and stagnant direction. As mentioned previously, it should be a state of P0 in terms of paranoid delusions and hallucinations, G0 in terms of grandiose delusions and hallucinations, and C0 in terms of catatonic delusions and hallucinations.

The details of them are described as follows:

P0 = No action should be taken so that I cannot be discovered by the persecuted others.
G0 = No action is needed as they do not dare to do any threat. They simply run away.
C0 = The oppressive others are changing and moving. Better watch carefully before taking any action. Inappropriate actions can be wrong and damaging.

That means P0, G0 and C0 all are inert concealment mechanisms formed by the unembodied self, external, false self and inner, false self. They are also inert visible mechanism in which the individual only respond to the oppressive environment in a very simple, naïve, and inert ways.

The static and stagnant response of alogia (speech), anhedonia (social relationship), avolition (will to do anything), and blunt affect (emotion) implies that the oppressive others are present and the individual cannot do or do not necessary to do anything to defend from their oppression. Thus, being inert is the most suitable way to face a prevailing, oppressive environment. For paranoid delusions and hallucinations, when they turn into forms of negative, psychotic symptoms, they become "no action should be taken so that they cannot be discovered by the persecuted others (P0)". For grandiose delusions and hallucinations, when they turn into forms of negative, psychotic symptoms, they become "no action is needed as the oppressive others do not dare to do any threat (G0)." They simply run away. For catatonic delusion and hallucinations, when they turn into forms of negative, psychotic symptoms, they become the oppressive others who are changing and moving. Better watch carefully before taking any action. Inappropriate actions can be wrong and damaging (C0). In other words, the individual visualize him- or herself in a very naïve, simple, and passive ways. This type of passive and inert visibility has several advantages:

1. The oppressive and abusive others in the immediate environment may come to a conclusion that the individual is non-threatening, easy to control and manipulate. Thus, they may not increase their control and oppression on the individual with prevailing negative symptoms.
2. The individual can save his or her mental and energy to avoid unnecessary struggle in combating the oppressive others. The inert, passive, and naïve mode of visibility, after the unnecessary struggle in positive, psychotic symptoms, should be the best way for minimal survival within a very oppressive and abusive, immediate, social and physical environment.

Psychotic, Negative Symptoms and Self-Destruction versus Self-Preservation Dilemma

The third dilemma is self-destruction and self-preservation. This dilemma starts with individual's inherent instinct to destroy and to preserve one's own self and that of others in facing danger and threat in the external environment. With psychotic, positive symptoms, individuals are involved heavily in a delusive self-destruction mechanisms in which they try to destroy themselves mentally so that the oppressive others cannot destroy them. In a way, this is the only delusive way to preserve the individual's own inner self such as self-image, self-identity, and autonomy. This is also a way to destroy oneself in order to destroy others.

There are different stages in self-preservation and self-destruction in the development of schizophrenia.

Stage 1: *No need* for the development of self-destruction versus self-preservation (Self-destruction is only limited to inherent sex and aggressive drives that are under control by the individual).

Stage 2: *Initial development* of self-destruction versus self- preservation (The individual may internalize negative comment from the external, oppressive environment)

Stage 3: *Gradual development* of self-destruction versus self- preservation (The individual tends to absorb and act according to the demands of others' oppression and criticism. But it is too painful and unbearable. Thus, he or she tries to dissociate his or her own sense of reality to lessen his or her negative feelings and inner pains).

Stage 4: *Externalization* of self-destruction versus self-preservation by rebellion of the oppressive others so as to preserve one's autonomy and substance. (The individual destroys his or her un-embodied self in order to diminish the influence of oppressive others. In doing so, he or she also diminishes his or her external parts of self-images and identities).

Stage 5: *Internalization* of self-destruction versus self-preservation by *diminishing the unembodied self and the development of the false self* (The individual dissociates him- or herself from the painful reality completely by diminishing his or her unembodied self and build up a false self. The individual is largely withdrawn from the participation in normal, social interaction and daily activities.

Stage 6: *Intense development* of self-destruction and self- preservation: *Full development of false self* (The full representation of the false self can be a full manifestation of psychotic symptoms. Others may perceive the individual as seriously insane and mad).

Stage 7: *Overwhelming development* of self-destruction and self- preservation: Destruction and *splitting of the false self and real self* (The individual regards the false self as a foreign lifeless body that should be rejected. The residual but diminished unembodied self and false self becomes a delusive negative reality).

As mentioned above, in the process of psychotic self-fragmentation, the individual's self system is gradually divided and split into an unembodied self, an outer, false self, an inner, false self and an inner, real self. In each type of this self-splitting, there should be a self-destruction versus self-preservation dilemma. The dilemma can be briefly described as follows:

1. In the splitting the real self and the unembodied self, the individual destroys the unembodied self to preserve the embodied self (stage 4).
2. In the splitting of embodied self into real self and false self, the individual destroys the false self to preserve the real self (stage 5 and stage 6).
3. In the splitting of the real self into inner, real and inner, false self, the individual destroys the outer, false self and inner, false self to preserve the inner, real self (stage 7).

In fact, the unembodied self, outer false self, and inner false self are all destroying the self system so as to preserve the remaining self system. The unembodied self is actually a detachment and dissociation from the external environment. That means, the individual destroys the vitality of the self system in the reception of the external, oppressive environment. Instead of perceiving others as bullying, oppressing, abusing and isolating him or her, the individual simply detaches his or her mind from others. He or she does not hear, see, smell and touch anything, object, person, or words in the immediate social environment. The false self is attempting total destruction of the interpretation or arousal of inner feelings, memories, and will power to respond to oppressive environment. He or she does not feel angry, humiliated, inferior, lonely, helpless, and fearful in facing abuse, oppression, domination, and isolation by oppressive others. The outer false self is attempting destruction of the inherent, natural, and spontaneous responses such as the urge to speak (alogia), feel (blunt affect), interact (anhedonia), and act (avolition) to oppressive others.

The inner false self actually represents a destruction of inner trigger, sparkling, connection, and accumulation of similar experiences and memories in responding to the external, oppressive environment. In doing so, the individual has no urges to, but also does not warm up to, or is very unmotivated to speak to (severe alogia), or interact with others (severe anhedonia), to do anything (severe avolition), and to express his or her emotion (severe blunt affect).

Conclusion

In conclusion, this chapter is a full discussion on the relationship between negative and positive symptoms in people with schizophrenia. In clinical situation, psychotic, negative symptoms have a full connection with positive symptoms. There are paranoid-oriented, grandiose-oriented and catatonic alogia, blunt affect, avolition and anhedonia. In paranoid, positive symptoms, individuals engage in delusive perception, thought, and action to avoid being persecuted (P+). In paranoid-oriented, negative symptoms, they can manifest in a stagnant (P0) and/or negative (P-) ways. P0 means that no actions, including talking (alogia), emotional response (blunt affect), will power and deeds (avolition), and social interaction (anhedonia) should be taken so that the individual cannot be discovered by delusive, persecuted others. P- implies that even if the individual has taken every action, there is still no way to avoid being persecuted, so it is better to remain stagnant and do nothing in verbal expression (alogia), social interaction(anhedonia), will power and determination (avolition), and emotional expression (blunt affect).

There is also grandiose-oriented blunt affect, avolition, anhedonia, and avolition. In positive, grandiose, positive, psychotic symptoms (G+), individuals affirm that they are powerful enough to diminish related threats in forms of active, grandiose self-identity, delusions and hallucination. However, in negative symptoms, the grandiosity turns into a stagnant (G0) withdrawn, and negative condition (G-). In G0, the individual concludes that no action, including expression (alogia), emotional response (blunt affect), power over things (avolition) and social interaction (anhedonia) are needed as the oppressive other do not dare to make any threat to him or her. The oppressive others simply get away because of the prevailing power of him or her. In G-, the individual affirms that he or she needs to conceive his or her powerfulness and existence so as to diminish the oppressive others suddenly. Thus, he or she needs to conceal his or her verbal expression (alogia), will power and action (avolition), emotional response (blunt affect) and social interaction (anhedonia).

Similarly, in positive, symptom-oriented, catatonic schizophrenia, the individual fully believes that he or she needs to store up and/or concentrate his or her psychic energy and has a very keen observation in forms of catatonic stupor before he or she can fight back or defend him- or herself from oppressive others. In negative symptoms, catatonic delusion, and hallucination exist in a stagnant and withdrawn ways. In the stagnant way, the individual assumes that the oppressive others are changing and moving. Thus, it is better to watch carefully before taking any action including talking (alogia), will power to do anything (avolition), interpersonal relations (anhedonia), and emotional response (blunt affect). Inappropriate actions can be wrong and damaging. In a withdrawn way, the individual assumes that the oppressive others are moving and changing. Being inert in action (avolition), speech (alogia), interpersonal relation (anhedonia) and emotional response (blunt affect) are the only ways to disguise oneself from the attack of oppressive others.

Psychotic negative symptoms also represent the process of self-fragmentation and self-integration. *In the process of self-fragmentation*, psychotic negative symptoms exist in all stages of self-fragmentation. In stage 1 of dissociation, the unembodied self represents a dissociation of the mind and body and a separation of real self from reality. In stage 2 of splitting where the dissociation fails, within positive symptoms, the false self and unembodied self merge together making the individual become inert, passive, and withdrawn from external reality. In stage 3 of molar fragmentation of personality in which the self system further splits into inner, real self, inner, false self and unembodied self. The inner false self, outer false self and unembodied self merge together and form negative symptoms. The individual has no emotional response (blunt affect), no interest in doing anything (avolition), including interpersonal relationship (anhedonia) or even speak any words (alogia) with any person, issue, and object in reality. In stage 4 of molecular fragmentation of thoughts within each fractured parital self system, negative symptoms prevail. Apart from alienation from reality, the individual also represses his or her unpleasant and traumatic experiences in adulthood and in adolescence. He or she is deeply absorbed in his or her blunt affect, avolition, anhedonia, and alogia. In stages 5 and 6, there is further fragmentation of all these fractured parital self systems. There is an intensification of clients' negative symptoms, and individual's experiences in childhood are also repressed. Apart from being heavily absorbed in negative symptoms, the individual appears as a child with dependent, regressive, and id-oriented behaviors. Finally, in stage 7, the self- fragmentation of all these partial self systems can be continual until reparation is impossible. That means, individuals suffer from severe negative symptoms in which they do not say any words, do nothing, have poor hygiene. behave like a babies, and are totally dependent on others. Similar situations also occur in self-splitting versus self-cohesion dynamic forces. The more vigorous the self-splitting is, the stronger is the need to have self-cohesion. In negative symptoms, the false self and the unemboided self are split out from the original self system and serve to make the concealed but residual self system cohesive and surviving. Regarding self-concealment versus self- visibility dynamic force, negative symptoms also occur in forms that are very detached and dissociated from the external, oppressive environment as well as normal ego and social functioning. As mentioned above, the split unembodied self, outer false self and inner false self also serve as concealment of the residual inner real self system from the external oppressive environment as well as inner, traumatic experiences and memories. That means there are three types of concealment within psychotic, negative symptoms. They are external concealment (the unembodied self), internal concealment (inner false self) and intermediate concealment (external false self). Together with this are three types of visibility, external concealed visibility, internal concealed visibility, and intermediate concealed visibility. However, in negative symptoms, the camouflage turns into a static and stagnant way. There are also inert visible mechanisms in which the individual only responds to the oppressive environment in very simple, naïve, and inert ways. In self-destructive and self-preservation dilemma, unembodied self, outer false self and inner false self are all destroyed as part of the self system to preserve the remaining self system. The false self is a total instruction or interpretation of arousal of inner feeling, memories, and will power to respond to oppressive environment. He or she does not feel angry, humiliated, inferior, lonely, helpless and fearful in facing abuse, oppression, domination, and isolation by oppressive others. The individual has no urges to, but also not warms up to, or is very unmotivated to, speak (severe alogia), to interact with others (severe anhedonia), to do anything (severe avolition), and to express his or her emotion (severe blunt affect).

All these have strong implications for the recovery of people with chronic schizophrenia. Related professionals should beware that within stagnant negative symptoms such as alogia, anhedonia, avolition, and blunt affect, they do not imply that paranoid, grandiose, and catatonic delusion and hallucinations vanish. Instead, they turn inward, they are repressed, and they are concealed. People with severe, negative symptoms do not turn into an empty vacuum. Instead, they conceal themselves and try to be invisible. They destroy external activities to preserve internal activities. They split their self into false selves so that they can integrate their fragile, inner, true self. Also, the longer the concealment, destruction, and splitting is, the more severe negative symptoms become. That means, related professionals should never repress or control positive symptoms by inappropriate, heavy dosages of antipsychotic medication and turn them into negative symptoms. Nor should they impose a very institutionalized service setting to intensify secondary, negative symptoms. Instead, people with severe negative symptoms are similar to those with positive symptoms. They also need a very supportive, social environment with caring, genuine and very accepting caregivers. The dilemma between positive and negative symptoms enables professionals to have an accurate, dynamic, substantially and effective intervention for clients with chronic schizophrenia.

REFERENCES

Arieti, S. (1974). *Interpretation of Schizophrenia (2nd edition)*: Completely Revised and Expanded, London: Crosby Lockwood Staples.

Kirkpatrick, B., Fenton, W.S, Carpenter, Marder, S. R. (2006). "The NIMH-MATRICS consensus statement on negative symptoms," *Schizophrenic Bulletin*, 32(2): 214–219.

Laing R. D., (1960). *The Divided Self*, London: Tavistock Publication.

AUTHOR CONTACT INFORMATION

Kam-shing Yip
Professor
Department of Applied Social Studies,
Hong Kong Polytechnic University,
Hung Hom, Kowloon, Hong Kong
Email: kam-shing.yip@connect.polyu.hk

INDEX

T

U

V

W